THE PRACTICAL PROGRESSIVE

ACKNOWLEDGEMENTS

With thanks to all of the contributors for their insights.

And with special thanks to **Bernard Schwartz** whose generous support made this guide possible.

THE PRACTICAL PROGRESSIVE

How to Build a Twenty-first
Century Political Movement

Erica Payne

PublicAffairs
New York

Copyright © 2008 by Erica Payne

Published in the United States by PublicAffairs™,
a member of the Perseus Books Group.

PublicAffairs books are available at special discounts for bulk
purchases in the U.S. by corporations, institutions, and other
organizations. For more information, please contact the
Special Markets Department at the Perseus Books Group,
2300 Chestnut Street, Suite 200, Philadelphia, PA 19103,
call (800) 810-4145, ext. 5000, or e-mail
special.markets@perseusbooks.com.

A CIP catalog record for this book is available from the
Library of Congress.

ISBN-13: 978-1-58648-719-5
First Edition

10 9 8 7 6 5 4 3 2 1

CONTENTS

GUIDE TO INFORMATION GRAPHICS

At-a-glance information for each organization is represented by the icons below:

mailing address

 phone number

 fax number

 contact person

@ email address

website address

organization founding date

2008 operating budget

type of organization (LLC, 501(c)(3), PAC, 527...)

LETTER FROM THE EDITOR

Over the last several years, fueled by entrepreneurial zeal and common purpose, progressives built an array of new organizations—think tanks, legal advocacy organizations, watchdog groups, leadership development efforts, civic participation vehicles and media organizations—to challenge conservative dominance. During the same period, leaders of established organizations began to transform their institutions, developing fresh strategies and innovative tactics for a new political moment. These organizations, both old and new, are beginning to coalesce into an intellectual and communications infrastructure that, though not nearly complete, is showing signs of potent and enduring strength. I daresay anyone who threw up their hands after the 2000 election has missed one of the most invigorating periods of renewal and growth in progressive political history.

Almost none of the organizations in this book are traditionally "political," in fact many are charitable organizations. But all play critical roles in shaping the country's public policy conversation. The purpose of this guide is to underscore the importance of this infrastructure and to highlight some of its strongest elements. In the first part of the book, I give an overview of the progressive infrastructure and offer suggestions for future investment. Then Jerry Hauser and Alison Green of The Management Center provide their thoughts on the characteristics of exceptional organizations. And finally, with the help of my Tesseract Group colleagues and the important research of progressive strategist Rob Stein, we present a brief history of the conservative infrastructure.

With this backdrop, we come to the heart of the book—the organizations. Each of the groups featured in this book was recommended by a progressive expert. These experts—writers, organization leaders, donors, advisors, and activists were asked *"if you were named chief progressive strategist, which 5—10 groups would you consider absolutely critical to our success?"* The groups they selected were then asked to create a profile in their own words. You will find the results in the pages that follow.

Our country faces serious challenges. During this time of debate progressives must understand the myriad ways they can help restore the country's philosophical ballast. And elections, while absolutely critical, are only one piece of a much larger puzzle. With that in mind I offer you **The Practical Progressive**: a thinking person's guide to creating meaningful, sustainable change in the public sector.

Erica Payne

THE EXPERTS

Eric Alterman

Paul Begala

Sergio Bendixen

Wes Boyd

Joe Conason

Kelly Craighead

Gail Furman

Alison Greene

Jerry Hauser

Gara LaMarche

Brian Mathis

Alexis McGill

Rob McKay

Minyon Moore

George Mursuli

John Podesta

Sasha Post

Andrew Rich

Cecile Richards

Bernard Schwartz

Frank Smith

Rob Stein

Katrina vanden Heuvel

Maureen White

THE PROGRESSIVE INFRASTRUCTURE

by Erica Payne

In 2000 a bitterly divided Supreme Court sent George W. Bush to the White House.

In 2002 in an historic election,[1] Republicans gained control of the Senate, increased their majority in the House and won nationwide control of state legislatures. It was the first time since the Civil War that a president's party took a majority of Senate seats away from the other party in an off-year election. It was the third time in 100 years that the president's party gained seats in the House in a midterm election. And it was the first time since 1952 that Republicans controlled state legislatures.

In 2004 Republican ascendancy continued with President Bush's re-election and Republican gains in the House and Senate. Bush campaign manager Ken Mehlman claimed the Republican Party was "in a stronger position...than at any time since the Great Depression."[2] Pundits foretold a looming era of GOP control.

By 2006 it was over. Bush's approval ratings plunged. Democrats regained control of the House and Senate. And today, Democrats are positioned to make substantial gains at all levels of government.

What happened? Did the pendulum swing or was it swung?

To answer the question, we have to first understand that much of politics has nothing to do with "politics." Underneath today's electoral contests is a fierce argument about policy and power. Candidates, elected officials and party committees are the public faces of this conflict, but the struggle is far deeper than a single election.

After the 1964 Goldwater defeat, conservative philanthropists began to build a set of ideologically-aligned institutions—academic centers, think tanks, legal advocacy institutions, watchdog groups, single issue groups, community organizations and media vehicles—to change the intellectual and political climate of the country. In the last 40 years, this "infrastructure" has supported and promoted conservative ideology so effectively, that it ultimately assured its political dominance. This infrastructure provides right and far-right conservatives with idea generation, legislation drafting, litigation, message dissemination, voter registration, investigative reporting, media monitoring, public relations, lobbying, policy analysis, mobilization, mass communications, direct marketing, human resources and other capacities that are critical to influencing the national "conversation" and as such the political dynamic.

[1] Barone, Michael. "Bush's midterm triumph is reminiscent of JFK's." *Wall Street Journal*. Nov. 9, 2002.
[2] Harris, John. "'04 Voting: Realignment—Or a Tilt?" *Washington Post*. Nov. 28, 2004.

In 2002 progressives began to wake up to this enormous structural disparity. We began to understand that our candidates were losing not because they were bad candidates but because they were structurally outmatched. We were sending David to fight Goliath without a slingshot. So we began to build new institutions outside of politics and to transform old organizations to meet the challenge. Fully half of the organizations in this book were created in the last 6 years, and many of the older institutions have been significantly restructured.

Since 2002 the **Progressive Infrastructure** has changed the Iraq debate, raised the minimum wage, stopped social security privatization, prevented the disenfranchisement of hundreds of thousands of voters and pushed the "culture of corruption" to the center of the public debate. It exposed substandard body armor, out of control mercenary armies, White House visits by Jack Abramoff, illegal political activity by right-wing churches, unseemly emails from Mark Foley, Republican plants in the White House press corps and missing White House emails. It forced the retirement of UN Ambassador John Bolton and six members of Congress, including Tom Delay. It published op-eds, magazine articles, white papers, voter guides and books. It produced commercials, YouTube videos and documentary movies. It argued in front of the Supreme Court and testified in front of Congress. It registered millions of voters and recruited thousands of volunteers.

The **Progressive Infrastructure** includes virtually no elected officials, candidates, candidate committees, state parties or national parties. Most groups in the infrastructure are strictly non-partisan, many are charitable organizations. With them, we can restore our country. Without them, we will not. Here's why.

Like any other business, politics has a **value chain**—a set of activities that converts *raw materials* into *finished products* and then *markets* and *distributes* those products to end *customers* in the *market*. Look at Nike. Nike buys raw materials like canvas and rubber, then converts these materials into shoes that it distributes and sells to customers. Along the way, Nike's marketing team develops the "swoosh" and clever slogans like "Just Do It" and then the company selects Michael Jordan as its spokesman.

The same thing happens in politics. Raw materials, like philosophical principles and economic theories, are transformed into specific policies that are marketed and distributed to candidates and advocacy groups or directly to voters. For example, a philosophy about fairness and the dignity of work combined with an economic theory about wealth creation and capitalism may be turned into a specific policy to raise the minimum wage. Good marketers translate the policy into a "Living Wage" campaign which is "sold" to voters either through the candidates (wholesale) or through ballot initiatives (retail). Voters then "buy" the product (elect the candidate or pass the ballot initiative).

Nike does *not* ask Michael Jordan to design the tennis shoes or to develop the "swoosh" and we shouldn't either. For years progressives searched endlessly for exactly the right Michael Jordan but we spent no time at all designing a better tennis shoe. The infrastructure is about the shoe …and the swoosh…and everything in between.

The **raw materials** of shoes are canvas and rubber. The raw materials of public policy are political and social philosophies, economic theories, legal rationales, constitutional interpretations, ideas about the role of governments, etc. They are typically developed in academia. In *A Conflict of Visions: Ideological Origins of Political Struggles*, conservative philosopher Thomas Sowell argues that competing social theories start with two distinct subjective visions or "gut feelings" about how the world works. One is the "constrained" vision, which views man as unchanged, limited and dependent on evolved social processes. The other is the "unconstrained" vision, which argues for man's potential and perfectibility, and the possibility of rational planning for social solutions. Sowell believes these conflicting attitudes are the root causes of clashes over equality, social justice and other issues.

Sowell's theory is interesting. What is more interesting is the support Sowell and other theorists receive from conservative philanthropists and how connected he and his work are to subsequent steps in the conservative value chain. Sowell is a Rose and Milton Friedman Fellow at the **Hoover Institute** at Stanford University. He is the recipient of the **American Enterprise Institute's** Francis Boyer Award. His books are marketed through the **Conservative Book Club**. His ideas are taught at the **Leadership Institute**. And he is a regular columnist for the conservative **Townhall.com**.

Understanding the importance of raw materials to the conservative value chain, conservatives have made major investments in academia, particularly in the field of law and economics. Progressives, though no strangers to university funding, have not made the strategic connection between the raw materials developed in academia and the finished products developed elsewhere. Progressive leaders see academic research as disconnected and impractical. For their part, progressive-minded academics fear that being connected to policy-making will soil their academic credentials. A well known progressive academic and columnist told me her tenure committee strongly urged her against writing a column as it would likely discredit her among her fellow intellectuals. These factors rob us of intellectual capital just when we need it the most.

Luckily we are beginning to correct this imbalance. And a few highly strategic funders have recognized that academic research is a critical long-term imperative. Enterprising entrepreneurs are re-connecting academics with policy professionals. In addition, many think tanks—the next step in the value chain—have begun to make a more concerted effort to reach out to academics. And finally, academics seeing the grave challenges we face—and the harm wrought by a one-sided intellectual debate—have begun to weigh in more often on the public conversation.

Transforming these raw materials into **finished products and marketing** them is typically done in think tanks. Think tanks identify ideas with potential resonance, translate them into specific policies and then develop marketing campaigns to promote them.

Social security privatization, welfare reform, "activist judges" and "strict constructionist" constitutional interpretation, preemption and the "death tax" are just a few of the finished products developed and marketed by organizations in the conservative value chain. Social security privatization[3] for example, began its rise thirty years ago as an academic paper by a Harvard Law School student. **The Cato Institute** recognized the power of the idea, and, with a $5,000 grant, turned the idea into a book. Cato then marketed the concept through

a conference and a follow-up paper calling for "guerilla warfare" against social security. Cato joined forces with the **Heritage Foundation** and the **American Enterprise Institute (AEI)** to drive the idea into the public debate. Several years later George W. Bush became a leading "spokesman" for the idea, "selling" this product during his first run for president. Similarly, welfare reform began as an idea which was explored by Charles Murray in the conservative journal *The Public Interest*. The 1984 article attracted the attention of **The Manhattan Institute**, a conservative think tank. With $30,000 of research support from the Olin Foundation and $25,000 of marketing support from the Smith Richardson Foundation, Murray turned the idea into a book called *Losing Ground*. The book was marketed effectively to political candidates and the public. Twelve years later this once-radical idea became a cornerstone public policy proposal for a *Democratic* president.

For many years conservative institutions like the Heritage Foundation, AEI and the Cato Institute had little competition. But things are starting to change. Founded four years ago, the **Center for American Progress (CAP)** has quickly become a dynamic hub for progressive product development and marketing. A multi-issue think tank, CAP credits include "strategic redeployment" and the framework for the health care proposals of all

[3] Birnbaum, Jeffrey. "Private-Account Concept Grew From Obscure Roots." *Washington Post*. Feb. 22, 2005.

three major Democratic presidential candidates. CAP's rapid response and media booking capacities generated over 5,000 press mentions so far this year. The CAP blog is one of the top 25 blogs on the internet. One of my experts put it this way: "We used not to have a response, and now we do."

On the legal front, the **American Constitution Society (ACS)** is working to counter the conservative **Federalist Society**. **ACS** is promoting liberal constitutional interpretation in its 127 law school chapters and 30 lawyer chapters across the country in an effort to counter the stranglehold conservative ideology has on the courts. And **The Brennan Center for Justice at NYU Law School,**[4] long respected for constitutional litigation, especially on campaign finance reform, is developing ideas around presidential power, checks and balances, electoral system reform and the judicial system. Brennan has greatly enhanced its communications capacity, bringing several senior communications experts into its senior management. In another long-neglected area, the national security arena, the **National Security Network** and the **Truman Project** are developing policy analysis, publishing papers and providing media training and booking for progressive national security/foreign policy experts. Economic powerhouses **Center for Budget and Policy Priorities** and the **Economic Policy Institute (EPI)** have

also begun to focus more attention on marketing. EPI, for example, has formed a strategic alliance with the **Campaign for America's Future Institute**, a major marketing capacity. In addition, both institutions have expanded their operations to include work in several key states.

There are several ways to **market** ideas: blogs, news articles, op-eds, radio and television appearances, documentary films, forums, expert briefings, etc. One of the most effective ways to launch a big idea is through a book. The conservative **Manhattan Institute** puts it this way: "Books are central to our approach. We make every effort to ensure that our authors are published by respected trade publishers and that their books receive as much review attention and publicity as possible. Nothing allows us to make a sustained, comprehensive argument more effectively."

Think of a book as a big loaf of bread. Some people want to eat the whole loaf, others want a slice with peanut butter and others just want a tiny crumb. A book can launch a big idea (loaf) that is then promoted through an article or an op-ed (slice) and then highlighted through a news show in a 15 second sound bite (crumb). **The Nation Institute** understands the power of books so well it created its own publishing arm, most recently supporting Jeremy Scahill's exposé on the country's largest mercenary

---

[4] The Brennan Center for Justice is a client of The Tesseract Group.

army. *Blackwater* won the coveted George Polk Book Award, and Scahill's subsequent Congressional testimony helped propel legislation that would ban U.S. government security contracts with Blackwater and other private military companies. The newly launched **Progressive Book Club** is focused on strategically marketing progressive books across the country. Of course, books aren't the only way to launch ideas. *Democracy: A Journal of Ideas* is a quarterly publication that offers readers shorter form arguments around important ideas.

Progressives have a variety of potential customers, and several organizations specialize in **distributing** products to these various customers. While it is not entirely accurate in the world of ideas to differentiate between marketing and distribution, I do so here in order to highlight some of the organizations that specialize in moving ideas to specific audiences.

Recognizing the incredible potential in the progressive-leaning single women market segment, **Women's Voices. Women Vote** brings rigorous testing to a variety of efforts to give women "20 million reasons to vote." **ACORN** specializes in reaching low and moderate income families. It is one of the nation's largest community organizations with more than 350,000 member families organized in 850 neighborhood chapters in over 100 cities. **US Action** works with like-minded community groups across the country. **Democracia** specializes in

Latinos, the fastest growing group in the country, many of whom are new unaffiliated citizens. **Catholics in Alliance for the Common Good, Sojourners,** and **Faith in Public Life** work in different but complementary ways to reach communities of faith, a once conservative stronghold. **Vote Vets** focuses on security-minded individuals and the military communities. Political powerhouse **Moveon.org** helps citizens "find their political voice" and engages them in a meaningful way in the political process. **Third Way** specializes in "wholesale" distributing, working closely with a variety of elected officials particularly on security and cultural wedge issues.

Of course a sales effort is only as good as the list that supports it. **Catalist** combines a comprehensive national database of all voting-age individuals in the United States with the tools and expertise needed to use the database effectively. The organization currently boasts a client list of dozens of the country's leading political organizations.

The groups mentioned, and others in this book, have created a permanent capacity for progressives to communicate their values and to distribute ideas 365 days a year every year.

A few years ago, progressives started to do a lot of collective hand wringing about the fact that we were "merely" an assortment of interest groups. This hand-wringing, while understandable, was misplaced.

The problem was not the single issue groups, but rather the fact that we didn't have anything *but* single issues groups. We were missing intellectual and policy foundations, and communications capacity. These missing elements are coming together now and the combination is proving potent. In addition, several of the single issue groups are now working together much more effectively, for example, maximizing their marketing dollars by coordinating activities through **America Votes**, a "table" where the various groups meet and share information.

In addition, single issue groups like the women's movement, the labor movement, the civil rights movement and the environmental movement are, at their heart, not interests, but *ideals* expressed through different lens. The women's movement revolves around the integrity of the individual and personal domain. The labor movement is really about fairness and the dignity of work. The civil rights movement is about justice and participation. And putting a bow on the whole exercise is the environmental movement which works to keep things going so that what we don't achieve in this generation, we will have a chance to achieve in the next.

Despite our best efforts, there are several potential supporters we will never reach individually. The political **"market"** for most Americans is mainstream media. For anyone still under the illusion that mainstream media is a "liberal" institution, please read Eric Alterman's *What Liberal*

Media? or David Brock's *The Right Wing Noise Machine,* or watch **Brave New Films' *Out-Foxed**. This informative documentary shows how easy it is to change the public debate. All you have to do is buy your own network, staff it with journalistically-lax ideologues, feign balance by countering your beefy conservative commentators with inept, no-name liberals and then spend billions of dollars building market share.

Another way to change the public debate is to strategically invest in niche media with journalistically-sound investigative reporting capacities, understanding that by amplifying well-researched, credible stories effectively in niche media, we can drive stories into the mainstream. **The Nation Magazine, The American Prospect**, and others have very strong (though underfinanced) investigative capacities. Important stories uncovered through these platforms are amplified through the **Huffington Post**, **Daily Kos**, **Air America Radio** and other media vehicles. If you doubt the value of this strategy, consider the fact that the investigative reporting of the political blog **Talking Points Memo** led directly to the resignation of Attorney General Alberto Gonzales.

Recognizing both the importance of investigative reporting and the fact that most Americans get their news from local newspapers, **The Center for Independent Media (CIM)** trains state-based bloggers in the art of investigative reporting, aggregates their content into a single state-based portal blog and then amplifies the content into the major state-wide news outlets. CIM is now active in Iowa, Colorado, Minnesota, New Mexico, Michigan and Washington, DC. **Progressnow.org**, another state-focused organization, amplifies important stories into its internet based communities in states across the country.

Investigative reporting isn't the only tool. **Citizens for Responsibility and Ethics in Washington (CREW)** uses research, litigation and media outreach to bring unethical conduct to the public's attention. CREW credits include writing the ethics complaint against Congressman Tom Delay, suing the Executive Office of the President and the National Archives and Records Administration for missing emails and serving as lead counsel in the lawsuit of Valerie Plame Wilson and former Ambassador Joseph Wilson against Vice President Dick Cheney, "Scooter" Libby, Karl Rove and others.

But uncovering new information is not enough; in order to create a fair market of ideas, we must also stop the flow of *mis*information. **Media Matters for America (MMFA)** is an internet-based media watchdog group that monitors, analyzes and corrects conservative misinformation in the U.S. media. Among its successes, MMFA revealed Don Imus' "nappy headed hos" comment, exposed White House "correspondent" Jeff Gannon as a conservative plant, discredited the book *The Truth*

About Hillary Clinton, prevented Sinclair Broadcasting (which reaches 25% of American households) from airing the anti-John Kerry film *Stolen Honor* and exposed the conservative slant of Sunday news programs through its report "If It's Sunday, It's Conservative."

The real function of these organizations and others like them is to ensure transparency in the marketplace of ideas. Providing good information about the halls of power is one of the essential roles of the progressive infrastructure.

People often complain that politics is a personality contest, and there is some truth to this. But what they miss is that while politics is a personality contest, it isn't a *personal* personality contest.

Nike picked Michael Jordan not because he could *sell* the product, but because he *was* the product. What better person to tell you to "Just Do It," than someone who himself just did it? Michael Jordan is Nike personified. Similarly, George W. Bush is an effective spokesman for conservatism because he is the perfect embodiment of its products. His affected Texas swagger is the preemption doctrine brought to life. His tax policy of "if you inherit it, you deserve it" is hand-in-glove with his own history. He was literally born to "privilege," executive and otherwise. George Bush didn't win because people "wanted to drink a beer with him." John Kerry didn't lose because he was a "French flip-flopper."

George Bush won because he embodied the product he was selling. John Kerry lost because he didn't.

To find the right people for the top of the ticket, we need to build a pipeline of authentic progressives in down-ballot races. **Progressive Majority's** mission is to elect "progressive champions." Progressive Majority recruits and trains progressives to run for office at the state and local levels and has elected 259 people and helped flipped control of four state legislatures and 27 local governments. **Emily's List**, which focuses on pro-choice Democratic women, has helped elect 69 pro-choice Democratic women members of Congress, 13 senators, 8 governors and 364 women to state and local office.

These and other candidates are our Michael Jordans and while we shouldn't expect them to *make* our product, we should expect them to *represent* our product. Finding candidates that embody our best ideals relies on us identifying those ideals, developing the intellectual foundations to support them, creating specific policies to realize them and effectively marketing those policies and the ideals they represent. In short, it requires a value chain.

Business expert Michael Porter, who first popularized the concept of the value chain, believed competitive advantage stemmed both from the ability to perform particular activities and from the ability to manage the linkages between these activities effectively. By the same token, progressives can create a competitive advantage by arranging our thinkers, writers, policy makers, marketers and candidates into a *system* that effectively transforms theories into policies, policies into messages and messages into political power.

The government of the United States has millions of employees, offices around the world and a budget of $3 trillion dollars. It is the single most powerful entity in the world. It can ensure freedom, protect the weak, explore new worlds, create industries, transform economies, cure disease, spread prosperity, re-build war torn nations and even reach the moon. If we can change the leadership of that government, we can change the world.

Just Do It.

LOOKING AHEAD: SUGGESTIONS FOR FUTURE INVESTMENTS

By Erica Payne

Progressives woke up to the need for an infrastructure just a few short years ago. Since then, we have made tremendous progress. But there's much left to do, most of which can be summed up in a single word. More. More thinkers, more writers, more books, more ideas, more messages, more speakers, more leaders, more outreach, more funders, more...

Raw Materials: The raw materials of public policy are political philosophies, economic and social theorems, legal rationales for constitutional interpretation, concepts about the role of government and the role of markets, ideas about individual responsibility to self and others, etc. Funding "pure" research may be less satisfying in the short term than underwriting a media buy, but over the long term, there is no more critical investment. **Find the best brains. Fund them.**

Kill the RFP: There is no way that any funder would have ever thought to issue a Request for Proposal (RFP) looking for two people in their underwear to start a petition drive to censure the President and MoveOn. Even if a progressive funder *had* written such an RFP, there is no way they would have known to send it to Wes Boyd and Joan Blades (the founders of MoveOn.org). As a result, the funder would <u>not</u> have supported one of the most successful new political organizations of the last 50 years. Funders often try to decide what they want to fund and then find someone to do it, to create a bucket and then fill it. But the best entrepreneurs have ideas you never thought of. The best venture capitalists meet dozens of entrepreneurs and read hundreds of business plans. They don't write RFPs. **Kill the RFP; fund entrepreneurs.**

Marketing: Having received a collective whooping from Frank Luntz and other conservative marketing geniuses, progressives have finally embraced marketing fundamentals and integrated them effectively into all of their policy dissemination strategies. *Ha!* Just because every progressive on the planet has read (the back cover of) *Don't Think of an Elephant* by George Lakoff and *The Political Brain* by Drew Westen does not mean they understand marketing. **Embrace the value of marketing and integrate it into policy development from the beginning.** Also, inadequately prepared spokespeople do their issues more harm than good. **Commit to media training and book experts on television only if they have an effective media presence.**

Human Resources: The primary asset of the progressive movement is human capital. The effective development and deployment of that talent is critical. We currently lack any kind of centralized human resource capacity. As such, placement is ad hoc (email: *"desperately seeking a talented* person in policy, development, operations, press"). In addition, functional silos, non-competitive compensation, and other factors cause us to lose some of our most talented professionals in their late 20s and early 30s, prior to their most productive working years. While there are a few promising new leadership development organizations, they largely focus on volunteer recruitment or college/ early career recruitment, which is not sufficient for our current needs. In the short term, we should concentrate on mid-career recruitment and retention where the need is greatest and the return is immediate. **Create a stand-alone organization to serve as a boutique Monster.com for the progressive movement.** Every person in the movement should be catalogued and tracked throughout their career. Persons of particular talent should be flagged, their careers monitored to ensure cross discipline training, appropriate relationship development with movement leaders, heightened compensation, etc to ensure their retention within the movement. **Identify the best talent and cultivate it.**

Further, campaign and campaign committee employees are often paid as contract workers and, as such, many don't receive health benefits. Legions of progressives lose their jobs every November only to be rehired several months later as another campaign season gets underway. We need to bring progressive values to progressive organizations and **level out the business cycles for career**

progressives. At a minimum we should provide health insurance that continues across cycles.

And finally, strong foundations make strong houses. Strong intellectual fundamentals make strong leaders. **Train people in the philosophical and theoretical roots of progressivism.**

Mergers and Acquisitions: The mantra of the last five years has been "let a thousand flowers bloom." Entrepreneurial spirit has created an array of organizations in various issue and functional specialty areas. But not all specialty areas require a separate organization. Many of the groups, particularly those with budgets under $1-2 million, may be more effective as part of a larger institution. A savvy major donor should **analyze the movement as a whole and use financial incentives to encourage organizational mergers** where such activity would create cost savings and the potential for greater impact.

Funding: It almost goes without saying that the progressive infrastructure detailed in these pages is dramatically under-financed compared to its conservative counterpart. Rather than bemoan our relative institutional poverty, we should try to understand and address its root causes. First, many progressive institutions are funded by foundations, rather than individuals. Because foundations tend to give project-specific funding rather than general support grants, progressive institutions lack the flexibility they need to be most effective. Encourage foundations to **give multi-year, general support funding. And encourage progressive organizations to reject foundation project funding if the project is "off-mission."**

Second, progressives have not translated political donors into movement donors. There are about 4,000 people who have given the DNC $10,000 or more during the last two years. Of these, only a small percentage has ever written a check to one of the organizations in this book. The question is why? First, many political donors are unaware of the importance of infrastructure. And second, with some exceptions, the political leadership of the progressive movement has not extended its capital to encourage funding of infrastructure organizations.

In 2002 progressive strategist Rob Stein developed a PowerPoint presentation[5] that detailed the evolution of the conservative intellectual infrastructure *(a paper partially based on this research follows)* and shared his finding with several movement leaders and funders. His research catalyzed a group of major funders to build a donor cooperative. **The Democracy Alliance (DA)** is now the single largest funder of progressive infrastructure. DA Partners have

invested over $100 million in infrastructure organizations and the group is almost single-handedly responsible for highlighting the need for infrastructure in the progressive movement. But one effort is not enough. We must **increase support of cross-movement funding mechanisms, donor recruitment and educational efforts.**

---

[5] For more information on Stein's research see *The Conservative Infrastructure*, a paper of The Tesseract Group, which is based on Stein's work.

IDENTIFYING HIGH PERFORMING ORGANIZATIONS

*by Jerry Hauser and Alison Green
of The Management Center*

In selecting organizations to support, funders should consider strategic factors like the role groups play within the progressive infrastructure and how potential grantees fit with the funders' own areas of interest. Beyond broader strategic considerations, though, funders need to look closely at the performance of the organizations themselves and their ability to deliver consistently outstanding results over time. We believe that funders should seek out and fund organizations that are, or have the potential to become, truly high-performing organizations, and they should leave the rest behind.

We have worked with numerous nonprofit organizations, including some included in this guide.[6] This experience has highlighted several key characteristics shared by high-performing organizations:

- **Leadership** that focuses on results rather than appearances and that exhibits relentless determination in the pursuit of impact;
- **Concrete goals** that provide a meaningful measuring stick against which progress is judged;
- **Execution-oriented management** to turn goals and plans into reality and to minimize the gap between what is supposed to happen in theory and what actually happens in practice;
- **Rigorous people practices** to attract and retain the very best employees and, importantly, to lose the rest; and
- **Performance-oriented cultures** to set a high bar for performance and a premium on learning from experience and improving over time.

Groups don't have to be perfect in all these dimensions, but the more evidence you see of strength in these areas, the more likely it is that the organization will make meaningful change, now and in the future.

What follows is a brief description of each of the key characteristics as well as top line ways to evaluate organizational commitment to extent to which organizations demonstrate each dimension if we were a donor with limited time.

The Prerequisite: Relentlessly Determined Leadership

We have yet to see an organization thrive in the long run without a leader who brings an intense, even obsessive, determination to get results. This determination then exhibits itself in a number of ways. Effective leaders constantly worry about the real impact of their work, rather than appearances. They are often perfectionists and, until they learn how to delegate effectively, may be described by others (or themselves) as control freaks, because they can't stand to see things not go as well

---

[6] The Management Center had no hand is selecting the groups for *The Practical Progressive*.

as possible. When they run into roadblocks that might deter the average person, they persist—and persist, and persist—until they find a way past the obstacle. Because they are determined to be successful, they make hard decisions that may be unpopular (such as abandoning a strategy that isn't producing results) or personally painful (such as letting go a loyal but lower-performing subordinate). They are also fairly ruthless when it comes to identifying ways the organization could perform better, and, again because they are so committed to results, they tend to model a deep commitment to learning from experience and adapting their approach to make it as effective as possible. Leaders need to have other traits—they must be reasonably strong critical thinkers, they must be able to communicate orally and in writing in a way that inspires the confidence and "followership" of others, they must exercise good judgment and they must have at least some ability to see the forest beyond the trees in order to establish a vision for the future—but in our experience, the quality that best differentiates truly effective leaders from the rest is their absolute determination to make an impact:

What to ask to assess leadership:
- What led you to start (or come to lead) this organization?
- What are you trying to achieve this year? What are you worried about? What are you doing about it?
- What are some of the biggest obstacles you've hit in the last couple of years? What did you do to address them?
- Tell me about a difficult decision you had to make recently.
- How would the people around you describe you?

The Four Practices

Even with the relentless drive and other leadership prerequisites in place, great leaders rarely start out as great managers. However, with a bit of help they can put into place four important management practices that we've seen help translate their drive and determination into strong results over time.

Practice #1: Adopting Ambitious Goals and Clear Plans

High-performing organizations establish concrete goals for what they will accomplish and then develop plans for how they will get there. Their goals are neither vague ("promote better housing for low-income residents") nor unrealistic ("secure high-quality health care for all residents by the end of next year"). Rather, strong goals establish a clear finish line that lies at the intersection of ambition and realism ("by the end of 2008, double the number of on-the-record supporters for our housing bill in the state senate from 12 to 24 so that we are in position to get it passed in 2009").

Plans stem from the goals and focus the attention of the staff so that everyone knows where energy should and should not go ("we will mobilize at least 5 influential citizens in each of our target 18 state senatorial districts; we will not conduct direct mail campaigns to build our base"). At the more detailed level they establish who will do what by when ("Kathy will meet with heads of each allied organization to develop list of targeted 'influentials' to pursue by Feb. 1"). Plans also change over time in light of progress, whereas goals generally remain fixed. ("We realized we also need broader pressure to get additional senators on board, so we will focus on generating editorials in both of the statewide newspapers.") Finally, organizational goals and plans align with more specific ones assigned to heads of departments, and those goals and plans then translate to the individual staff member level.

Having seen organizations with goals that sounded impressive but real-world results that were not, we'd add one final note: goals are only as powerful as they are genuinely-held. That is, goals need to represent what the leaders of the organization truly believe would represent meaningful progress. They should not merely predict results that would have come about no matter what, having been put on a page simply to satisfy funders. Rather, goals need to represent serious growth in impact, and leaders of the organization must be deeply committed to doing what it takes to reach them.

What to ask to assess goals:
• What were your goals for last year? To what extent did you achieve them?
• What will success look like for you this year? Why is that important?

How hard will it be to get there?
• How were those goals developed? Were there targets you considered setting, but ultimately rejected? (You're looking for rigorous back-and-forth and debate, not just pro forma process.)
• What's an example of a goal you didn't meet? (A group that truly stretches itself likely won't meet all goals, but you're looking for evidence that it re-strategizes in such a case.)
• If I were to ask your head of communications (for instance) what her goals are, what would she say?

Practice #2: Managing for Execution

Even the most compellingly articulated goals and plans can fail to drive action unless they're accompanied by strong day-to-day management practices. In order to ensure that goals are translated into action and lead to results, organizations must carry out the day-to-day work effectively—which often leads managers to adopt a relatively hands-on management style. This means they reach agreement with their staff about outcomes on the front-end, they get their hands dirty and check in periodically (before it is too late) to see how work is proceeding along the way and to help their staff adapt tactics as needed, and they reflect on lessons at the end and hold staff accountable for results.

What to ask to assess management for execution:

- *Tell me about a project you undertook recently.*
  - *What was the vision for it?*
  - *What happened?*
  - *How did you ensure that happened? (You're looking for managers who leave little to chance: either they have good reason to rely on the person in charge of the project, or they keep their hands on things enough to ensure success.)*
  - *How do you know it happened?*
  - *What lessons did you take away?*
- (Depending on the above) Tell me about a particularly unsuccessful (or successful) project you undertook. What went wrong (or what worked)?

You can also get information about an organization's ability to execute by how it handles its interactions with you. Do staffers get back to you, and do what they say they're going to do? If you ask them to send you something, does it arrive promptly and in the form you requested? Is it well organized? While these may seem like small details, you can often extrapolate from these sorts of things into how the group operates on a larger level.

Practice #3: Committing to Great People

Rigorous people practices are critical for building a team of talented staffers who can propel organizations to the highest levels. This means that rather than simply posting openings on popular websites and selecting the best from whoever happens to apply, organizations proactively identify and aggressively recruit individuals who would be outstanding. It also means going to great lengths to retain high-performers, often offering them rapidly-increasing responsibility over time. Finally, and least commonly, it means quickly transitioning out staff who don't meet a high bar for performance—not only the egregiously weak (like those who can't get to work on time or who miss critical deadlines) but also the mediocre, like the communications director who can draft a press release but can't do anything beyond the basics to actually get a story placed.

What to ask to assess people practices:

- How would you describe the bar for performance here?
- Who are your best people? What are you doing to retain them?
- *Tell me about your most recent high-level hire. How did you go about searching for the person? You're looking for active headhunting, not just mass marketing and taking whatever applicants come along.*
- When was the last time you fired someone or coached someone out? How many people have you fired in the last two years? Why? *You're looking for an organization that fires people who don't perform at a high standard.*

Note that the lesson above about judging an organization from your own interactions applies here as well. Beyond the leader, are you impressed with the caliber of the staff with whom you come into contact?

Practice #4: Inculcating Cultures of Performance

In high-performing organizations, messages about "how we do things here" come through loud and clear, beginning at the top with the organization's leadership. These messages are transmitted through the hundreds of daily signals that managers send in their actions and words. While each organization will have its own unique values, top-performing organizations place a heavy emphasis on achieving results and on constantly improving over time.

What to ask to assess culture:

- How would you and other people who work here describe the culture? *Listen to references to high standards and a constant striving for excellence.*
- What are some examples of how that plays out? *For instance, a high-performing organization might tell you that staffers know that if they do a mediocre job on a project, they'll need to redo it, that halfhearted work won't be accepted and they'll be held accountable for their performance.*
- What's an example of when something happened that wasn't consistent with the culture, and what happened?
- What kind of person wouldn't fit in here?

What You Are NOT Looking For

Just as we have found certain characteristics and practices to be essential, we have also found a number of traits that, contrary to conventional wisdom, do not differentiate high performing organizations from others. Given that, we would caution against letting either the presence or absence of these have a significant impact on your funding decisions. Among others, beware of being overly swayed by the following:

Charismatic leaders: Strong leaders do not need to be charismatic, as long as they are able to inspire "followership," meaning that people in and around the organization respect their determination, judgment and ability to get things done.

Formal staff development programs: At strong organizations, staffers get developed and grow significantly. Rather than through formal programs, mentorships or large investments in "on the side" staff training, the real growth most commonly happens via pursuit of ambitious goals and reflection with a manager who holds staff members to a high standard and gives feedback based on what is and is not leading staff members to reach their goals.

Low staff turnover: Strong organizations believe ih "good turnover," the coaching out of employees who aren't meeting a high bar and the retention of high performers. Often, in fact, little or no turnover is a bad sign, since no one is perfect in hiring, and no turnover can mean that an organization does little to correct hiring mistakes.

Hands-off management and an emphasis on employee autonomy: At strong organizations, managers are likely to be hands-on in making sure that they're on the same page as their staff, in monitoring the execution of the work, and in creating accountability—because, frankly, things need to get done. Staff empowerment comes from having great people with clear responsibility for ambitious goals who are held accountable for reaching those goals, but "empowerment" is often not an end in itself.

As you make your funding decisions, we encourage you to look for evidence of the factors we describe here, and then to take one final step—consider what can be changed and what cannot in an organization and its leadership. We have seen that it is possible for leaders to learn skills like developing solid goals and plans, delegating well, recruiting top talent, and having tough conversations with low performers. We have also discovered that there are certain qualities that simply cannot be taught—caring that goals represent meaningful progress and not merely nice-sounding deliverables for a donor, being motivated by results and working hard to achieve them, modeling and holding others to high standards and regularly reflecting on and learning from experience. In making your decisions, look first for evidence of the non-teachable qualities. Then, support these organizations and their leaders as they develop the skills they need to get great results over time.

THE CONSERVATIVE INFRASTRUCTURE

*With Brittany Charlton,
Jonathan Milgrom
and Jennifer Romanek
of The Tesseract Group*

*This paper draws on the extraordinary
research of former Clinton
Administration official Rob Stein
who provided an early and critical
analysis of the conservative intellectual
infrastructure and its "money matrix."
Stein's important work helped galvanize
progressive.funding, long-range
planning and catalyze progressive
institution building. Stein is the Founder
of the Democracy Alliance and serves
on the Board of the organization.*

Impetus for Change:
LBJ versus Goldwater

Following the death of President
John F. Kennedy and his succession
by Lyndon B. Johnson in 1963,
the Democratic Party experienced
an immense popularity. In 1964,
Republicans searched desperately
for a candidate strong enough to run
against the incumbent Democrat
Johnson. Nelson Rockefeller and Barry
Goldwater emerged from the pack.[1]

The two candidates embodied different
political outlooks which mirrored
the intense polarization that had
developed between moderate and
conservative Republicans in preceding
years. Rockefeller, a moderate who
found his support primarily in the
Northeast, espoused the ideology of

more liberally-minded conservatives,
supporting initiatives to expand
government infrastructure and social
welfare programs. Goldwater, on
the other hand, embraced highly
conservative ideals and drew his
support from Middle America, favoring
low taxes, small federal government,
individual rights, business interests
and opposing social welfare programs.
Although they came from the same
party, the two candidates represented
very different political platforms.[2]

The Republican Primary and National
Convention illuminated the rift that had
developed in Republican thought. With
a 51% to 49% victory in California,
Goldwater eked out the Republican
nomination. At the Republican National
Convention, Rockefeller's speech
embracing moderate ideals was
met with "boos" from conservative
Republicans in the San Francisco
convention hall.[3] So goes the idiom,
a house divided cannot stand.
Goldwater resoundingly lost the
presidential election to Johnson, with
the Electoral College voting 486—52
in Johnson's favor.[4] The enormity of
this victory sent chills through the
conservative elite and convinced
them a strategy change was in order.

Blueprint for Power:
The Powell Memo

After the 1964 defeat, conservative
business leaders grew increasingly
fearful that the free enterprise system
was under attack. At the behest of
Eugene Sydnor, Jr., Director of the
U.S. Chamber of Commerce, Lewis
Powell crafted a strategy memo to

counter this perceived challenge. At the time, Powell was a corporate lawyer for the Phillip Morris Corporation and board member of eleven corporations. It was two months prior to Powell's nomination by President Nixon to the U.S. Supreme Court.[5]

The memo, dated August 23, 1971, says, "survival of what we call the free enterprise system…lies in… organization, in careful long-range planning and implementation, in consistency of action over an indefinite period of years, in the scale of financing available only through joint effort, and in the political power available only through united action and national organizations."[6] In the memo, Powell cautioned that the American free enterprise economic system was "under broad attack…[by] Leftists and other revolutionaries."[7] He found liberal influences on college campuses particularly disconcerting, citing a study which demonstrated that 50% of college students "favored socialization of some basic U.S. industries," and enumerating prominent college professors who embraced liberal ideals.[8] Powell suggested that liberal students would, after graduation, seek employment "in the centers of real power and influence in our country namely: with the news media, especially television, in government as staffers and consultants at various levels, in elective politics, as lecturers and writers and on the faculties at various levels of education."[9] His fear was that, so situated, they would then shift the American political paradigm even further to the left.

Powell believed corporate America was neither "trained nor equipped to conduct guerilla warfare" with the burgeoning progressive movement. According to Powell, business leaders were simply trained to "be good citizens." In a rallying cry, he said, "the time has come—indeed it is long overdue—for the wisdom, ingenuity and resources of American business to be marshaled against those who [oppose] it."[10] In Powell's eyes, it was time for an all out, no-holds-barred war between corporate conservatives and the liberal establishment.

Powell's memo laid out a plan of coordinated attack believing that "independent and uncoordinated activity by individual corporations, [although necessary, would] not be sufficient. Strength [laid] in organization, in careful long-range planning and implementation, in consistency of action over an indefinite period of years, in the scale of financing available only through joint effort and the attainment of political power available only through united action and national organizations."[11] In other words, Powell understood that organizing a conservative infrastructure was integral to regaining and maintaining widespread influence.

The Powell Memo provided a blueprint for the creation of a set of institutions that together could change the public debate. To combat liberal influences on college campuses, Powell suggested that the National Chamber of Commerce establish a staff of reputable scholars to create ideology, a staff of cogent speakers to articulate the message of the scholars, a speakers bureau composed of upper echelon American businessmen to address students as guest lecturers on college campuses and a panel of academics to evaluate liberal biases in college-level textbooks. Powell urged the National Chamber of Commerce to pressure colleges and universities to balance their faculties among liberal and conservative professors.[12]

To combat liberal influences in the general public, Powell suggested that the National Chamber of Commerce monitor television networks for liberal bias and provide feedback to the Federal Communications Commission, create incentives to encourage greater publication from conservatives in scholarly journals, distribute pro-corporation documents to news stands and devote ten percent of American businesses' budgets to general corporate advertisement of the "overall purpose."[13] To combat liberal influences in court, like the American Civil Liberties Union, Powell suggested that the National Chamber of Commerce assemble a team of highly competent lawyers funded by corporate America. Lastly, he advised corporations to exert greater influence on stockholders through shareholder reports and by assembling a national organization of stockholders via the Chamber of Commerce.[14]

The Beginning

In 1973, just two years after Powell passed along his recommendations to Sydnor, two Washington aides, Paul Weyrich and Edwin Fuelner, discussed the ideas expressed in the Memo with renowned conservative beer baron Joseph Coors. After describing in vivid, fear-mongering detail the impending crash course of the American economic system, Weyrich and Feulner received a $250,000 grant from Coors to build a conservative think tank. The think tank was called the Heritage Foundation.

Though Weyrich and Feulner did not officially launch the Heritage Foundation until Coors' donation in 1973, the pair had been planning for Heritage while working on Capitol Hill. The men decided that Republicans needed a research organization possessing what Feulner called a "quick response capability."[15] A few months later, Colorado Republican Senator Gordon Allott, then Weyrich's employer, told Weyrich that Joseph Coors had been "stirred" by Lewis Powell's "call to arms against the critics of free enterprise and had become convinced that business was 'ignoring' a crisis."[16]

Officially, the mission of the Heritage Foundation is to "to formulate and promote conservative public policies based on the principles of free enterprise, limited government, individual freedom, traditional American values and a strong national defense."[17]

The think tank has played a central role in conservative politics, producing a steady flow of policy guidelines and suggestions aimed at presenting right-wing positions in a salient, saleable manner.

Weyrich served as Heritage's first president in 1973. After only a year in that capacity, he moved on, forming the Committee for the Survival of a Free Congress with backing from the Coors fortune.[18] The committee sought to influence the electoral process through fundraising, outreach, education, recruitment and grassroots organizing and kept Weyrich enormously prominent in the conservative infrastructure. In 1977, Feulner assumed control of Heritage. Feulner proved to be an extraordinary promoter and fundraiser who appreciated the mobilizing power of ideas. In his first four years at the Heritage Foundation, Feulner raised Heritage's annual budget from $1,008,557 to just over $7.1 million.[19] Feulner was not only able to lure support from tremendously wealthy family foundations like the John M. Olin Foundation and the Smith Richardson Foundation, but also from Fortune 500 corporations and banks including General Motors, Ford Motors, Procter and Gamble, Chase Manhattan Bank, Dow Chemical, the Reader's Digest Association, Mobil Oil, Pfizer and Sears.[20]

In addition to developing Heritage's substantial endowment, Feulner also established Heritage's innovative style, focusing on producing article-length policy recommendations on current legislative and foreign policy issues known as "backgrounders." This novel system revolutionized the way that information penetrated the policy process, as it ensured that arguments bolstering the conservative party could be rapidly sent and easily digested by politicians, public officials and journalists. In the words of Heritage Foundation President Edwin J. Feulner, "We don't just stress credibility....We stress an efficient, effective delivery system. Production is one side; marketing is equally important."[21] These backgrounders grew increasingly important towards the end of the 1970s. When the Reagan administration and Senate Republicans took power in 1980, Heritage incorporated current backgrounders into a massive compilation known as the *Mandate for Leadership*.

The 1,077 page, twenty-volume *Mandate* represented a set of 2,000 policy recommendations which served as a roadmap for Reagan's presidency. These recommendations included rolling back minority programs, dramatically increasing military spending and cutting taxes. In 1984, just before Reagan's re-election, Heritage published *Mandate for Leadership II*, which recommended privatization of social security and denial of special educational funding for the handicapped. In 1985, following Reagan's first term and subsequent reelection, Heritage claimed that, between 1981 and 1985, the Reagan administration enacted 60—65% of the suggested policies from the first *Mandate for Leadership*.[22]

Throughout the 1980s and early 1990s, the Heritage Foundation functioned as the key architect and advocate of the "Reagan Doctrine," under which the United States government supported anti-Communist resistance movements in such places as Afghanistan, Angola, Cambodia and Nicaragua. Heritage's foreign policy analysts provided guidance to anti-communist rebel forces, including the Nicaraguan contras and Jonas Savimbi's Unita movement in Angola, and to dissidents in Eastern bloc nations and Soviet republics. Ultimately, Heritage managed to win both covert and overt United States support for so-called "wars of liberation" against Soviet-aligned states around the world. Throughout the late 1980s and early 1990s, Heritage's support for the contras and Angola's Savimbi proved extremely influential with the United States government, including the Central Intelligence Agency, the Defense Intelligence Agency and the National Security Council. Disturbingly, after Heritage presented its case for armed support for these movements, U.S. support followed.[23] The Heritage Foundation played an instrumental role in advancing and upholding Reagan's controversial description of the former U.S.S.R. as an "evil empire" whose defeat, as opposed to mere containment, was the most pertinent avenue of foreign policy to pursue. This policy served as the justification for the Star Wars anti-ballistic missile defense system which the Heritage Foundation still pursues today.[24]

Following the collapse of the Soviet Union in 1991, Heritage advised Newt Gingrich and other conservatives on the development of the *Contract with America*, which was credited with helping to produce a Republican majority in Congress. The *Contract* represented a pact of principles that directly challenged both the political status-quo in Washington and many of the ideas at the heart of the Clinton administration, which was then assuming office after George H.W. Bush's defeat. As such, while Heritage is still officially a non-partisan think tank, it is often credited with supplying many of the ideas that ultimately ended the Democrats' forty year reign of Congressional control in 1994.[25]

Elements of the Conservative Infrastructure

The most important thing to understand about the Heritage Foundation is that it is only one of a myriad of similarly well-funded organizations developing and promoting conservative economic and legal theory. These organizations include:[26]

- Heritage Foundation: $32.9[27] million annual budget
- American Enterprise Institute: $17.6 million annual budget
- Cato Institute: $17.6 million annual budget
- Hoover Institution: $30.6 million annual budget

- Manhattan Institute:
  $8 million annual budget
- Hudson Institute:
  $7 million annual budget
- Reason Foundation:
  $4.8 million annual budget
- Freedom Works:
  $3.8 million annual budget
- Pacific Research Policy Center:
  $4 million annual budget
- Citizens Against Government Waste:
  $5 million annual budget
- National Center for Policy Analysis:
  $4.9 million annual budget
- Competitive Enterprise Institute:
  $4 million annual budget

The American Enterprise Institute (AEI) is an extremely influential, pro-business right-wing think tank that predates Heritage, having been founded in 1943 by asbestos manufacturer Lewis Brown. AEI is intimately connected to the power brokers of the neoconservative movement. Irving Kristol, widely regarded as the movement's founder, is a Senior Fellow at AEI. Other current or former AEI staff who are prominent neoconservatives include Michael Novak and Richard Perle. AEI has emerged as one of the leading architects of the second Bush administration's public policy, and over twenty AEI alumni and current visiting scholars and fellows have served either in a Bush administration policy post or on one of the government's seemingly vast array of panels and commissions. Former United States Deputy Secretary of Defense Paul Wolfowitz is a visiting scholar, and

Lynne Cheney, wife of Vice President Dick Cheney and former chairman of the National Endowment for the Humanities, is a senior fellow.[28]

The Cato Institute is a non-profit think tank with strong libertarian leanings, oftentimes on behalf of its anti-regulation corporate funders like the tobacco industry. Cato advocates policies that advance "individual liberty, limited government, free markets and peace." This translates into policy proposals in favor of abolishing the minimum wage, corporate welfare and trade barriers, diminishing federal government involvement in the marketplace and in local and state issues and enhancing school choice via vouchers.[29] Cato's legacy dates back to its founding in 1977, at a time when the conservative movement was heavily influenced by libertarian ideals. However, Cato's relationship with today's Republican Party is more tenuous than in the past, as power has shifted from staunchly anti-government leaders like Barry Goldwater and Ronald Reagan, to pro-interventionist neoconservatives like George W. Bush. In recent years, Cato's non-interventionist foreign policy views, and strong support for civil liberties, have frequently led them to criticize those in power, Republican and Democrat. Cato scholars opposed President George H. W. Bush's 1991 Gulf War operations, President Clinton's interventions in Haiti and Kosovo and President George W. Bush's 2003 invasion of Iraq. On the other hand, Cato scholars supported the 2001 invasion of Afghanistan as a response to the terrorist attacks of September 11, 2001. Cato scholars have been similarly critical of recent perceived infringements upon American's civil liberties, speaking out against the USA Patriot Act, imprisonment of so-called "unlawful enemy combatants" and the Bush Administration's aggressive assertions of unilateral executive authority.[30]

The Hoover Institution on War, Revolution and Peace at Stanford Universitywas founded in 1919 by Herbert Hoover. The Hoover Institution is especially influential in the American neoconservative movement, and has, throughout George W. Bush's term, represented the "conservative think tank President Bush looks to for ideas."[31] Hoover boasts its strong ties between right-wing ideologues, right-wing think tanks and right-wing policy makers, and many of its scholars have worked for various Republican Presidential Administrations, including Nixon, Ford, Reagan, George H.W. Bush and George W. Bush. With eight current Hoover Fellows sitting on Bush's Defense Policy Board, as well as several current and former associates like Donald Rumsfeld and Condoleezza Rice serving in the country's highest policy-making posts, the influence of Hoover is difficult to overestimate.[32] While it is best known for its focus on foreign and defense policies, "Hoover...has focused particular attention on tax policy, promoting the flat tax for well

over a decade and organizing policy briefings and conferences on the issue...It was, according to one well-placed journalist and author, one of four leading policy institutions that pulled the nation's economic policy debate to the right in the early 1980s."[33]

Today's Conservative Message Machine

The network of conservative message makers, advocates, elite journals, professional networks and legal/media monitors enjoy a combined annual operating budget of around $400 million.[34] Together, these elements constitute a value chain that develops, promotes and distributes conservative public policy. Ideas formulated by think tanks are disseminated first to elite journals such as the *Weekly Standard*, *National Review* and *American Spectator*.[35] These ideas cover the policy landscape, with some of the "top hits" including:

• "Blueprint for America"
• Less government/lower taxes
• De-regulation
• "Defund the Left"
• Chilling The "Liberal" Media
• "Contract With America"
• Welfare Reform
• "Death" Tax
• "Compassionate Conservatism"
• School Vouchers
• Social Security Privatization
• Military "Preemption" Doctrine

After gaining traction in the elite journals, ideas then flow to those mass media outlets that form part of the conservative infrastructure, including Fox Television News, Scarborough Country MSNBC, The Rush Limbaugh Show, Radio America, *The Wall Street Journal* editorial page, *The Washington Times* and websites such as Townhall.com and AnnCoulter.org. Also important here are groups in charge of liberal media mongering. These include:

- Center for Study of Popular Culture:
  $2.8 million[36] annual budget
- Media Research Center:
  $6 million annual budget
- Accuracy in the Media:
  $1.3 million annual budget
- Center for Media and Public Affairs:
  $1 million annual budget

Legal advocacy groups play an important part in the machine, monitoring judiciary hearings and providing support for conservative causes, further reinforcing the machine. The most important of the groups are:

- Center for Individual Rights:
  $2.1[37] million annual budget
- Pacific Legal Foundation:
  $6.5 million annual budget
- Institute for Justice:
  $4.7 million annual budget
- Landmark Legal Foundation:
  $1.1 million annual budget
- Mountain States Legal Foundation:
  $2.1 million annual budget
- Washington Legal Foundation:
  $3.2 million annual budget

- Judicial Watch:
  $14.3 million annual budget
- Federalist Society:
  $3.6 million annual budget

Additionally, conservative organizations monitoring the liberal media, primarily the Media Research Center, progress the conservative cause by networking with think tanks and legal advocacy groups to diminish the productive propagation of liberal messages.[38]

The $400 million tab incurred by the aggregate of think tanks and universities, elite journals, mass media outlets, legal advocacy groups and liberal media monitors is picked up by wealthy donors and philanthropic foundations.[39] At the heart of this financial support are nine billionaire family foundations including:

- Scaife Family (4 Foundations):[40]
  assets of $305 million
- Bradley Foundation:
  assets of $496 million
- Koch Family (3 Foundations):
  assets of $52 million
- Smith Richardson Foundation:
  assets of $436 million
- John M. Olin Foundation:
  assets of $55 million
- Earhart Foundation:
  assets of $52 million
- Castle Rock Foundation (Coors):
  assets of $55 million
- McKenna Foundation:
  assets of $15 million
- JM Foundation:
  assets of $21 million

Over a seventeen-year period from 1985–2001, these foundations made total grants of $1,659,000,000, of that over $650,000,000 went to the conservative infrastructure. With steady, generous, multi-decade support, these nine billionaire families change the public policy climate of the country. In addition to the nine billionaire families, a few hundred wealthy conservatives are responsible for most of the funding of the conservative infrastructure. The contributions are encouraged by the movement's "investment bankers," leaders like Grover Norquist, Paul Weyerich and Irving Kristol, and by several coordinating groups that help direct and motivate top donors. The most critical of these include:[41]

• The Philanthropy Round Table
• Capital Research Center
• Council for National Policy

The Philanthropy Round Table, for example, serves as a consortium of individual, foundational and corporate donors, including the Coors Foundation that funds conservative causes.[42] The Capital Research Center (CRC) is a non-profit organization, whose supposed purpose is "to study non-profit organizations, with a special focus on reviving the American traditions of charity, philanthropy and voluntarism." The CRC also investigates what the organization deems "viable private alternatives to government regulatory and entitlement programs."[43] From their own mission statement, the sole purpose of the CRC is to restore "traditional American values of individual responsibility and free choice," in other words, the same sentiments echoed in the Powell memo on free enterprise.

Of particular note is the secretive Council for National Policy (CNP), which may be the most influential of the conservative network. "[F]ew people, outside its members, seem to know what the group is, what it does, how it raises money and how interlocked it has become in the matrix of conservative activism."[44] CNP was reportedly conceived in 1981 "by at least five fathers, including the Reverend Tim LaHaye, an evangelical preacher who was then the head of the Moral Majority." Paul Weyrich, a familiar name from the Heritage Foundation, "took responsibility for bringing together the best minds of conservatism, and his imprint on the group's mission is unmistakable: It provided a forum for religiously engaged conservative Christians to influence the geography of American political power."[45] Limited intelligence suggests that this invitation-only society, which meets at thrice-yearly conventions, operates as an arm of the hard right, utilizing its secret meetings to plan its strategy for implementing the radical agenda. It is here, they say, that organizers and activists meet with the financial backers who put up the money to carry out their agenda.

One anecdotal example of the influence exerted by this underground conservative complex is the 1999 CNP meeting in San Antonio, which featured then-GOP presidential candidate George W. Bush as a keynote speaker. Reports on the gathering suggest that "Bush promised the CNP to implement its agenda and vowed to appoint only anti-abortion judges to the federal courts."[46] Soon afterwards, having secured the confidence of critical CNP members, Bush won the Republican Party nomination.

Conclusion

While the conservative movement may have suffered some electoral setbacks in very recent history, it remains one of the most powerful forces in American political life. Combating this well-funded, well-coordinated machine is the work of this generation of progressive leaders.

THE ORGANIZATIONS OF THE PROGRESSIVE INFRASTRUCTURE

21st Century Democrats

ACORN

Advancement Project

Air America

Alliance for Justice

America Votes

American Constitution Society

American Progressive Caucus Policy Foundation

American Prospect

Brave New Films

Brennan Center for Justice at NYU Law

Bus Project

Campaign for America's Future

Catalist

Catholics in Alliance for the Common Good

Center for American Progress

Center for Budget and Policy Priorities and it's State Fiscal Analysis Initiative

Center for Community Change

Center for Independent Media

Center for Progressive Leadership

Century Foundation

Citizens for Tax Justice

Color of Change

CREW

Daily Kos

Democracia

Democracy Alliance

Democracy for America

Democracy: A Journal of Ideas

Demos

Drum Major Institute

Economic Policy Institute and it's Earn Network

Emily's List

FairVote

Faith in Public Life

Free Press

The Gathering

Gill Action

Hamilton Project

Huffington Post

Human Rights Campaign

Human Rights First

Lawyers Committee for Civil Rights Under Law

Leadership Conference of Civil Rights

League of Conservation Voters

League of Young Voters

Media Matters for America

Minnesota 20/20

Mom's Rising

MoveOn

NARAL

The Nation

The Nation Institute

National Congress of Black Women

National Council of La Raza

National Security Network

New Ideas Fund

Planned Parenthood

Progress Now

Progressive Book Club

Progressive Majority

Progressive States Network

Project Vote

Public Campaign

Pushback Network

Rock the Vote

SEIU

Sierra Club

Sojourners

Sunlight Foundation

The Roosevelt Institution

Third Way

Truman Project

USAction

Vote Vets

Western Progress

Women's Voices. Women Vote.

Young Democrats of America

Young People For

2008 ESTIMATED ORGANIZATIONAL BUDGETS

< $500,000
ColorOfChange.org

Daily Kos (noted as "peanuts" in profile)

The New Ideas Fund

$500,000–$1 MILLION
Bus Project

Democracy: A Journal of Ideas

FairVote

Faith in Public Life

Minnesota 2020

The Gathering

Roosevelt Institution

$1–$2MILLION
Catholics in Alliance for the Common Good

Citizens for Tax Justice

Drum Major Institute for Public Policy

National Security Network

Progressive States Network

Truman National Security Project

Western Progress

$2–$5 MILLION
Alliance for Justice

American Prospect

Center for Independent Media

Center for Progressive Leadership

Citizens for Responsibility and Ethics in Washington

Democracia USA

Democracy for America

Free Press

Hamilton Project

League of Young Voters

The Nation Institute

ProgressNow

Pushback Network

Third Way

Vote Vets

Young People For the American Way

Young Democrats of America

$5–$10 MILLION

21st Century Democrats

Advancement Project

American Constitution Society

Brennan Center for Justice

Campaign for America's Future

The Century Foundation

Demos

Economic Policy Institute

Lawyers' Committee for Civil Rights Under Law

Leadership Conference on Civil Rights

League of Conservation Voters

Progressive Majority

Public Campaign

Rock the Vote

Sojourners

The Sunlight Foundation

$10+ MILLION

ACORN

America Votes

Center for American Progress

Center on Budget and Policy Priorities

Center for Community Change

Human Rights Campaign

Human Rights First

MoveOn

NARAL

National Council of La Raza

Project Vote

Sierra Club

The Nation

USAction

Women's Voices. Women Vote

NO ANSWER

Air America Radio

American Progressive Caucus Policy Foundation

Brave New Films

Catalist

Emily's List

Gill Action Fund

Huffington Post

Media Matters for America

MomsRising.org

National Congress of Black Women

Planned Parenthood Federation of America

Progressive Book Club

SEIU

ORGANIZATIONAL FOUNDING YEAR

FOUNDED POST-2002

American Progressive Caucus Policy Foundation (2008)

Brave New Films (2008)

Minnesota 2020 (2007)

Western Progress (2007)

Center for Independent Media (2006)

Hamilton Project (2006)

MomsRising.org (2006)

National Security Network (2006)

Progressive Book Club (2006)

The New Ideas Fund (2006)

The Sunlight Foundation (2006)

Vote Vets (2006)

Catalist (2005)

Catholics in Alliance for the Common Good (2005)

ColorOfChange.org (2005)

Democracy Alliance (2005)

Democracy: A Journal of Ideas (2005)

Faith in Public Life (2005)

Gill Action Fund (2005)

Huffington Post (2005)

Progressive States Network (2005)

Pushback Network (2005)

Third Way (2005)

Truman National Security Project (2005)

The Gathering (2005)

Air America Radio (2004)

Center for Progressive Leadership (2004)

Democracia USA (2004)

Democracy for America (2004)

Media Matters for America (2004)

Roosevelt Institution (2004)

Women's Voices. Women Vote (2004)

Young People For the American Way (2004)

America Votes (2003)

Center for American Progress (2003)

CREW (2003)

Free Press (2003)

League of Young Voters (2003)

ProgressNow (2003)

Daily Kos (2002)

FOUNDED PRE-2002

American Constitution Society (2001)

Bus Project (2001)

Demos (2000)

Advancement Project (1999)

Drum Major Institute for Public Policy (1999)

Progressive Majority (1999)

USAction (1999)

MoveOn (1998)

Brennan Center for Justice at NYU Law (1997)

Public Campaign (1997)

Campaign for America's Future (1996)

FairVote (1992)

American Prospect (1990)

Economic Policy Institute (1986)

21st Century Democrats (1985)

Emily's List (1985)

National Congress of Black Women (1984)

Project Vote (1982)

Center on Budget and Policy Priorities (1981)

Human Rights Campaign (1980)

Rock the Vote (1980)

Alliance for Justice (1979)

Citizens for Tax Justice (1979)

Human Rights First (1978)

Sojourners (1971)

ACORN (1970)

League of Conservation Voters (1970)

NARAL (1969)

Center for Community Change (1968)

The Nation Institute (1966)

Lawyers' Committee for Civil Rights Under Law (1963)

National Council of La Raza (1968)

Leadership Conference on Civil Rights (1950/1969)

SEIU (1921)

The Century Foundation (1919)

Planned Parenthood Federation of America (1916)

Young Democrats of America (1932)

Sierra Club (1892)

The Nation (1865)

Twenty-First Century
Democrats

1731 Connecticut Ave NW
2nd Flr
Washington, DC 20009

☎ 202-626-5620
🖨 202-347-0956
✖ Mark A. Lotwis
@ mark@21stdems.org

💻 21stcenturydems.org
⚷ 1985
📊 $5,700,000
🖧 527 with a Federal PAC

Mark A. Lotwis
Executive Director

Mark A. Lotwis was appointed Executive Director in 2007. Mark is responsible for overseeing the PAC's day to day operations including supervising and hiring staff, fundraising, financial compliance and managing all political, communications and field operations. Mark first joined 21st Century Democrats in 2006 as Executive Vice President.

Previously, Mark was a Partner at Strother Duffy Strother (2004-2006), and a Partner and Senior Vice President at MacWilliams, Robinson & Partners (1998-2004). At both firms, Mark served as a media consultant to numerous Democratic Members of Congress, state and local candidates, environmental organizations and labor unions.

Mark proudly served as Chief of Staff for Rep. Ted Strickland (D-OH) from 1997 to 1998. During the 1994 and 1996 election cycles, Mark served as the Western Field Director and Campaign Planning Director (respectively) at the Democratic Congressional Campaign Committee (DCCC). Mark also managed the successful 1992 re-election campaign of Rep. Louise Slaughter (D-NY). Mark's career in public service began when he was elected Chairman of the Board of Directors of the New Jersey Public Interest Research Group. Mark has a Ph.D. in Political Science from The American University.

What does your organization do and how does it do it?
Our mission is three fold:
• to elect populist progressive Democrats seeking office at the local, state and federal level who will stand up for America's working families and be leaders inside the Democratic Party on Capitol Hill, State Houses,

counties and cities across the country.

- to train the next generation of field organizers who go on to careers in progressive politics and provide the human capital to build the progressive movement.
- to foster our *"21st Century Leaders"* network of the best and brightest progressive elected officials, community activists and campaign operatives.

Our strategy is built on:
- training young campaign staff in field organizing;
- creating comprehensive and accountable grassroots field programs designed to elect progressive candidates on the state and federal level; and
- placing field organizers on the ground in key competitive elections and in battleground states to persuade and identify voters and to turnout the Democratic vote.

How will your organization impact the public debate in 2008?
We will play a key role in winning elections of progressive Democrats by placing trained field organizers and field managers in targeted campaigns. These field organizers will recruit thousands of volunteers and identify 500,000 new Democratic supporters by knocking on one million doors and making two million phone calls.

Our *"21st Century Leaders"* list of the rising stars in the progressive Democratic community will become an explicit alternative to centrist Democratic organizations for up and coming progressive elected officials.

What is your 2008 operating budget?
$5.7 million

Looking out 2-3 years, how would you like to grow/change your organization?
Our legal status as a 527 with a federal PAC allows us to help elect progressives at the state and federal level. In order to maintain our involvement in federal elections, we are required by the Federal Election Commission to pay for our programs on a 50% non-federal ("soft")—50% federal ("hard") split of funds. In the future, we seek to raise more federal money by growing our online fundraising. This in turn will enable us to deliver more political punch to elect progressive Democrats to Congress, and to elect more state legislators who will control redistricting after the next census.

What do you need to do that?
We need an additional financial investment of $500,000 per year in our online communications and marketing programs to build our email activist list and our online fundraising of federal dollars. This investment would allow us to reach millions of progressive activists to support our programs and our endorsed candidates.

21st Century delivers "progressive ground troops." They "don't mess around."

How will your organization change if progressives win in November? If they lose?

Win or lose in 2008, we will expand our training of field organizers to add to our existing network of 4,400+ progressive activists who will become future staff and candidates advancing the progressive agenda. We will expand our *"21st Century Leaders"* network of progressive elected leaders to become mentors to new up and coming progressive candidates who will be the next generation of leaders across America.

If you had to offer some advice to fellow progressives what would it be?

The Democratic Party has lost the last two Presidential elections (and numerous U.S. House, Senate and state legislative elections) because of a misallocation of campaign budgets on negative 30 second TV ads on broadcast TV (that few watch anymore)—leaving limited resources for fundamental field organizing and execution of field programs to have face to face conversations between people.

This reliance on TV advertising has left no lasting progressive infrastructure. The time has come to build the future human capital needed to sustain the progressive movement by training new generations of field organizers and placing them in the field to win critical elections.

Please list your board of directors and their affiliations.

Robert Arbour
President, Triple Net Equities, Inc

Andrew Clubok
Partner, Kirkland & Ellis, LLP

William Combs
Private Democratic Consultant

Jere Glover
Attorney, Brand Law Group

Victoria Hopper
Executive Producer, Easy Rider Productions

Mitch Kaplan
Partner, Kaplan, Stahler, Gumer & Braun Agency

Vincent Panvini
Political Director, Sheet Metal Workers

James Rosapepe
President, Patuxent Group;
State Senator, Maryland

Jim Scheibel
Executive Director, Ramsey Action Program

Mikaela Seligman
Principal, The OCL Group

Liz Smith
Political Director, American Federation of Teachers

ACORN

2-4 Nevins St
Brooklyn, NY 11217

 718-246-7900
 718-246-7939
Steven Kest
@ skest@acorn.org

 acorn.org
 1970
 $50,000,000
Non-profit but not
tax-exempt corporation

Maude Hurd
President

Maude Hurd is the President of ACORN, the Association of Community Organizations for Reform Now, the nation's largest community organization of low-and moderate-income families. Hurd first joined ACORN in 1982, when her neighborhood ACORN chapter marched into City Hall and with bags full of trash collected in their neighborhood and won a clean up program covering 700 vacant lots.

Since she was elected ACORN President in 1990, Hurd has led campaigns for better housing for first time homebuyers, living wages for low-wage workers, reforms from subprime lenders and comprehensive immigration reform.

In 2006, Hurd traveled the country to help launch successful ballot initiative campaigns to raise the minimum wage in several states. Hurd lives in Dorchester, Mass., and works there as a substance-abuse prevention specialist.

What does your organization do and how does it do it?
ACORN, the Association of Community Organizations for Reform Now, is the nation's largest and most successful community organization of low and moderate income families, with more than 400,000 members organized into over 1,000 neighborhood chapters in 110 cities and 41 states across the country. Since 1970 ACORN has been

ACORN is an "indispensable piece" of the progressive puzzle. Their "effective" work represents the "fundamentals of democratic ideals."

building solidly rooted and powerful community organizations that are committed to social and economic justice, and have taken action and won victories on thousands of issues of concern to our members. Our priorities include: decent and affordable housing, for first time homebuyers and tenants; living wages for low-wage workers; an end to predatory financial practices; public schools that work for all students; and a path to citizenship for new immigrants to this country. ACORN achieves these goals by building community organizations that have the power to win changes— through direct action, negotiation, legislation and voter participation.

How will your organization impact the public debate in 2008?
ACORN is running the nation's largest voter registration program, with a goal of registering 1.2 million new low income, African-American and Latino voters this year. Later this fall we will run a massive door-to-door get-out-the-vote program, using trusted messengers to encourage over 2 million neighbors to go to the polls. These voters are demanding that the candidates address issues such as stopping home foreclosures, providing universal health coverage and helping immigrants become citizens.

What is your 2008 operating budget?
$50 million

Looking out 2-3 years, how would you like to grow/change your organization?

In recent years ACORN has been on a significant growth trajectory, doubling the number of offices we are in over the last four years. Over the next 2 years our plan is to increase our membership density within these communities, reaching a membership total that surpasses 1 million, on our way to 5 million members by the middle of the next decade. For poor people especially, there is power in numbers, and ACORN is completely focused on building power for our members and constituency.

What do you need to do that?
We are aggressively recruiting and training full-time community organizers who can build our organization and develop leadership within the neighborhoods where we work. To achieve our membership growth goals, we plan on doubling the number of community organizers who work for ACORN, from 400 to 800.

How will your organization change if progressives win in November? If they lose?
Regardless of whether progressives win or lose, ACORN will remain focused on the same program and goals. We'll play more offense if progressives win, more defense otherwise—but we'd be doing our constituency a disservice if we stopped fighting aggressively on our issues even with progressives in the White House and controlling Congress.

If you had to offer some advice to fellow progressives what would it be?

Message and ideas are important. Communication strategies are important. Inspirational leaders are important. But there can be no long-lasting progressive change without the bottom-up engagement of millions of lower income Americans, and that engagement can only be built through community organizing. We encourage fellow progressives to join us in helping create a culture of democratic participation by supporting the work of community organizations.

Please list your board of directors and their affiliations.
ACORN's board is composed of local grassroots ACORN leaders: two elected representatives from each of our state boards, which in turn are made up of the elected chairpersons of our neighborhood chapters.

 advancementproject.org

📠 202-728-9558 justdemocracyblog.org

1730 M St, NW   ✂ Sabrina E. Williams   ⌐ 1999

Ste 910   @ swilliams@   📊 $6,262,783

Washington DC, 20036 advancementproject.org ⬚ 501(c)(3)

Judith Browne-Dianis Esq. (l)

Penda D. Hair Esq. (r)
Co-directors

Judith Browne-Dianis
Judith Browne-Dianis has an extensive background in civil rights litigation, which includes fighting to protect the rights of displaced Hurricane Katrina survivors. She was instrumental in securing a victory in Kirk v. City of New Orleans, which barred the city from bulldozing homes without first giving home owners opportunity to challenge the demolition. Through litigation, public speaking and field work, Browne-Dianis staunchly advocates justice and equity for displaced New Orleans residents. She also served as co-counsel in NAACP v. Katherine Harris, et al., representing the Florida State Conference of the NAACP and black Floridians in a lawsuit to remedy voting rights violations related to the November 7, 2000 election.

A graduate of Columbia University School of Law and a recipient of the distinguished Skadden Fellowship, Browne-Dianis began her civil rights career at the NAACP Legal Defense and Educational Fund, Inc. (LDF), practicing law in the areas of housing, education, employment and voting rights. In its 30th Anniversary issue in 2000, *Essence* magazine named Browne-Dianis one of "30 Women to Watch" and, in the same issue, featured her in an article defining the Black agenda for the millennium.

Penda D. Hair
Penda D. Hair—an aggressive racial justice advocate with 20 years of civil rights experience—has a stellar record of victories both in and out of court. A leader in the national struggle to protect affirmative action, Hair developed crucial Fair Housing Act amendments, argued major civil rights cases before the U.S. Supreme Court and won the most extensive

THE PRACTICAL PROGRESSIVE

redistricting remedy ever imposed in a litigated voting rights suit.

She is the author of the Rockefeller Foundation's report on innovative civil rights strategies, *Louder Than Words: Lawyers, Communities and the Struggle for Justice* (2001) and former Washington, DC office director of the NAACP Legal Defense and Educational Fund, Inc. A 1978 Harvard Law School graduate, Hair also served as a clerk for U.S. Court of Appeals Judge Wilfred Feinberg and former Supreme Court Justice Harry A. Blackmun. In 1998, The American Lawyer named Hair one of the top public interest attorneys under age 45.

What does your organization do and how does it do it?
Advancement Project, a policy, communications and legal action group committed to racial justice, was founded by a team of veteran civil rights lawyers. Our mission is: *"To develop, encourage and widely disseminate innovative ideas, and pioneer models that inspire and mobilize a broad national racial justice movement to achieve universal opportunity and a just democracy!"*

Advancement Project partners with community organizations bringing them the tools of legal advocacy and strategic communications to dismantle structural exclusion. From Advancement Project's inception, we have worked "on-the-ground," helping organized communities of color dismantle and reform the unjust and inequitable policies that undermine the promise of democracy. To implement our theory of change, Advancement Project provides direct, hands-on support for organized communities in their struggles for racial and social justice, providing legal and communications resources for on-the-ground efforts; nationally, we actively broaden and extend the practice of community-centered racial justice lawyering through training, networking, creation of tools and resources, media outreach and public education.

How will your organization impact the public debate in 2008?
Advancement Project will address the historic legacy and political effects of discrimination and economic exclusion that perpetuate racial disparities in most aspects of American political and social life. These disparities impede the development of open society in which all people have an equal opportunity to participate democratically, and to support their families adequately. Accordingly, we will attempt to impact the public debate in 2008 by promoting progressive solutions to reducing the marginalization of low-income communities of color.

The Advancement project employs "innovative" and "fresh" ways to empower disenfranchised communities.

What is your 2008 operating budget?
$6,262,783.

Looking out 2-3 years, how would you like to grow/change your organization?
Advancement Project will remain committed to dismantling structural exclusion. History has shown that successful movements for social change have by necessity, involved grassroots mobilization by and with people refusing to accept the status quo. Thus, we are convinced that even today, structural exclusion can be dismantled through the multiracial collective action of organized communities and the civic participation of its members. Advancement Project will continue to remain at the forefront of building this critical movement by providing strategic council, legal expertise and communications assistance.

What do you need to do that?
The decline in unrestricted funding in the foundation community is a critical, but missing element in racial justice and other mission-driven initiatives. Only with unrestricted funds can organizations maintain crucial infrastructure, and thereby, ensure the sustainability, growth and capacity of projects, especially those built on partnerships between experts and community-based partners. Equally important, unrestricted funds provide the flexibility that is essential to respond to emergencies, such as the aftermath of Hurricane Katrina.

How will your organization change if progressives win in November? If they lose?
Racial and social justice grassroots organizations/coalitions will be uniquely poised to fill the current void and regain public support for an agenda to advance racial and social justice if progressives win in 2008. However, Advancement Project understands that the pace of change is likely to be slow as we are introducing new paradigms or rearranging old ones that are entrenched in our society regardless of who wins in November. To accomplish this requires sustained effort. Conservative policy advocates have understood the importance of this patient approach for decades.

If you had to offer some advice to fellow progressives what would it be?
The populist language of the civil rights movement too often has been either seized by the opponents of equal justice or replaced by a legalese that lacks broad public appeal. We must find ways to recapture the public's attention that allows us to argue our issues in a persuasive and compelling way in the court of public opinion. We must develop a viable and modern apparatus with which to break into the marketplace of ideas and the public discussion on race and ethnicity. We believe progressives of all races and ethnicities must have access to the discussion.

Please list your board of directors and their affiliations.

Gerald Torres, Esq.
University of Texas

Molly Munger, Esq.
Co-Director, Advancement Project
(Los Angeles Office)

Stephen R. English, Esq.
Co-Director, Advancement Project
(Los Angles Office)

Jose (Joe) Alvarez
Northeast Regional Director,
American Federation of Labor-
Congress of Industrial
Organizations (AFL-CIO)

Harry Belafonte
Acclaimed Entertainer
and Social Activist

Angela Glover Blackwell
President, PolicyLink

Bonifacio (Bonny) Garcia, Esq.
Partner, Burke, Williams
& Sorenson, LLP

Penda D. Hair, Esq.
Co-Director, Advancement Project

Johnnie Johnson
Executive Director, Drew Community
Voter's League

Bill Lann Lee, Esq.
Partner, Leif, Cabraser, Heimann
& Bernstein

Michael Lawson, Esq.
Partner, Skadden, Arps,
Slate,Meagher & Flom

William Lynch
President, Bill Lynch Associates, LLC

Connie Rice, Esq.
Co-Director, Advancement Project
(Los Angeles)

Sheila Thomas
Employment Attorney, Private Practice

641 6th Ave
4th Flr
New York, NY 10011

☎ 212-871-8100

🖨 212-871-8108

✂ Mark Green

@ mgreen@airamerica.com

🖳 airamerica.com

🕮 March 31, 2004

🏢 For Profit

Mark Green
President

Mark Green is president of Air America Radio and of the New Democracy Project, a public affairs institute. He is the author or editor of 21 books, including the best-selling *Who Runs Congress?* (1972) and *The Book on Bush* (2004), as well as most recently of *Losing Our Democracy* (paperback 2007).

He was the elected Public Advocate for New York City from 1994-2001 and the City's Democratic nominee for mayor in 2001. He teaches at New York University, appears weekly with Ed Koch and Al D'Amato on NY1's "Wise Guys" show, is seen regularly on MSNBC'S "Hardball," and co-hosts Air America's weekend radio program "7 Days in America" with Arianna Huffington.

What does your organization do and how does it do it?
Air America Radio is an American radio network specializing in progressive talk. The network started programming on March 31, 2004 with Al Franken as its well-known host. The network specializes in presentations and monologues by on-air personalities, guest interviews, calls by listeners and news reports. Air America believes in fair and unbalanced news, that is if balance means arguing why the world may be flat, evolution only a theory and saddle in cahoots with Al-Qaeda, we'll stick with fairness.

How will your organization impact the public debate in 2008?
With the ability to reach an audience of some two million people via its radio network and web presence, Air America Radio's progressive views will no doubt have a major impact on the public debate for 2008.

Looking out 2-3 years, how would you like to grow/change your organization?

Air America Radio is optimistic about the future of progressive politics in America and is capitalizing on the public's growing appetite for news, information and opinion that reflect a progressive point of view. Along with growing its radio audience with new affiliates in new markets, Air America will also be expanding and modernizing the distribution of its content by way of the Internet. It will relaunch a redesigned website at the end of March, 2008, on the occasion of its fourth anniversary.

What do you need to do that?
Air America will be seeking new capital investment, additional affiliates and more readers on-line.

How will your organization change if progressives win in November? If they lose?
We'll keep analyzing news events with humor from a progressive viewpoint, no matter who's president, though it will be a nice change to do it with a president not looking for more countries to invade on false pretenses.

If you had to offer some advice to fellow progressives what would it be?
Know that we're in the mainstream and they're in the extreme.

Air America is the "only" progressive broadcast outlet. After a rocky start, the group is "changing the airwaves" and "challenging right wing radio dominance."

ALLIANCE FOR JUSTICE

11 Dupont Circle NW
2nd Flr
Washington, DC 20036

📞 202-822-6070
📠 202-822-6068
✖ Brenda Soder,
Director of Communications
@ Brenda@afj.org

💻 afj.org
afjjusticewatch.blogspot.com
🔑 1979
📊 $4,500,000
⚎ 501(c)(3)

Nan Aron
Executive Director

A leading voice in public interest law for over 30 years, Nan Aron is president and founder of Alliance for Justice. Nationally recognized for her vast experience in public interest law, the federal judiciary and citizen participation in public policy, she has appeared as an expert in such media outlets as *The New York Times*, *The Wall Street Journal*, *The Washington Post*, *USA Today*, the *Los Angeles Times*, *The Nation*, *Vanity Fair* and National Public Radio. She is also a frequent guest speaker at universities, laws schools, corporations, nonprofits and foundations.

Prior to founding Alliance for Justice, Nan was a staff attorney for the ACLU's National Prison Project, where she challenged conditions in state prison systems through lawsuits in federal and state courts. As a trial attorney for the Equal Employment Opportunity Commission, she litigated race and sex discrimination cases against companies and unions in federal and district courts.

What does your organization do and how does it do it?
Alliance for Justice fights for progressive values through the advancement of a fair and independent judiciary, by strengthening the voice of nonprofits in their work to affect change and inspiring a new generation of progressive activists. Among AFJ's most noteworthy activities are the following:

• Monitors federal judicial nominations and compiles in-depth reports about nominees to the federal bench. These reports are shared with the public and Senate staff to ensure that each nominee receives a comprehensive hearing.
• Sends timely updates and action alerts to more than 40,000 members

of its Justice Action Network.

- Produces award-winning documentary films that engage and educate the public about the influence the Courts have on the lives of all Americans.
- Works to expose the politicization of the Department of Justice and the expansion of executive power at the expense of basic human rights.
- Offers nonprofits and foundations resources, training and technical assistance regarding the laws that govern participation in the policy process.

How will your organization impact the public debate in 2008?

Alliance for Justice will highlight the importance of the courts and the Bush administration's impact on the federal judiciary throughout the coming year. It will also emphasize the need to restore fairness and balance to the nation's courts and will provide the next administration with recommendations to meet this goal. Lastly, AFJ will host a September symposium in Washington, DC to explore the Bush legacy and the future of the courts after the election.

What is your 2008 operating budget?
$4.5 million

Looking out 2-3 years, how would you like to grow/change your organization?

In the coming years, Alliance for Justice will continue to develop and expand its current projects using cutting edge technologies and outreach tools. As AFJ pushes to

restore balance in our nation's courts, it will strengthen its reputation as the foremost clearinghouse, watchdog and progressive advocacy group on behalf of a fair and independent judiciary and continue to serve as a trusted source for members of the Senate and the public. In addition, AFJ is poised to become the first stop for nonprofits and foundations that are looking for expert advice and clarity regarding their electoral and policy activities.

What do you need to do that?

AFJ's growth and success will require a strong national base of supporters who can contribute a myriad of resources. From its "online" Justice Action Network to its "offline" group of trusted academic advisors, AFJ must continue to build its vast network of activists, donors, advocates and friends.

How will your organization change if progressives win in November? If they lose?

If progressives win in November, Alliance for Justice will quickly shift from a reactive agenda to a

This organization is "putting legal questions at the front of the agenda." They are "focused" on discussing the legal issues related to the poor.

proactive agenda. We will seek to restore the rights that were lost during the past eight years and work to restore fairness and balance to the nation's federal judiciary. We will also work to restore integrity to the Department of Justice.

If progressives lose this November, AFJ will continue its work opposing extreme judicial nominees, raising the importance of the courts among the public and Senators alike and monitoring the abuses of executive power.

If you had to offer some advice to fellow progressives what would it be?
Be educated, be innovative and be resilient. It isn't always easy, but it is always worth the fight.

Please list your board of directors and their affiliations.

President, Nan Aron
Alliance for Justice

Clay Hiles
Chair, Hudson River Foundation

Betsy Cavendish
Appleseed

Teri Chaw
National Employment
Lawyers Association

Sally Greenberg
Treasurer, National Consumer
Law Center

Anne Hess
Secretary

Sarah Kovner

Robert Raben
Vice Chair, The Raben Group

Norman Rosenberg

Judith Scott
SEIU

Diane Shust
National Education Association

Arnold Spellun
McLaughlin & Stern LLP

John Trasvina
MALDEF

Bradley Whitford

AMERICA √OTES

1401 New York Ave, NW
Ste 720
Washington, DC 20005

📞 202-962-7240
🖨 202-962-7241
✂ Anna Ekindjian, National
    Development Director
@ aekindjian@americavotes.org

🖥 americavotes.org
🔑 2003
📊 $20,083,166
🔗 527

Martin Frost
Director

Greg Speed
Executive Director (not shown)

Martin Frost
Congressman Frost represented the Dallas-Fort Worth area from 1979-2005 and departed Congress as the senior southern Democrat in the House. He served from 1999-2003 as Chair of the Caucus, the third highest elected leadership position for Democrats, and was the senior Democrat on the powerful Rules Committee.

In addition to his significant legislative accomplishments, Mr. Frost is considered a top electoral strategist. During the 1996 and 1998 election cycles, Mr. Frost chaired the Democratic Congressional Campaign Committee, where his ability to run campaigns and win was proven. The DCCC achieved a net gain of 14 House seats under his leadership.

As the President, Mr. Frost brings his unique perspective as an elected official, Democratic Party leader and organization-builder to America Votes. He is widely-regarded as an aggressive and inspiring fundraiser who donors have come to appreciate for his candor and persistence.

Mr. Frost is also called upon periodically to write for The Politico and appear on Fox News as a

America Votes is "essential." It's the "the one place" where the single issue groups "sit down and work together." They are well "coordinated" and "integrated."

political commentator. He is a graduate of the Georgetown Law Center, where he was a member of the law review, and University of Missouri-Columbia with a Bachelor of Journalism degree.

Greg Speed

Greg Speed is an expert manager, with a long history of overseeing successful electoral organizations, advocacy and political campaigns and political consulting businesses. As Executive Director, Speed's management expertise is invaluable to the coalition. He is widely respected for his ability to connect seemingly disparate ideas and people to work together toward shared goals. He has overseen budgets ranging from $1-20 million dollars and staffs ranging from 8-100 employees.

Prior to America Votes, Speed launched Envision Communications, where his clients included progressive organizations, labor unions, candidates and party committees. Having recently served as the National Communications Directors for Communities for Quality Education (2006) and the Democratic Congressional Campaign Committee (2004), Speed focused his consulting practice on strategic communications efforts designed to shape the public debate through grassroots community involvement, issue advocacy and voter education.

Speed's experience both in Washington and in the states instills confidence in America Votes' partners. He has held senior positions on congressional and legislative campaigns in numerous states, including Florida, Kentucky, Texas and Wisconsin.

Greg was raised in "Chicagoland" and received his B.A. in Political Science from the University of Wisconsin-Madison. He resides on Capitol Hill with his wife, Lona Valmoro, and their son Andrew.

How will your organization impact the public debate in 2008?
America Votes' partner organizations lead the progressive voter mobilization effort including field canvasses, mail and phone programs. Their work on the field side will echo the messages voters hear and see on television, radio and the internet.

As the coalition leader, America Votes (AV) coordinates all field voter contact, eliminates duplication, and provides a tremendous cost-savings to coalition partners and funders. Investments in America Votes strengthen the investments that organizations and individual donors make to existing organizations.

What is your 2008 operating budget?
$20,083,166

Looking out 2-3 years, how would you like to grow/change your organization?
America Votes will take responsibility for building progressive infrastructures in our states,

including coordinated planning tables, communications hubs, donor collaboratives and in-state media and field capacity. We'll also include more organizations that represent diverse populations to build the electoral power of people of color, women, young people and LGBT progressives.

In 2008 and 2010, we will mobilize the coalition to turnout the largest possible number of voters by contacting voters on issues that matter to them, bringing new people into the process and solidifying life-long progressive voters.

We will maximize the "off-years" to experiment with new technology, improve data on the shared voter file, and create voter models.

What do you need to do that?
Ours is a labor-intensive program and we need skilled staff to lead these efforts. We also need a diversified donor base committed to building permanent infrastructure in the states. Our nimble structure allows us to operate in more states with a robust budget during election years and sustain our operation in fewer states during off-years.

How will your organization change if progressives win in November? If they lose?
America Votes goes beyond defining success in terms of one election. No matter the outcome in November, we will continue coordinating organizations to prepare for the next election. We will work with our partners to ensure that progressive successes at the polls result in policy enactment. We will also maintain a permanent infrastructure in other ways, such as uploading data to the VAN, that will continue after November.

Redistricting after the 2010 census will impact electoral opportunities for our movement. Our 2008 priorities have been determined with an eye toward reapportionment, as many of our partners are focused on state legislative races. Whoever controls state legislatures after this election cycle will be in a strong position in these battles.

If you had to offer some advice to fellow progressives what would it be?
Diversify at all levels. We have the opportunity this cycle to run multiple campaigns and effect change up and down the ballot. With voter turnout at an all-time high, it would be a waste to focus on one contest; we can mobilize progressives for various reinforcing efforts. We also can bring new people into the process by prioritizing underrepresented communities—youth, people of color, women and LGBT progressives. A more diverse movement is a more progressive movement. Lastly, we can diversify our investments to support a broad range of organizations—c3, c4 and 527—that all play a critical role.

Please list your board of directors and their affiliations.

Mark Lotwis
21st Century Democrats

Zach Pollett
ACORN

Karen Ackerman
AFL-CIO

Larry Scanlon
AFSCME

Ed Coyle
Alliance for Retired Americans

Linda Lipsen
American Association for Justice

Liz Smith
American Federation of Teachers

Brad Woodhouse
Americans United for Change

Kristina Wilfore
Ballot Initiative Strategy Center

Paul Helmke
Brady Campaign to Prevent
Gun Violence United with
the Million Mom March

Robert Borosage
Campaign for America's Future

Deepak Bhargava
Campaign for Community Change

Greg Tarpinian
Change to Win

Juan Marcos Vilar
Civic Participation Campaign

John DeCock
Clean Water Action

John Hein
Communities for Quality Education

Rodger Schlickeisen
Defenders of Wildlife Action Fund

Arshad Hasan
Democracy for America

Ellen Malcolm
EMILY's List

Joe Solmonese
Human Rights Campaign

Kalyn Free
INDN's List

Gene Karpinski
League of Conservation Voters

Beth Sullivan
League of Education Voters

Billy Wimsatt
League of Young Voters

Brent Wilkes
LULAC

Eli Pariser
MoveOn.org Political Action

Barbara Leach
My Rural America

Gregory Moore
NAACP National Voter Fund

Nancy Keenan
NARAL Pro-Choice America

Brian Dautch
National Association of Social Workers

John Stocks
National Education Association

Ira Foreman
National Jewish Democratic Council

Simon Rosenberg
NDN

Mary Jean Collins
People For the American Way

Cecile Richards
Planned Parenthood Action Fund

Gloria Totten
Progressive Majority

Doug Phelps
Progressive Future

Michael Huttner
ProgressNow Action Fund

Anna Burger
SEIU

Carl Pope
Sierra Club

Jeff Blum
USAction

Ilana Goldman
Women's Campaign Forum

Page Gardner
Women's Voices. Women Vote

Karen Nussbaum
Working America

David Hardt
Young Democrats of America

AMERICAN CONSTITUTION SOCIETY FOR LAW AND POLICY

	✆ 202-393-6181	🖥 ACSLaw.org
	🖨 202-393-6189	🔑 2001
1333 H St NW	✄ Lisa Brown	📊 $5,100,000
11th Flr	@ lbrown@ACSLaw.org	🗂 501(c)(3)
Washington DC, 20005		

Lisa Brown
Executive Director

Lisa Brown is the Executive Director of the American Constitution Society. She was Counsel to the Vice President of the United States from September 1999 through January 2001, and Deputy Counsel from April 1997 through August 1999. In addition to advising the Vice President and his staff on legal matters, she handled civil rights issues, served on the Executive Board of the President's Committee for Employment of People with Disabilities and worked closely with the Vice President's Domestic Policy Office on a variety of legislative initiatives. She was an Attorney Advisor in the Office of Legal Counsel at the Department of Justice from June 1996 until April 1997. She graduated from the University of Chicago Law School in 1986, after which she clerked for the Honorable

John C. Godbold on the U.S. Court of Appeals for the 11th Circuit in Montgomery, Alabama.

What does your organization do and how does it do it?
The progressive counterpart to the conservative Federalist Society, ACS is developing the ideas and network to effectively counter the conservative legal movement by:
• Communicating compelling progressive analyses of law and policy—on issues ranging from voting rights, national security and racial equality to executive power, criminal justice and privacy—and disseminating this intellectual capital through:
• over 1,000 public programs (debates, conferences and speeches) a year all across America;
• regular briefings in Washington for Congress and the media;
• print and electronic publications that make complex legal concepts accessible to lay audiences; and
• Building a progressive legal network—ACS currently has student chapters in 162 law schools in 47

states, 28 lawyer chapters and thousands of other supporters— which is:

- Bringing together young and experienced lawyers alike who will fill positions of influence in law, public life and academia, and
- Preparing them to carry the progressive case into courtrooms, hearing rooms and newsrooms.

How will your organization impact the public debate in 2008?

ACS will host events, release publications and brief journalists and policymakers on vital legal and policy issues that should be addressed by a new Administration, including:

- Liberty, security and democracy issues (e.g. detainee treatment; national security policy);
- Voting issues (e.g. voter ID laws, voter registration and student voting rights);
- Policies and practices of the Department of Justice and other agencies; and
- Decision-making trends at the Supreme Court.

What is your 2008 operating budget?
$5,100,000

Looking out 2-3 years, how would you like to grow/change your organization?

To encourage broad application of progressive ideas, we would like to:

- deepen our communications capacity to reach more policymakers at the Federal and state levels;
- become a highly valued resource for

policymakers and journalists seeking rigorous yet accessible analyses of legal and policy issues; and

- expand our network by increasing membership, strengthening existing chapters and organizing new chapters.

What do you need to do that?

Additional resources and staff to do grassroots organizing, expand chapter-based activities, expand media coverage of our ideas and experts, and make more extensive use of electronic communications technologies.

How will your organization change if progressives win in November? If they lose?

The substance of our work will remain the same, because we are engaged in a long-term effort to change the way lawyers, judges, policymakers, law students and, indeed, all Americans, think about our laws and Constitution. This work is equally important regardless of who is in the White House. With a new, progressive Administration, the need for new ideas and approaches will provide important opportunities for ACS members to participate in the policymaking process.

ACS is the "progressive answer to the Federalist Society." One of "the most important strategic imperatives," their work is "absolutely critical."

If you had to offer some advice to fellow progressives what would it be?

In every policy area that progressives care about, the conservatives' success in reshaping the law and the courts has had an enormously detrimental impact. We would reiterate the core insight of a 1988 report to Attorney General Ed Meese entitled *"The Constitution in the Year 2000: Choices Ahead in Constitutional Interpretation:"*

"There are few factors that are more critical to determining the course of the Nation, and yet are more often overlooked, than the values and philosophies of the men and women who populate the third co-equal branch of the national government—the federal judiciary."

Please list your board of directors and their affiliations.

Frederick M. Baron
Baron & Blue

Stephen P. Berzon
Altshuler Berzon

Faith E. Gay
Quinn Emanuel

Pamela Harris
O'Melveny & Myers

Antonia Hernández
California Community Foundation

The Honorable Eric H. Holder, Jr.
Covington & Burling

Anne Irwin
Public Defender

Dawn Johnsen
Professor, University of Indiana
School of Law

Harriet Johnson
3L at University of Mississippi
School of Law

Donya Khalili
3L at University of Pennsylvania
Law School

Ron Klain
Revolution, LLC

Victor A. Kovner
Davis Wright Tremaine

Goodwin Liu
Professor, University of California
Berkeley Law School

William Marshall
Professor, University of North Carolina
Law School

Spencer Overton
Professor, George Washington
University School of Law

Robert Post
Professor, Yale Law School

Robert Raben
The Raben Group

Teresa Wynn Roseborough
MetLife

Theodore Shaw
NAACP Legal Defense Fund

Paul Smith
Jenner & Block

Geoffrey R. Stone
Professor, University of Chicago
Law School

Stephen Susman
Susman Godfrey

The Honorable Patricia M. Wald
Commission on the Intelligence
Capabilities of the United
States Regarding Weapons of
Mass Destruction

Roger Wilkins
Professor, George Mason University

AMERICAN PROGRESSIVE CAUCUS POLICY FOUNDATION

2652 South June St
Ste 305
Arlington, VA 22202

📠 703-606-2531
✂ Laura Kalick, 301-634-4950
@ KalickEOTC@aol.com
✂ Lorelei Kelly, 202-487-7728
@ loreleikelly@gmail.com
✂ Stephen Shaff, 301-209-1899 x115
@ Stephen@community-vision.com

🖥 apcpf.org
🔑 January 16, 2008
📊 under development
🔗 501(c)(3)

**Executive Director
under recruitment**

**What does your organization do
and how does it do it?**
The American Progressive Caucus
Policy Foundation (APCPF) is a
nonpartisan 501(c)(3) organization.
Our mission is to bring together the
collective wisdom and experiences
of progressives inside and outside of
Congress and Washington, D.C. to
promote peace and global security,
energy independence, environmental
sustainability, human rights, civil
liberties and the health and well-being
of us all.

We will serve as a unique and much-
needed progressive intersection
(including but not limited to Members
of the Congressional Progressive
Caucus) and to function as a
communications, fact-finding, research
and education hub for progressive
organizations, leaders and other public
policy-makers, issue advocates from
the national to the grassroots levels of
civil society, the media and the general
public inside and outside of Congress
and Washington, D.C.

We value our diversity and seek
broad engagement to advance a
progressive agenda to help attain our
preferred future and to form a more
perfect union.

**How will your organization impact
the public debate in 2008?**
• To provide unique and much-
needed intersection throughout
the progressive movement by
guaranteeing that progressives
inside and outside of Congress
from the national to the grassroots
levels meet together regularly,
communicate and coordinate more
fully, establish shared priorities,
work out efficient divisions of labor
and implement agreed-upon action
plans (e.g. Board of Directors to be
primarily comprised of leaders of
major progressive organizations,
civil society groups and networks of
grassroots and Netroot researchers,

policy analysts and concerned citizens as well as key progressive donors and strategists coupled with an Advisory Board of Progressive Caucus leaders from inside Congress plus progressive office holders at state and local levels);

- To host an annual strategic planning forum before or early on in each new session of Congress for progressives inside and outside Congress. Currently, there is no organized, systemic tie-in between the Congressional Progressive Caucus and very useful progressive conferences and gatherings inside and outside Washington, D.C.

What is your 2008 operating budget?
Under development.

Looking out 2-3 years, how would you like to grow/change your organization?
In addition to the two principal roles for 2008 described above, the APCPF is planning to fulfill the following additional roles within the growing progressive infrastructure with a view toward enhancing coordination and collaboration among progressives inside and outside of government from the local to the national levels.

- To function as a funnel for progressive policy-makers and their staff by translating concept papers/reports customarily provided by "think tanks" into workable proposals, talking points, briefs and multi-media materials. To do this, we need a small professional staff of experienced and new progressives who can help define

the art of the achievable and who can bring to the table insights gleaned from historical experience when progressives held greater power in Congress and other legislative bodies, but who can also pivot and provide what is needed when in the minority, and out of power, too;

- To serve as policy incubator, platform and echo chamber to develop and showcase progressive ideas in ways that can't be done when the mainstream media ignores progressive policy alternatives and progressives ourselves are too narrowly focused on the executive and judicial branches of government or particular candidates running for elective office (e.g. Not enough for progressive think tanks to focus disproportionately on winning in the next election cycle for the White House, Congress or fighting the next judicial branch appointment.);

- To raise funds and identify other resources to fuel on-going capacity for conducting progressive fact-finding hearings across the country, organizing public education forums and supporting timely, informative research on critical public policy issues throughout the country; and

The APPCF "forges key connections between Washington and the outside world."

- To develop and maintain critical contact information about on-going public education campaigns being waged by progressives from the community to the national levels of government on a wide range of public policy issues;
- To develop and extend an on-line platform to maximize benefits of using the Internet and other multimedia tools in connecting and expanding the 21st Century progressive movement, thus enabling a growing number of Americans individually and collectively to be better informed about public policy-making at all levels of their government and to take a more active role in shaping their preferred future;
- To publish an annual handbook of progressive organizations, publications and on-call academics for use by progressive elected officials and staff everywhere;
- To provide public speaking venues to utilize "progressive road show/speakers' bureau" of Congressional Progressive Caucus Members and counterpart policy-makers at state and local levels of government in conjunction with on-going public education activities and topical research.

What do you need to do that?

We need every interested progressive organization and individual to contribute to the development of the APCPF by sending tax deductible contributions, volunteering in-kind services to help with rapid development of the nonpartisan educational and research capabilities

of the APCPF and/or look at the other roles described above and communicate to us how you are able and willing to most effectively help develop this key missing link in rounding out the much-needed infrastructure to support progressive policy debate and intellectual capital.

How will your organization change if progressives win in November? If they lose?

We will accelerate our business and development plan in order to help advance progressive problem-solving and capacity-building hopefully in concert with a new Democratic President and increased Democratic majorities in the U.S. House of Representatives and U.S. Senate.

If you had to offer some advice to fellow progressives what would it be?

To share information and coordinate more freely with one another and come together to prioritize collectively and advance a short-list of progressive policy goals that can change from one year to the next as we achieve more of our preferred policy changes.

Please list your board of directors and their affiliations.

The APCPF Board is still expanding, but it includes the following so far:

**Caucus Co-Chair (volunteer),
U.S. Rep. Barbara Lee**
Congressional Progressive

**Caucus Co-Chair (volunteer),
U.S. Rep. Lynn Woolsey**
Congressional Progressive

Lorelei Kelly
The White House Project

Laura Kalick
Senior Consultant for Nonprofit Tax
Services with BDO Seidman LLP

Stephen Shaff
Founder and President of Community
Vision Consultants, a DC-based
affordable housing development and
social activist organization

Bill Fletcher
The Aurora Project

Joan Blades/Wes Boyd
Co-Founders, Moveon.org

Bob Borosage
Campaign for America's Future

Katrina Vanden Heuvel
The Nation

Conrad Martin
Fund for Constitutional Government

John Cavanagh
Institute for Policy Studies

Larry Mishel
President of the Economic
Policy Institute

Julie Bergman Sender
Executive Producer of Balcony Films

Joel Barkin
Executive Director of the
Progressive States Network

THE AMERICAN PROSPECT

2000 L St NW
Ste 717
Washington, DC 20036

☎ 202.776.0730
🖶 202.776.0740
✂ Andrew Green,
   Publishing Fellow
@ agreen@prospect.org

🖵 prospect.org
🔑 1990
📊 $3,500,000
🏛 501(c)(3)

Diane Straus Tucker
President/Publisher

Diane Straus Tucker, president and publisher, joined *The American Prospect* in December 2005 after a long career in publishing and a shorter one in practical politics, working with Howard Dean at the Democratic National Committee. For nearly two decades, Diane worked on the business side of publishing, most recently as group publisher of Manhattan Media, which publishes several weekly community newspapers in Manhattan as well as *Avenue* magazine. Earlier in her career, she was publisher of *The Westchester County Times*, Trader Publications and the *Cranford Citizen and Chronicle*. Before migrating to the business side she had worked as an editor at *The Village Voice* and *New York* magazine. She is past chair of the *Yale*

Alumni Magazine, having attended in the first class of women. And she won 13 national platform tennis championships.

What does your organization do and how does it do it?
The American Prospect is the vehicle through which progressive ideas gain traction. The Prospect is a leading progressive monthly magazine of politics and policy, complemented by a growing Web site and several influential blogs. Our work provides ammunition for progressive arguments, breaks news and amplifies the work of other progressive efforts. Perhaps most importantly, our print and online content offers deep critiques and policy proposals coupled with the necessary political framework to drive strategies for change. Additionally, we publish in-depth special reports on many of the issues of greatest interest—or profound concern—to enlightened, engaged liberals. These reports bring together the work of academic experts, journalists, legislative leaders and practitioners in a particular policy area. Finally,

as a magazine widely respected by the diverse progressive community, we are able to build broad strategic coalitions and function as a convener.

How will your organization impact the public debate in 2008?
As one of the leading voices of the progressive movement, *The American Prospect* is providing expert analysis on where various candidates stand on issues important to progressive voters. We are also agenda-shapers, pushing candidates and policy experts to expand their platforms and include more progressive ideas. These messages are amplified by a mainstream media that pick up our content and share it on a broader scale. Many of our senior editors and writers disseminate the *Prospect's* progressive ideas in their other roles as columnists and commentators for major newspapers, radio and television programs.

What is your 2008 operating budget?
$3.5 million

Looking out 2-3 years, how would you like to grow/change your organization?
Our organization is constantly expanding, specifically in our Web presence, and we anticipate that trend to increase in the next 2-3 years. We recently integrated Ezra Klein's widely read blog onto our site, where it joined our popular group blog "Tapped" (winner of 2007 Sidney Hillman Award for reporting

on social and economic justice). We expect to continue to grow our Web presence, solidifying our reputation as the premier site for a daily dose of progressive politics. On the print side, the magazine continues to expand its stable of intelligent and highly regarded authors, specifically through our Writing Fellows program. The program offers young, progressive writers a position in the magazine generating content for both print and online. We also recently introduced a Publishing Fellows program on the business side, offering young people interested in a career in publishing a unique opportunity to learn all facets of the *Prospect's* business side.

What do you need to do that?
In order to continue our contribution to the broader progressive landscape, the *Prospect* relies on funding from a host of sources, specifically foundations. We also continue to seek donors who understand that building a strong progressive infrastructure is just as important as supporting candidates and causes.

One of the most "eloquent, unflinching and sophisticated voices for the values of liberalism." *The American Prospect* is "terrific."

How will your organization change if progressives win in November? If they lose?

When progressives win the November 2008 election, it will mark a dramatic shift in the *Prospect*'s role. Rather than fighting from the outside for progressive change, we will be holding candidates' feet to the fire and expecting them to deliver on promises made. It's an exciting opportunity to serve as the voice of this country's hopeful and excited progressive base as we start enacting necessary policies. If progressives lose we will maintain our role as a champion of progressive policies.

If you had to offer some advice to fellow progressives what would it be?

In the short term, our advice is succinct. In the words of co-founder Paul Starr in a recent op-ed piece, "keeping the election focused on the manifest failures of conservative Republican leadership" is the best way to ensure victory for progressives in the fall.

For the longer term, we endorse the words of a former *Prospect* editor who argued in our pages two years ago that American progressives must return to their philosophical roots. Historically, "liberalism was built around the idea—the philosophical principle—that citizens should be called upon to look beyond their own self-interest and work for a greater common interest." We progressives, in other words, need a big, animating idea that distinguishes us from the failed policies of conservatism.

Finally, we offer concrete and specific advice to our fellow progressives in the pages of our magazine and on our web site and blogs. Any progressive organizations with good ideas should not hesitate to contact us to discuss potential partnerships.

Please list your board of directors and their affiliations.

Board Chairman, Ben Taylor
former editor and publisher,
The Boston Globe

**President and Publisher,
Diane Straus Tucker**

Senior Editorial Group

**Robert Kuttner
(founding co-editor)**

**Paul Starr
(founding co-editor)**
Princeton University

**Harold Meyerson
(executive editor)**

Other board members

Maria Echaveste
Nueva Vista Group

Danny Goldberg
Gold Village Entertainment

Jehmu Greene
Project Vote

10510 Culver Blvd
Culver City, CA 90232

📞 310-204-0448
🖨 310-204-0174
Nichole Wicks
@ nichole@bravenewfilms.org

🖥 bravenewfilms.org
🔑 January 1, 2008
501(c)(4)

Robert Greenwald
Founder

Robert Greenwald is a filmmaker and political activist. Greenwald is the director/producer of several documentaries: "Iraq for Sale: The War Profiteers," "Wal-Mart: The High Cost of Low Price," and "Outfoxed: Rupert Murdoch's War on Journalism." Brave New Films (BNF), Greenwald's new media company, uses online viral videos to educate, influence, and empower viewers to take action around issues that matter. Greenwald and BNF are at the forefront of the battle to create a just America. Now with over 14 million views, Brave New Films uses quick-strike video campaigns that challenge corporate media with the truth and empowers political action.

What does your organization do and how does it do it?
Brave New Films creates campaigns around issues that matter and pushes them out through the internet to a large coalition of groups. The campaigns consist of bloggers, a website and viral videos, with an action ask attached which helps motivate people to take action. BNF has created a quick-strike capability that challenges corporate media with the truth and empowers political action nationwide. BNF is pioneering the way social activism is being done for the 21st century. No other group has the ability to combine new media, activism and filmmaking with as much effectiveness as BNF. With over 14 million views our online guerilla campaigns have successfully pressured, mobilized, informed and challenged better reporting ("No Savage" was successful in getting 10 prominent advertisers to drop sponsorship of Michael Savage's radio show), accountability from our public officials ("The Real Rudy" prompted

a NYC council investigation into the first responder radio contract) or even shape the public discussion.

How will your organization impact the public debate in 2008?
By bringing relevant issues to the forefront and revealing the story behind the mainstream media's reporting of certain issues. As the country becomes increasingly involved in the people who will be running the country after November, we hope to continue reminding everyone that the issues are important. We will be focusing on issues that matter including economic disparity, the war and immigration.

Looking out 2-3 years, how would you like to grow/change your organization?
We would like to continue to create and distribute hard-hitting campaigns that result in action and victories. However, in addition to this programmatic work, we're taking our formula further by implementing a network with live programming which will be webcast. This programming is the next step to challenge, inform and mobilize a diverse and young generation.

What do you need to do that?
We have developed the technology and need to continue to grow our donor base and further develop funding partnerships.

How will your organization change if progressives win in November? If they lose?

Regardless of who wins or loses, it is BNF's fundamental goal to hold our public officials accountable, and keep policy-makers informed about pressing issues that matter. We will continue to educate and empower people to take action for a more just world.

If you had to offer some advice to fellow progressives what would it be?
The media landscape is constantly changing, having the ability to have quick access to information, breaking stories and being able to disseminate this information for your constituents will be crucial—new media has that ability.

They have "tapped into the media savvy world" in the name of progressive issues. And are "overwhelmingly effective."

BRENNAN CENTER FOR JUSTICE

161 Avenue of the Americas
12th Floor
New York, NY 10013

📞 212-998-6730
📠 212-995-4550
✂ Cathy Toren, Director
      of Development
@ cathy.toren@nyu.edu

🖥 brennancenter.org
🔑 1997
📊 $7,900,000
🏛 501(c)(3)

Michael Waldman
Executive Director

Waldman is a nationally known public interest lawyer, government official, teacher and writer. He became director of the Brennan Center in October 2005. Waldman served as Director of Speechwriting for President Bill Clinton from 1995-99. Previously, he was Special Assistant to the President for Policy Coordination (1993-1995). He was the top administration policy aide working on campaign finance reform, and drafted the administration's public financing proposal. He is the author of six books, including *POTUS Speaks* (2000), *My Fellow Americans* (2003) and *A Return to Common Sense: Seven Ways to Save Our Democracy* (June, 2008). He has been a lecturer at Harvard's

JFK School of Government, a partner in a law firm and executive director of Public Citizen's Congress Watch.

What does your organization do and how does it do it?
The Brennan Center is a nonpartisan public policy and law institute that focuses on fundamental issues of democracy and justice. A singular institution—part think tank, part public interest law firm, part advocacy group—the Brennan Center combines scholarship, legislative and legal advocacy, and communications to win meaningful, measurable change in the public sector. We believe that America's government is broken—that we must repair and renew the great systems of American democracy. So we fight to renew our electoral system, pressing for universal voter registration and public financing of campaigns. We seek to hold the executive branch accountable through restoration of checks and balances. And we seek reform of our judicial system, by guaranteeing access to lawyers for the poor and fair and impartial judges.

How will your organization impact the public debate in 2008?
We combine skilled communications advocacy with core policy and legal work. In 2008 our key focus is to make sure the elections are fair, that citizens can register and vote and their votes are counted. We will publish a new book on democracy reform, issue a proposal for universal voter registration, seek support for our proposal to restore checks and balances in the fight against terrorism, and expand our campaign finance reform efforts.

What is your 2008 operating budget?
$7.9 million.

Looking out 2-3 years, how would you like to grow/change your organization?
The Brennan Center has built on core legal and policy strengths to become a dynamic force for reform. We hope to build on that strength in several ways. We seek to expand our work on issues of democracy and justice, adding policy analysts to our legal team. We will expand our thriving communications operation, seeking to move public opinion and policymakers. We will augment organizational infrastructure, including much needed administrative support. And we are committed to expand our new Washington, D.C. office, to deepen our impact on national policy. In all these ways, we hope to grow in staff, budget and impact to become the flagship progressive organization, at the center of the fight to renew core public institutions.

What do you need to do that?

Building on our supporters in the philanthropic, legal and business community, we urgently need to expand our sources of unrestricted funding. Such funds enable us to build the organization, including communications and lobbying, with maximum strategic flexibility. We hope to move to half the organization's funds coming from organization-wide gifts, up from about one third today.

How will your organization change if progressives win in November? If they lose?
If progressives prevail, there will be a rare opportunity to advance system reforms, especially in voting, campaign finance and Constitutional protections in the fight against terrorism. Our work is respected by all three likely presidential candidates. We would view our role both as a source of policy research and argumentation, and as a watchdog to ensure that progressive democracy reforms are part of the governing agenda. If progressives lose in 2008,

The Brennan Center is "playing a central role in the drive to renew American democracy." It has "national quality communications" and "political savvy" to boost the "intense" brainpower. "It's one of progressives' defining organizations."

there will be an urgent need to fight back, as with our successful fights against disenfranchising voter laws, in courts and states as well as nationally. And we will focus more on public persuasion and on policy development.

If you had to offer some advice to fellow progressives what would it be?
In basic ways, our government is broken. Needed changes go beyond a single administration or even new policies. We must make democracy reform a central goal of progressive politics. It must come early in a new term. It will be very hard to meet key challenges, from climate change to health care to economic instability, if we do not rebuild our democracy. Similarly, we cannot assume that a progressive victory alone will change America. Without a strong infrastructure of think tanks, advocacy groups and media institutions, even a sympathetic president and Congress will find it hard to overcome the forces of stasis and special interest influence.

Please list your board of directors and their affiliations.

James E. Johnson, Chair
Partner, Debevoise & Plimpton LLP;
Former Under Secretary of the Treasury

Patricia Bauman
President & CEO, Bauman Family Foundation

Nancy Brennan
Executive Director, Rose Kennedy Greenway Conservancy

Zachary W. Carter
Partner, Dorsey & Whitney LLP

John Ferejohn
Professor, NYU School of Law & Stanford University

Peter M. Fishbein
Special Counsel, Kaye Scholer LLP

Gail Furman
Psychologist

Susan Sachs Goldman

Helen Hershkoff
Professor, NYU School of Law

Samuel Issacharoff
Professor, NYU School of Law

Robert Johnson
Economist/Philanthropist

Thomas M. Jorde
Professor Emeritus, Boalt Hall School of Law, UC Berkeley

BUS PROJECT

PO Box 15132
Portland, OR 97293

☏ 503-233-3018
🖶 503-233-7209
✂ Lucy Palmersheim
@ Lucy@busproject.org

🖳 busproject.org
☞ 2001
📊 $840,000
🖧 501(c)(4) with affiliated
501(c)(3) and state PAC

Jefferson Smith
Founding Chair

Jefferson Smith is the Founding Chair of the Bus Project and has become one of the Northwest's foremost spokespersons on voter mobilization and engaging new people in the political process. He's an Oregon native, graduate of the University of Oregon and magna cum laude graduate of Harvard Law School. He clerked for the Honorable Judge Goodwin of the 9th Circuit Court of Appeals before turning down offers from across the country to return home to Portland to work as a lawyer and public advocate. A column headline from *The Oregonian* labeled Jefferson as having the "Vision, Youth To Help Us Find A New Path," he was named by *Portland UpClose* as one of the "Top 20 to Watch." *The Oregonian* also dubbed him "a brilliant speaker." In

that capacity, Smith has presented for national progressive organizations such as the Take Back America Conference, Campus Progress, Young People For and the Young Democrats of America.

What does your organization do and how does it do it?
The Bus Project engages young volunteers to drive political change in the short term, develop the next generation of progressive leaders and impact the issue environment over the long term. A few of our programs:
- We fill our bus with volunteers and take Bus Trips to swing districts to knock thousands of doors for progressive candidates.
- Young people register and turn out their peers to vote with innovative, effective events like Trick or Vote—a multi-state costumed get-out-the-vote canvass that increases voter turnout in urban, youth-dense communities. In Oregon, Trick or Vote has engaged over 1,000 volunteers, and holds the title as the largest volunteer canvass in the state's history.
- Our freewheeling Candidates Gone

Wild debates introduce thousands of young people to local and statewide candidates and increase voter participation by 25%.

- PolitiCorps, the political bootcamp for young activists, trains 24 college-aged students from around the nation each year, and has sent 85% of graduates directly into the progressive workforce.

How will your organization impact the public debate in 2008?
The Bus Project is Oregon's leading direct voter contact engine. In 2008, we will engage volunteers to complete 25,000 hours of service and leverage that energy to register 20,000 voters, make 150,000 voter contacts, send action alerts to 100,000 progressives and place 50 young leaders in the progressive workforce. This year we will share our model by leading the Bus Federation—a coalition of five state-based organizations engaging young voters in the West.

What is your 2008 operating budget?
$840,000 (including affiliated 501(c)(3) and state PAC)

Looking out 2-3 years, how would you like to grow/change your organization?
We hope to expand our impact by:

- Engaging even more volunteers in our grassroots voter contact work
- Further targeting our work to communities with the greatest need
- Launching PolitiCorps Young Professionals, a progressive leadership training program for twenty-and-thirty somethings

What do you need to do that?
We are currently seeking resources to launch a new-and-traditional media campaign to increase awareness and bring in new volunteers, and are working with researchers to conduct studies of our work that will help us determine where to target our efforts to maximize our impact.

How will your organization change if progressives win in November? If they lose?
The Bus Project is working to help build a 20-year progressive movement that will provide social justice infrastructure for the future. Given that frame, the results of a single election are relevant, but not dispositive—scant majorities will be unable to accomplish the needed change. So if progressives win bare majorities in 2008, the task is obvious–create bigger victories and help foment the process that will help create and reward courageous action on behalf of elected officials. If progressives lose, we need to keep doing year-round grassroots voter

The "quintessential" success story of local political motivation. The Bus Project "keeps it fresh" and "gets people excited" about government participation.

contact work around key issues. Win or lose, we need to work to build lingering institutions.

If you had to offer some advice to fellow progressives what would it be?
We need to work to advance a new progressive era and build a 60% progressive consensus around the idea that we're stronger together than we are apart. We should focus not only on short-term political victories, but on developing leaders and building infrastructure to promote and sustain our work for decades to come.

Please list your board of directors and their affiliations.

Co-Chair, Representative Ben Cannon

Co-Chair, Helena Huang

Joseph Baessler

Brent Barton

Ryan Christensen

Lew Frederick

Ian Greenfield

Nolan Lienhart

Sarah Masterson

Benjamin Matasar

Jake Oken-Berg

Sara Ryan

Andrew Scott

Jefferson Smith

R.P. Joe Smith

CAMPAIGN for AMERICA'S FUTURE
— ourfuture.org

1825 K St NW
Ste 400
Washington, DC 20006

☎ 202-955-5665
🖨 202-955-5606
☓ Anne Snouck-Hurgronje,
@ Foundation Relations Manager
asnouck@ourfuture.org

💻 ourfuture.org
☞ March 25, 1996
📊 $5,000,000
🗂 501(c)(3) and 501(c)(4)*

Robert Borosage (l)

Roger Hickey (r)
Co-directors

Robert Borosage
Robert co-directs America's Future and most recently directed our Straight Talk initiative. He writes widely on political, economic and national security issues for a range of publications, including *The New York Times*, the *Los Angeles Times*, *The Huffington Post* and *The Nation*, where he is a contributing editor. He is the founder and chair of Progressive Majority. He was the founder and Director of the Campaign for New Priorities, involving over 100 organizations in the call to reinvest in America in the post-Cold War era.

He has served as an issues advisor to progressive political campaigns, including those of Senators Carol Moseley-Braun, Barbara Boxer and Paul Wellstone. In 1988, he was Senior Issues Advisor to the presidential campaign of Reverend Jesse L. Jackson.

Roger Hickey
Roger co-directs America's Future and is director of our Health Care for All Civic Engagement program. He is a leading national figure on Social Security reform and is spearheading our efforts to gather an active coalition to achieve quality affordable health care for everyone in America. A decade ago, he was one of the founders of the Economic Policy Institute, a Washington think tank that looks at

This group is "a permanent and effective" campaign for progressive values.

*The Institute for America's Future is a 501(c)(3) organization. The Campaign for America's Future—IAF's sister organization—is a 501(c)(4) organization.

economics from the point of view of working Americans. Hickey served as the EPI's Vice President and Director of Communications, helping to establish the international reputation of the Institute. In the early 1970s, Hickey was co-founder of the Public Media Center, a public interest ad agency in San Francisco that continues to produce advocacy advertising for labor, environmental and citizen organizations.

What does your organization do and how does it do it?
The Campaign for America's Future is the strategy center for the progressive movement. Our goal is to forge the enduring progressive majority needed to realize the America of shared prosperity and equal opportunity that our country was meant to be. In an era of growing insecurity and glaring inequality, our strategic focus is on kitchen-table issues of concern to all Americans — jobs, education, health care, energy costs and retirement security. These concerns define a common ground that can move this country from social and racial battle grounds to a shared economic agenda.

We pursue this mission with three basic strategies — detailing elements of a compelling progressive economic agenda; convening and educating progressive leaders; and incubating campaigns on defining issues.

How will your organization impact the public debate in 2008?
CAF has launched two major new initiatives for 2008. Its economic war room is providing briefings for progressive leaders and political activists, and continued resources for activists on how to argue about an economy in trouble. Second, CAF is pulling together a major coalition around health care for all, spearheading the efforts to drive that issue into the debate and then push for reforms over the next years.

CAF will also focus agenda and strategy for progressive activists and organizations through its Take Back America Conference and its on-going Tuesday Group coordination sessions.

What is your 2008 operating budget?
$6 million

Looking out 2-3 years, how would you like to grow/change your organization?
In an era of reform, CAF will seek to expand its capacity to develop bold, strategic reform ideas. We will continue to drive strategic initiatives — like Apollo on jobs and new energy, and the fight on Social Security — into the debate. Our new initiatives are on health care for all and on a new strategy for sustainable growth in the global economy.

CAF will also seek to expand its efforts to help provide strategic coordination of message and agenda — through the Tuesday group, Take Back America and strategic roundtables.

With our new web site, we aim to provide progressives with a central, interactive hub for progressive agenda and strategy.

What do you need to do that?
No surprise. We need more resources, more public intellectuals, expanded event and coordination capacity and a strengthened board structure. The Health Care for All Initiative will require significant resources to fuel the coalition able to overcome massive industry resistance. The global economic strategy will require skilled coordination of a network of scholars and legislators, providing both public platform and a political strategy.

How will your organization change if progressives win in November? If they lose?
CAF is part of building an independent progressive agenda and capacity. If Democrats win in November, progressives will have to mobilize independently to help define and drive reforms, to provide support where merited and challenge where needed. CAF will help nurture, guide and contribute to that independent capacity. We will be central to the effort to hold the administration and Congress accountable.

If conservatives win, CAF will expand its efforts to indict the on-going failure of conservatives, while developing alternatives that show what could be. We will join with progressive leaders in the Congress to develop defining issue campaigns that can help educate Americans to these realities.

If you had to offer some advice to fellow progressives what would it be?
The conservative era is bankrupt. The question is what comes next. Progressives need to be mobilizing for bold reforms that help consolidate a governing majority. And at the same time, we need fundamentally new thinking to address stark new challenges. We need to get out of our defensive crouch, remove the shackles on our imaginations, and challenge the narrow limits of our current debate.

Please list your board of directors and their affiliations.

Institute for America's Future

Warren Beatty
Mulholland Productions

Susan Bianchi-Sand
United American Nurses

James Forman, Jr.
Georgetown University Law Center

Maria Jobin-Leeds
Access Strategies Fund

Robert Johnson
Impact Artist Management

John Sweeney
AFL-CIO

Margery Tabankin
The Streisand Foundation

Katrina vanden Heuvel
The Nation

Antonio Villaraigosa
Mayor of Los Angeles

Scott Wallace
Wallace Global Fund

Roger Wilkins
George Mason University

Campaign for America's Future

Lara Bergthold
Act III Productions

Jeff Faux
Economic Policy Institute

Leo Gerard
United Steelworkers

Al Meyerhoff
Coughlin, Storia, Geller,
Rudman and Robbins LLP

Eli Pariser
MoveOn.org

1101 Vermont Ave NW
Ste 900
Washington, DC 20005

📟 202-962-7200
🖨 202-962-7201
✂ Laura Quinn
@ lquinn@catalist.us

🖥 catalist.us
🔑 April 2005
📊 $5,000,000
🏛 LLC

Laura Quinn
CEO (above)

Harold Ickes
President (not shown)

Laura Quinn
Laura Quinn is a founding partner of QRS Newmedia, Inc., which specializes in communication technology design and integration services. Founded in 1996, QRS clients have included the Democratic Presidential campaigns in 1996, 2000 and 2004; a wide of range of progressive political campaigns, organizations and non-profits; and other corporate and academic institutions. QRS's technology renovation for the Democratic National Committee in 2003-04 included complete IT, telecom and media system overhauls, as well as construction of a national voter file and new internet marketing systems, that helped the DNC increase their donor base more than five-fold and to out-fundraise the Republican National Committee for the first time in history.

Prior to these endeavors, Ms. Quinn served as Deputy Chief of Staff for Vice President Al Gore; as Director of the Democratic Technology and Communications Committee for Democratic Majority Leader Tom Daschle in the U.S. Senate; as Communications Director for U.S. Senator Jay Rockefeller and in senior staff roles and consulting for progressive political organizations and campaigns.

Harold Ickes
Harold Ickes' nearly fifty years ofcommitment and accomplishments fighting for progressive causes have

Catalist is providing "all the data" for "all the groups;" they are "the mother of all lists."

earned him trust, respect and friendship of unusual breadth and depth in the progressive political community. He is a founding partner of The Ickes & Enright Group, a Washington DC consulting firm. Prior to this, Mr. Ickes served as Assistant to the President and Deputy Chief of Staff for Political Affairs and Policy to President Clinton, managing a number of the President's key policy initiatives. He was also an architect of the President's 1996 re-election campaign (the first successful re-election campaign of a Democratic president since FDR), the 1996 Democratic National Convention and the 1997 Presidential Inaugural.

Prior to serving in the White House, Mr. Ickes was a partner in the New York law firm of Meyer, Suozzi, English & Klein, P.C., specializing in election and union-side labor law. He rejoined the law firm as partner in 1998 and serves as co-chair of its thirty-member Labor Law and Government Affairs Departments.

What does your organization do and how does it do it?
Catalist's mission remains central in all our work: to build and operate a robust, enhanced national voter file database that a variety of progressive organizations can use to improve communications, organizing, and fundraising to produce measurable increases in civic participation and electoral gains.

Fundamentally we're in the business of transforming the way progressive organizations communicate and campaign by providing clean,

extensive and affordable data on America's voting-age population. In addition, we also provide 24/7 customer support through a dedicated, field-tested staff. Our growing client list reflects a diversity of progressive enterprises—both national and state-based, large and small, membership and issue focused, political and not-for-profit.

Access to our data comes through a range of subscriptions, offering Pollster, Fundraising, Grassroots, Academic, National and State-by-State subscriptions. A subscription includes a unique instance of our "Q-tool" which allows our customers to run queries based on their immediate needs. Through our analytics team we also provide cutting edge targeting models and analysis that help our clients fully harness our data's potential to build grassroots support.

How will your organization impact the public debate in 2008?
We will be working extensively throughout the cycle with America's largest progressive campaign efforts, providing data services and support. Catalist's client organizations are already putting our voter data and services to work in their planning, targeting and early organizing for 2008 civic engagement and election work. We expect to be one of the fundamental reasons for the advancement of progressive causes in November by providing progressive political, advocacy and not-for-profit organizations

unprecedented access to voter data and data infrastructure.

Looking out 2-3 years, how would you like to grow/change your organization?
Catalist will constantly be updating and expanding the breadth of information on our voter file as the first priority for development. Another key area will be continuing to develop our innovative interface, analysis and visualization tools to expand how our data is used by customers and aid in their strategic planning. Finally, system development with a focus on capacity enhancement in the anticipation of dramatic increases in customer load as we move further along in the cycle.

We continue to be excited about company progress and the prospects ahead—for increasing Catalist's value to investors and clients alike—and for helping our clients find, persuade and mobilize more voters in 2008.

What do you need to do that?
Catalist, from the start, has been a coordinated effort on behalf of progressives to begin this much-needed element for success. We have been able to build, benchmark and test our systems under real-world, multi-user, multi-state stresses thanks to early capital investment. Continued investor support will be a vital part of making sure that Catalist is capable of maintaining and expanding our services, while offering them at affordable prices to the progressive community.

How will your organization change if progressives win in November?
Regardless of the turnout in November, the need for our product will remain as many of our clients transition from election work to issue advocacy on vital reform legislation such as healthcare, climate change, immigration, energy policy and more. This election season will be a crucial test of our system and provides an incredible opportunity to help elect a progressive president and add to progressive majorities in congress.

But in many ways Catalist's fullest potential will be realized beyond this election cycle. We will be vigilant in fine tuning business practices and products based on what we've learned from this cycle, to ensure services that enhance our customers ability to communicate at the individual level—to mobilize broad national support for progressive policies and reforms, and increase the strength of the progressive community by helping them identify, communicate with, and recruit new donors and members.

If you had to offer some advice to fellow progressives what would it be?
Data-driven marketing and campaigning, and the data analytics (data mining) that goes with it, is a process that answers the questions that are fundamental to the strategy of any advocacy organizations or

campaign. Which voters support your cause or candidate? Which voters are undecided? Which voters care about a particular issue? Which voters will vote at all? Most important of all, which voters will respond if you reach them? Data is the raw material of political "microtargeting," because it is the means to start developing a person-by-person view of the electorate. It is critical that progressives continue to share and swap data over time. Data and data systems are more like language than widgets—the more people who use them, the more valuable they become. Progressives need to understand that sharing and swapping data strengthens everyone.

Please list your board of directors and their affiliations.

Patricia Bauman
The Bauman Foundation

Albert Dwoskin
A.J. Dwoskin & Associates

Robert Hauptman
SEIU

Harold Ickes
Ickes-Enright Group

Tom Novick
M+R Strategies

Michael Podhorzer
AFL-CIO

Laura Quinn
Catalist Chief Executive Officer

Vijay Ravindran
Catalist Chief Technology Officer

Michael Warren
Stonebridge International LLC

Catholics in Alliance
FOR THE COMMON GOOD

1730 Rhode Island Ave NW
Ste 915
Washington, DC 20036

202-429-9680
202-429-9686
Alexia Kelley
akelley@catholicsinalliance.org

catholicsinalliance.org
July 2005
$1,500,000
501(c)(3)

Alexia Kelley
Co-founder/Executive Director

Alexia Kelley is co-founder and Executive Director of Catholics in Alliance for the Common Good, an organization dedicated to expanding Catholic voters' awareness and support for social justice and the common good. She is the co-author of two books, *A Nation for All: How the Vision of the Common Good Can Save America from the Politics of Division* (Jossey-Bass, June 2008), and *Living the Catholic Social Tradition* (2004). Prior to launching the Alliance, Kelley worked for 10 years at the US Catholic Church's anti-poverty program (Campaign for Human Development), and has worked in the environmental movement and on social justice issues for the Quakers.

Kelley has a B.A. in Religion with honors from Haverford College and a Master of Theological Studies from Harvard Divinity School with a focus on Religion and Culture.

She is a board member for the Providence Hospital Foundation, an advisory board member for Faith in Public Life, and a founding board member of Language, Education and Technology Center.

What does your organization do and how does it do it?
Catholics in Alliance for the Common Good works to expand support among Catholic citizens for social justice and the common good, and related issues of health care access, economic justice and poverty elimination, environmental stewardship and peace-building. To accomplish this mission, the

This group is "refocusing the religious debate" onto "the social good."

PAGE 99

Alliance conducts robust media/communications activities, operates a field program in 6 states and provides strategic support to the US Catholic social justice movement. Multi-faceted media campaigns include creative ad campaigns directed to Catholics and all Americans, a national progressive Catholic media commentators' bureau and 15 state bureaus and an upcoming book on the common good, *A Nation for All*. All Alliance programs are operated in collaboration with 20 national Catholic and interfaith social justice organizations that comprise the Alliance. A national July 2008 Convention for the Common Good will bring this movement together before the November elections to mobilize Catholics around a "platform for the common good."

How will your organization impact the public debate in 2008?
Throughout 2008 our national and state media and field campaign "Campaign for the Common Good" is implementing public education advertising campaigns with aggressive media and field support to amplify the common good message in our voter education materials, our movement's "platform for the common good," and publishing our book. These and other national and local media interventions and issue forums will continue to move the values debate towards social justice and the common good.

What is your 2008 operating budget?
$1.5 million

Looking out 2-3 years, how would you like to grow/change your organization?
Over the next three years, Catholics in Alliance would like to expand field operations, and maintain permanent field organizers in the Midwest and Southwest. We would also like to expand our media capacity, with a focus on hiring permanent netroots and internet organizers who would amplify our field and media outreach through coordinated efforts in new media and online organizing. We envision several satellite media/field bureaus in key states that consistently interject the social justice voice into regional media markets and organize state and regional social justice leaders and campaigns in support of a social justice agenda nationally.

What do you need to do that?
To expand our field and media outreach, we need secure and ongoing funding outside of election years, in order to maintain permanent field and media staff in our key states; and to enhance capacity at our headquarters to support and coordinate field staff and to provide training for participating organizations.

How will your organization change if progressives win in November? If they lose?
If progressives win in November, our focus will shift to providing

strong field and media support to the progressive faith movement (in collaboration with the larger progressive movement) that will mobilize grassroots and message support to ensure and hold to account legislative and policy victories for universal health care, economic justice, a responsible end to the war in Iraq and action on climate change. If progressives lose, we will continue aggressive field and media movement-building efforts, recognizing that without a strong movement on the ground, and a penetrating media message, we will never win on our issues politically or legislatively.

If you had to offer some advice to fellow progressives what would it be?

Progressives should more actively engage people of faith as allies in the struggle for universal health care, living wages, environmental stewardship and justice for immigrants. For many years, progressives wrote off most religious Americans as political allies and sought little collaboration in service of the common good. This is changing, and progressives should continue to build on nascent alliances on these issues and as a broader progressive movement. There is a hunger among progressive Catholics and others to collaborate with the larger progressive movement, and to broaden the narrow debate over faith and politics in America.

Please list your board of directors and their affiliations.

Chair, Ambassador Elizabeth Frawley Bagley
Former Ambassador to Portugal (1991-93); Board of Directors of Vital Voices International, the National Democratic Institute for International Affairs; Member of President's Advisory Commission on Public Diplomacy

Treasurer-Secretary, Francis Xavier Doyle

Fr. William J. Byron
President, St. Joseph's Preparatory School

Prof. Jennifer Mason
Associate Professor, University of Notre Dame School of Law

Ms. Melba Novoa
Executive Director emeritus, The National Catholic Council for Hispanic Ministry

Prof. David O'Brien
Professor of Roman Catholic Studies, College of the Holy Cross, Center for Religion, Ethics and Culture

Mr. David Robinson
Executive Director, Pax Christi USA

Mrs. Agnes Williams

Ms. Alexia Kelley (non-voting)
Executive Director, Catholic Alliance for the Common Good

Center for American Progress
Center for American Progress Action Fund

1333 H St NW
Washington, DC 20005

📞 202-682-1611
🖨 202-682-1867
✂ Debby Goldberg
@ dgoldberg@
americanprogress.org

🖥 americanprogress.org
🗓 March 25, 1996
📊 CAP (c-3): $26,300,000; CAP
Action Fund (c-4): $3,500,000
🔗 501(c)(3) and 501(c)(4)

John D. Podesta
President and CEO

John Podesta is the President and Chief Executive Officer of the Center for American Progress. Podesta served as Chief of Staff to President William J. Clinton from October 1998 until January 2001, where he was responsible for directing, managing and overseeing all policy development, daily operations, Congressional relations and staff activities of the White House. He coordinated the work of cabinet agencies with a particular emphasis on the development of federal budget and tax policy, and served in the President's Cabinet and as a Principal on the National Security Council. A frequent guest of Sunday morning news programs, Podesta is known for his straight talk, acerbic wit and fierce defense of the Clinton Administration— which he also served from 1997 to

1998 as both an Assistant to the President and Deputy Chief of Staff. Earlier, from January 1993 to 1995, he was Assistant to the President, Staff Secretary and a senior policy adviser on government information, privacy, telecommunications security and regulatory policy.

Podesta is currently a Visiting Professor of Law on the faculty of the Georgetown University Law Center, a position he also held from January 1995 to 1997. He has taught courses on technology policy, congressional investigations, legislation, copyright and public interest law. Podesta is considered one of Washington's leading experts in technology policy, and has written a book, several articles and lectured extensively in these areas.

Podesta has held a number of positions on Capitol Hill including: Counselor to Democratic Leader Senator Thomas A. Daschle (1995-1996); Chief Counsel for the Senate Agriculture Committee (1987-1988); Chief Minority

Counsel for the Senate Judiciary Subcommittees on Patents, Copyrights, and Trademarks; Security and Terrorism; and Regulatory Reform; and Counsel on the Majority Staff of the Senate Judiciary Committee (1979-1981). In addition, in 1988, Podesta founded with his brother Tony, Podesta Associates, Inc., a Washington, D.C. government relations and public affairs firm.

A Chicago native, Podesta worked as a trial attorney in the Department of Justice's Honors Program in the Land and Natural Resources Division (1976-1977), and as a Special Assistant to the Director of ACTION, the federal volunteer agency, (1978-1979). He has served as a member of the Council of the Administrative Conference of the United States, and the United States Commission on Protecting and Reducing Government Secrecy.

Podesta is a 1976 graduate of Georgetown University Law Center, and a 1971 graduate of Knox College.

What does your organization do and how does it do it?
American Progress advances a progressive vision for America through its ideas and action. As a multi-issue think tank, our team of policy experts offers key insights and practical solutions on a range of ideas. We help frame the national ideas debate by: publishing policy papers that offer innovative approaches; convening experts who add their points of view to the debate; and, advocating on behalf of our ideas with influencers around the country.

We spend as much time and resources on the "selling" of our work as we do on its development—that is, we have built a communications and outreach infrastructure that makes sure our ideas are disseminated, advocated for and enacted. Our target audiences include: Capitol Hill, where we engage members of Congress and staffs to advance legislative priorities; state and local leaders who welcome policy innovation; mainstream and new media outlets; and, activists and advocates around the country.

How will your organization impact the public debate in 2008?
We will work to ensure that issues most important to the American people, ones where progressives have real ideas and solutions, are advanced in the public debate. We will pave the way for important conversations on health care, economic mobility, energy and global warming and our nation's security by offering practical progressive ideas and analysis coupled with scrutiny of and pushback against failed conservative ideas and actions— all in real time.

This group is "the central hub of the modern progressive movement."

What is your 2008 operating budget?
Center for American Progress (c-3): $26.3 million; Center for American Progress Action Fund (c-4): $3.5 million

Looking out 2-3 years, how would you like to grow/change your organization?
As we work to frame a progressive national agenda and create a narrative and a brand around what it means to be progressive, the Center for American Progress hopes to deepen our portfolio of policy expertise, strengthen our outreach and advocacy capabilities, build a community of supporters from around the country who believe in our vision and our mission, and build an endowment that ensures the organization's future.

What do you need to do that?
We need to broaden our audience of core supporters who can lend policy expertise, networks of influence and financial support.

How will your organization change if progressives win in November? If they lose?
CAP/CAPAF will continue to play a central role in the development and marketing of progressive ideas and values regardless of the outcome in 2008. Should progressives score notable victories up-and-down the ballot, we would expect to serve as a central source for transition and governing ideas, personnel decisions and on-going issue advocacy campaigns at both the federal and state levels. We would also expect to help drive the larger progressive movement's efforts to move its major priorities in 2009 and beyond—restored economic security and mobility, universal health care, poverty reduction, national energy transformation and the end of the war in Iraq.

If you had to offer some advice to fellow progressives what would it be?
Take the time and care to ensure that all of the new voters and activists who have entered the system this election cycle become core parts of the progressive movement for years to come. We are on the cusp of a significant realignment of our politics away from the conservative policies and coalitions of the past. We are moving towards a progressive majority that could significantly transform American politics the way Theodore and Franklin Roosevelt and the women's suffrage and civil rights movements did in the twentieth century. But like all significant moments in our history, we need to solidify a enduring coalition in order to make these changes possible. The millions of young people and new voters who are energizing our current politics need a permanent home that welcomes them, encourages their participation, and makes the best use of their ideas and beliefs about the future.

Please list your board of directors and their affiliations.

Carol Browner
The Albright Group

Senator Tom Daschle
Alston & Bird, LLP

Richard Leone
The Century Foundation

Peter Lewis

Cheryl Mills
New York University

Aryeh Neier
Open Society Institute

John Podesta
Center for American Progress

Marion Sandler
Sandler Foundation

Hansjörg Wyss
Synthes-Stratec

Jose Villarreal
Akin Gump Strauss
Hauer & Feld, LLP

Center on

Budget
and Policy
Priorities

820 First St NE
Ste 510
Washington, DC 20002

📞 202-408-1080

🖨 202-408-1056

✂ David Simmons, Director of
Development & External Affairs

@ Simmons@cbpp.org

💻 cbpp.org

🔑 1981

📊 $16,413,000

🏛 501(c)(3)

Bob Greenstein
Founder/Executive Director

Greenstein is the founder and Executive Director of the Center on Budget and Policy Priorities. He is an expert on the federal budget and a range of domestic policy issues, including low-income assistance programs, tax policy and Social Security.

Greenstein has written numerous reports, analyses, op-ed pieces and magazine articles on budget- and poverty-related issues. He appears on national television news and public affairs programs and is frequently asked to testify on Capitol Hill. His ideas on fiscal issues and domestic policy are sought by federal policymakers, journalists, and leaders of organizations involved in these issues.

In 1996 Greenstein was awarded a MacArthur Fellowship; the MacArthur Foundation cited the Center as "a model for a non-partisan research and policy organization." In 1994 he was appointed by President Clinton to serve on the Bipartisan Commission on Entitlement and Tax Reform. Prior to founding the Center, Greenstein was Administrator of the Food and Nutrition Service at the U.S. Department of Agriculture, where he directed the agency that operates the Food Stamp Program and other federal food assistance programs.

A recent Washington Post profile of the Center observed, "For the past 25 years...Greenstein & Co. have been there for every hearing, every amendment and every budget reconciliation, ensuring that the interests of the poor and working class are considered."

What does your organization do and how does it do it?
The Center combines the skills of a high-caliber national research institute with those of a high-performing

strategic policy organization. Both functions are dedicated to improving government policies toward low- and middle-income Americans and ensuring that government has the resources to meet its responsibilities and address critical needs.

The Center has a proven track record of affecting policy debates by producing credible analyses used by journalists and policymakers, developing innovative policy ideas, building coalitions, and conducting sophisticated media outreach.

A critical part of the Center's mission is to help other nonprofits, both in Washington D.C. and across the country, engage more effectively in policy debates over budget priorities and reducing poverty and inequality. For example, for more than a decade the Center has nurtured the growth of the State Fiscal Analysis Initiative (SFAI), a network of state policy organizations in more than 30 states that promote sound policies to improve the lives of low- and moderate-income families.

How will your organization impact the public debate in 2008?
By issuing trenchant and timely analyses, conducting media outreach, educating policymakers, journalists, and other non-profits, and collaborating with other groups, the Center will help shape and inform debates on budget priorities, tax policies, low-income programs, and measures to address the weakening economy.
This work will be critical not only in terms of policy outcomes this year, but also in helping to lay the groundwork for policy improvements that may be possible under a new Administration in 2009.

What is your 2008 operating budget?
$12,342,000 for core Center operations and $4,071,000 that is granted to state-based organizations for a total of $16,413,000. This figure does not include our International Budget Project or the DC Fiscal Policy Institute project. is granted to the organizations in the SFAI network for a total of $16,413,000. This does not include our International Budget Project or the DC Fiscal Policy Institute project.

Looking out 2-3 years, how would you like to grow/change your organization?
Upcoming federal and state policy debates will help determine the degree to which the nation meets the needs of vulnerable Americans, fosters economic opportunity, and raises sufficient revenue to sustain a high-quality public sector. The Center would like both to help build up non-profit policy institutes in the states and to expand its analytic and outreach capacity to help organizations that represent the interests of low-income families to

CBPP is the "authoritative voice" on fiscal responsibility. They are at the "heart" of progressive economic policy.

participate more effectively in policy debates.

Also, while the Center is known for its ability to make complex policy issues accessible to policymakers, the media, and other nonprofits, we would like to make greater use of web-based and other technologies to expand our audience to include more of the general public.

Also, while the Center is known for its ability to make complex policy issues accessible to policymakers, the media, and other nonprofits, we would like to make greater use of web-based and other technologies to expand our audience to include more of the general public.

What do you need to do that?
The Center's efforts would benefit from additional resources to enhance our analytic and communications capacity. As importantly, resources are needed to strengthen the infrastructure of state networks, such as SFAI, to strengthen their voice in state and federal policy decisions, in part through expanded coalition-building and outreach. Many of these groups operate on small budgets and would benefit from additional policy analysts, outreach staff, and communications professionals.

How will your organization change if progressives win in November? If they lose?
Regardless of who wins, the Center will have extensive work to do

to help shape important budget debates and secure positive outcomes in issues ranging from health care to climate change.

The years 2009-2010 may present the best opportunity in decades to secure major policy advances. The Center will help a new Administration develop sound policy ideas that are effective, politically pragmatic, and make progress in addressing problems of poverty and inequality, among others. On the other hand, the years 2009-2010 also could bring threats of substantial cuts in important domestic programs. In that case, the Center would help to lead a national, broad-based effort to safeguard government's ability to deliver services to those who need them.

If you had to offer some advice to fellow progressives what would it be?
Progressives must participate in federal and state debates over budget and tax issues, such as whether to make the Administration's tax cuts permanent. The outcomes of these debates will largely determine whether government has the needed resources to address significant needs in areas ranging from health care to environmental protection. This is especially true given the nation's serious long-term budget problems, which threaten to foreclose major new investments in these priorities.
To participate in these debates effectively, progressives need both

to build broad, "big tent" coalitions and to use various channels (the traditional media, the web, etc.) to educate the general public about the issues at stake, which Washington "spin" often obscures.

Please list your board of directors and their affiliations.

Henry J. Aaron
Senior Fellow, Brookings Institution

Kenneth Apfel
Director of the Management, Finance and Leadership Program of Public Policy at University of Maryland

Barbara B. Blum
Senior Fellow for Child and Family Policy, National Center for Children in Poverty, Columbia University

Marian Wright Edelman
President, Children's Defense Fund

David de Ferranti
Chair, Brookings Institution

James O. Gibson
Senior Fellow for the Center for the Study of Social Policy

Beatrix A. Hamburg
Visiting scholar, Cornell Medical College, Department of Psychiatry and Professor of Pediatrics and Psychiatry, Mt. Sinai School of Medicine

Frank Mankiewicz
Vice chair, Hill and Knowlton

Richard P. Nathan
Distinguished Professor of Political Science and Public Policy, director of the Nelson A. Rockefeller Institute of Government, and former provost of the Rockefeller College of Public Affairs and Policy, State University of New York in Albany

Marion Pines
Senior fellow, Johns Hopkins University Institute for Policy Studies

Sol Price
Founder and chairman of the board of The Price Company

Robert D. Reischauer
President, the Urban Institute

Audrey Rowe
President, AR Consulting

Susan Sechler
Senior Advisor, The German Marshall Fund

Juan Sepulveda, Jr.
Executive Director, The Common Enterprise/San Antonio

William Julius Wilson
Lewis P. and Linda L. Geyser University Professor, Harvard University

CENTER *for* COMMUNITY CHANGE

1536 U St NW
Washington, DC 20009

☎ 202-339-9300
🖨 202-387-4892
✂ Elizabeth Coit, Development
   Director, 202-339-9326
@ ecoit@communitychange.org

🖥 communitychange.org
🔑 1968
📊 $13,949,691
🏛 501(c)(3)

Deepak Bhargava,
Executive Director

Deepak Bhargava is Executive
Director of the Center for Community
Change. Mr. Bhargava previously
served as the Center's Director of
Public Policy. He also directed the
Center's National Campaign for Jobs
and Income Support.

During his tenure as Executive
Director, Mr. Bhargava has sharpened
the Center's focus on grassroots
community organizing as the central
strategy for social justice and on
public policy change as the key
lever to improve poor people's lives.
He conceived and led the Center's
work on immigration reform, which
has resulted in the creation of the
Fair Immigration Reform Movement
(FIRM), a leading grassroots network
pressing for changes in the country's

immigration laws. He has spearheaded
the creation of innovative new projects
like Generation Change, a program
that recruits, trains and places
the next generation of community
organizers, and the Community
Voting Project, which brings large
numbers of low-income voters into
the electoral process. Mr. Bhargava
has also overseen a dramatic internal
transformation of the organization over
the past years, resulting in a younger,
more diverse board and staff, a new
physical home at 1536 U Street and
greater focus of the organization's
work on strengthening and aligning
community organizations toward
policy change.

Mr. Bhargava has provided
intellectual leadership on a variety
of issues including the future of
the progressive movement in the
United States, poverty, racial justice,
immigration reform, community
organizing and economic justice.
He has written on these issues for
a range of publications including
The Washington Post, The Nation
and *The American Prospect.* His

strategy memo co-authored with Seth Borgos, "A Proposition for the Future," provided a roadmap for how the field of grassroots organizing and the Center needed to adapt to changing circumstances, and proved highly influential in the field. His groundbreaking article co-authored with Jean Hardisty, "Wrong About the Right" influenced how many progressives think about the strategies necessary to achieve lasting social change. Mr. Bhargava has testified before Congress on more than 20 occasions.

He serves on the boards of the Coalition for Comprehensive Immigration Reform, the Discount Foundation, the League of Education Voters, *The Nation* editorial board and the National Advisory Board for the Open Society Institute.

Born in Bangalore, India, Mr. Bhargava's family immigrated to the United States when he was a child. He grew up in New York City and graduated summa cum laude from Harvard University. He lives in Washington, D.C. with his partner Harry Hanbury, a documentary filmmaker.

What does your organization do and how does it do it?
The Center for Community Change strengthens the capacity of grassroots organizations working in low-income communities of color, and links them together in statewide and national coalitions to win progressive policy change. By creating and nurturing grassroots organizations, we engage constituencies that most national progressive organizations cannot reach or do not have the familiarity to support, with a focus on African Americans, new immigrants, low-income whites and Native Americans. We organize nationwide coalitions to raise a political and moral voice for social change, such as the Fair Immigration Reform Movement, the nation's premier grassroots coalition of immigrant rights organizations pressing for humane immigration laws. We help grassroots organizations engage in rigorous, systematic electoral programs by providing technical assistance, data and financial resources through our Community Voting Project. We train community organizers by providing paid internship and fellowship opportunities to promising young leaders through our Generation Change program.

How will your organization impact the public debate in 2008?
In 2008, we will register and mobilize 550,000 low-income voters; host scores of public forums that enable low-income people to ask policymakers about the issues that matter to them; build coalitions

This organization brings the debate back to the "moral fundamentals of democracy." Their ED, Deepak Bhargava, is a "dynamic leader for change."

that can push issues of health care, immigration and poverty into the national debate in 2008 and beyond; teach low-income grassroots groups how to project their message and showcase their work through the media; and convene grassroots leaders, policymakers, public intellectuals and others to develop an agenda for a new President and Congress.

What is your 2008 operating budget?
$13,949,691

Looking out 2-3 years, how would you like to grow/change your organization?
In the past five years, our organization has grown rapidly and we are mostly looking to stabilize in the next few years. We do, however want to: (a) broaden and deepen the network of field relationships we have built through the Campaign for Community Values; (b) develop stronger ties with other progressive organizations and allies; (c) become more tactically nimble, with greater capacity to respond to breaking opportunities; and (d) strengthen the reflective and analytical culture of the organization and grapple with the challenge of how governing power could be used creatively and accountably.

What do you need to do that?
Two things: Internally, we need to strengthen our communications, public policy and alliance-building capacities, which have not kept pace with the growth of our field relationships. Beyond that, we need

to generate more resources for our key field partners—those locally based organizations that engage and develop leadership at the community level. Without a vibrant community organizing sector, it will be impossible to achieve our own organizational goals or the broader goals of the progressive moment.

How will your organization change if progressives win in November? If they lose?
In response to the harsh political climate of recent years, we have directed most of our attention to long-term capacity building and strengthening the field. A progressive victory would open the door to achieving substantive policy changes for our constituents for the first time in nearly a decade. Taking advantage of that opening will require us to implement the changes described above (greater tactical mobility, cross-sectoral alliances, more policy and communications capacity, etc.) at an accelerated pace, with some potentially hard trade-offs between short-term opportunities and long-term commitments. If progressives lose, our organizational trajectory will be the same, but the pace is likely to be more measured.

If you had to offer some advice to fellow progressives what would it be?
(a) Think boldly, not just incrementally. We are looking at a transformative moment in American politics; let's not blow it by thinking small.
(b) Take ideas seriously, as the Right

did, but keep in mind that the best ideas grow out of the interplay of action and reflection. The current division of labor between an elite policy sector and a field in constant, repetitive motion serves neither well.

(c) Rather than accommodate our politics to the hyper-individualism of contemporary America, we need to talk explicitly about the ties of empathy, responsibility and common fate that bind people together. It's not an easy story to tell, but without a deeper sense of human solidarity we'll never get to the world we want.

(d) Take race seriously. The question for progressives is—"Is everyone on our bus?" or will we sidestep politically difficult issues like immigration reform or criminal justice or racial justice that impact the most vulnerable and disadvantaged people in our society?

Please list your board of directors and their affiliations.

Deepak Bhargava
Executive Director, Center for Community Change

Heather Booth
Director of Health Care Reform Campaign, AFL-CIO

Tom Chabolla
Assistant to the President, Service Employees International Union

Bill Dempsey
Director, Capital Stewardship Program United Food and Commercial Workers Union

Patty Dinner
Consultant

Sara Gould
President & CEO, Ms. Foundation for Women

Pronita Gupta
Director of Programs, Women Donors Network

Jonathan Heller
Project Director, Human Impact Partners

Alan Jenkins
Executive Director, The Opportunity Agenda

Madeline Lee
Consultant, Madeline Lee Consulting Services

Paulette Meyer
Chair, Equal Rights Advocates

Cecilia Munoz
Vice President, National Council of La Raza

Manuel Pastor Jr.
Professor, Geography & American Studies, Equity Director, Program for Environmental and Regional Equity, USC Department of Geography

Lenora Bush Reese
Consultant

Frank Sanchez
Senior Program Officer,
The Needmor Fund

Phil Tom
Associate, Small Church
& Community Ministry Office,
Presbyterian Church (USA)

Dorian T. Warren
Assistant Professor of International
& Public Affairs, Columbia University

CENTER FOR INDEPENDENT MEDIA

1825 Connecticut Ave NW
Ste 625
Washington, DC 20009

✆ 202-387-3670
🖶 202-37-3673
✂ David S. Bennahum
@ david@newjournalist.org

🖥 newjournalist.org
⌬ May 1, 2006
📊 $4,382,790
🖧 501(c)(3)

David S. Bennahum
Director

Bennahum is a former journalist and leading new media strategist, beginning with his role as a founding writer with *Wired* magazine in 1994, and a business career that included guiding online strategy for several Fortune 500 corporations and partnership in a New York-based private equity fund that invested in next generation wireless mobile services. For the past three years, David has focused his skills on the creation of long-term not-for-profit infrastructure, including working with David Brock to establish Media Matters for America in 2004, and working with Rob Stein to create the Democracy Alliance in 2005, where he served as Director of Strategy and Research.

What does your organization do and how does it do it?

The Center for Independent Media is a nonpartisan nonprofit organization that fosters diversity of ideas in the national debate through the advancement of independent media, with a primary emphasis on online journalism. The Center brings talented and diverse voices and ideas to the fore of our national discourse, through its Fellowships, publications, conferences and research. Programs emphasize the importance of citizen-driven journalism as a critical founding principle of our nation. Program participants adhere to the highest standards of journalism, follow the code of ethics adopted by the Society of Professional Journalists and are the recipients of numerous awards for excellence in journalism.

CIM is a "powerful alternative" to the big money news conglomerates. It is "the future."

How will your organization impact the public debate in 2008?

With over 16,000 stories broken since the first program launched in Colorado in July 2006, and dozens of stories having captured national and local media attention, the Center has demonstrated and perfected a scalable mechanism to produce quality citizen-driven online journalism that adheres to the highest standards of the profession, while diversifying the breadth of news available to the public. The Center's growth will be focused on expanding our programs in the two critical regions of the country where we currently operate: the Rocky Mountain / Southwest and Midwest.

What is your 2008 operating budget?

$4,382,790

Looking out 2-3 years, how would you like to grow/change your organization?

We aim to build the premier independent online news network in the public interest, capable of informing debate on the key issues of our time, thanks to the saliency and accuracy of the news we break. Much as NPR built an effective model around radio in the public interest, we aim to develop the news room and news media of the 21st Century, capable of leveraging the web as the primary vehicle for reaching a diverse audience with timely news and information.

What do you need to do that?

The Center seeks $5.5 million to expand operations to six additional states while operating its four current state programs and a national program in Washington, DC. These funds can be divided in two parts: $3.1 million to operate our current programs (4 states and Washington, DC), and $2.4 million of new support to expand to six additional states.

How will your organization change if progressives win in November? If they lose?

Regardless of electoral outcomes, the Center's news network will continue to hold government by the people, for the people, accountable for its actions, on the state and national level. The role of the news media, enshrined in our constitution, is to act in the interest of civic debate and robust democracy, by investigating the workings of those sent to office on behalf of the nation's citizens and informing the public with timely, accurate news reports. At a time when the news media has collapsed, especially in local markets, we will continue to fill the void they've left.

Please list your board of directors and their affiliations.

David Bennahum
(see page 115)

Eric Braverman
Associate Principal in McKinsey & Company's Washington, DC office.

John Bzorthwick
John Borthwick is an investor and entrepreneur in the process of creating a new early stage funding vehicle.

CENTER FOR PROGRESSIVE LEADERSHIP

1133 19th St NW
9th Flr
Washington, DC 20036
202-775-2003

☎ 202-318-0485

🖨 Peter Murray

✉ pmurray@
progressiveleaders.org

@ ProgressiveLeaders.org

🖥 August 2004

📊 501(c)(3)

🏛 CPL, a 501(c)(3): $3,500,000;
CPL Action Network,
a 501(c)(4): $600,000

Peter Murray
President

Peter Murray is the founder of the Center for Progressive Leadership (CPL), a national training institute dedicated to developing the next generation of progressive leaders. Mr. Murray has spearheaded the creation of CPL's core training curriculum, expansion in five state offices and development of CPL's national leadership programs.

Prior to joining CPL, Mr. Murray was the President and founder of the Empowerment Group, Philadelphia's largest minority and bi-lingual entrepreneurship training organization. Mr. Murray was also co-founder and Executive Vice-President of the I Do Foundation, a national social justice foundation, and CEO of Image Contractors, a community-based construction company in Philadelphia. For his leadership in the nonprofit sector, he received the Eli Segal Entrepreneurship Award in 2002, the Eugene Lang Community Service Award in 1999 and was selected for *Fast Company* magazine's 2002 "Fast 50," which honors 50 leaders from around the world who are reshaping their sectors.

What does your organization do and how does it do it?
The Center for Progressive Leadership (CPL) is a national political training institute that develops diverse leaders who can effectively advance progressive political and policy change.

CPL has trained over 4,000 diverse progressive leaders through intensive, nonpartisan leadership programs

Recruiting and training "top talent."

primarily in our state offices in Arizona, Colorado, Michigan, Ohio and Pennsylvania. CPL trains, mentors and coaches high-potential leaders at every level of political involvement, including:

- Organization Leaders
- Future Candidates and Elected Officials
- Campaign Professionals
- Community Organizers and Grassroots Activists
- Policy, Government and Media Leaders

The Center for Progressive Leadership's programs provide comprehensive, long-term leadership development through a variety of techniques including interactive workshops, mentorship, leadership coaching, field work and peer networking.

CPL targets leaders from communities which have traditionally lacked access to political power, including women, people of color and GLBT individuals.

CPL's programs support communities of leaders working together to bring about progressive change.

How will your organization impact the public debate in 2008?
In 2008, CPL is capitalizing on the new surge of progressive energy in our political system. Hundreds of thousands of Americans are engaging in progressive politics for the first time. Building on this groundswell of excitement, CPL is training thousands of new leaders in core political skills and placing them

in organizations and campaigns. CPL's training will boost field organizing efforts in 2008 and draw these newly engaged leaders into a lifetime of activism.

What is your 2008 operating budget?
$3.5 Million for the Center for Progressive Leadership (501c3) $600,000 for the Center for Progressive Leadership Action Network (501c4).

Looking out 2-3 years, how would you like to grow/change your organization?
The Center for Progressive Leadership's 2-3 year vision is one of strategic expansion into new states. The Center for Progressive Leadership is looking to establish 5 additional state offices by 2010. Potential targets include Florida, New Mexico, Virginia, North Carolina, Oregon and Wisconsin. With a total of 10 permanent state offices in 2010, CPL will be training thousands of promising leaders each year who will reshape politics from the grassroots up.

What do you need to do that?
Strong in-state support (partners, advisors and donors) and national funding for growth. Local support in target states from partner organizations, donors, elected officials and activists is crucial for CPL's success. CPL aims to expand to a $6.5 million budget by 2010, which will require significant new donor support at the national and state level.

How will your organization change if progressives win in November? If they lose?
Year in and year out, win or lose, the Center for Progressive Leadership will be recruiting, training, mentoring and supporting the next generation of progressive leaders.

If you had to offer some advice to fellow progressives what would it be?
"If you want one year of prosperity, grow grain. If you want ten years of prosperity, grow trees. If you want 100 years of prosperity, grow people."
—Chinese Proverb
Let's build 100 years of success for the progressive movement.

Please list your board of directors and their affiliations.

Raúl Grijalva
United States Representative, Arizona's 7th District

Kathleen Kennedy Townsend
Former Lieutenant Governor of Maryland; Assistant Attorney General of the United States; Founder of The Maryland Student Service Alliance

Tony Payton, Jr
Pennsylvania State Representative; 2006 CPL Pennsylvania Fellow

Jeffrey Navin
Managing Director, American Environics Strategies

Mike Lux
CEO of Progressive Strategies, LLC

Matt Dunne
Community Affairs Consultant at Google.com

THE
CENTURY
FOUNDATION

41 East 70th St
New York, NY 10021

📟 212-535-4441
🖨 212-535-7534
✳ Christy DeBoe Hicks,
   Vice President, Public Affairs
@ hicks@tcf.org

🖥 tcf.org
🗝 1919
📊 $5,200,000
🏛 501 (c)(3)

**Richard C. Leone
President**

Richard C. Leone is President of
The Century Foundation, formerly
the Twentieth Century Fund, a
public policy research foundation.
His analytical and opinion pieces
have appeared in *The New York
Times*, *The Washington Post*, the *Los
Angeles Times*, *Foreign Affairs* and
The Nation. Mr. Leone was formerly
chairman of the Port Authority of
New York and New Jersey and
State Treasurer of New Jersey.
He also was President of the New
York Mercantile Exchange and a
managing director at Dillon Read
and Co., an investment banking firm.
He is a member of the Council on
Foreign Relations and the National
Academy of Social Insurance.

**What does your organization do
and how does it do it?**
The Century Foundation, founded
by the progressive businessman
Edward A. Filene, is a nonprofit
public policy research institution.
Our efforts cut across many policy
areas, but focus particularly on
four basic challenges facing the
United States:
• persistent economic inequality
  combined with the shift to
  American households of financial
  risks previously borne by
  employers and government;
• the aging of the population;
• preventing and responding to
  terrorism while preserving civil
  liberties; and
• restoring America's international
  credibility as an effective
  and cooperative leader in
  responding to global security
  and economic dangers.

Our staff, fellows and contract
authors produce publications and
online analysis about a wide range of
issues. For example, Maggie Mahar,
author of *Money-Driven Medicine*,

writes extensively about health care reform; Richard Kahlenberg, author of *All Together Now*, is the nation's leading authority on socioeconomic integration in public schools; Greg Anrig, author of *The Conservatives Have No Clothes*, calls attention to the failure of right-wing ideas; Tova Andrea Wang is a widely sought after expert on election reform issues; Bernard Wasow writes about the economy, Social Security and taxes; and Jeffrey Laurenti focuses on restoring America's global leadership by rebuilding relationships with other countries and international institutions. Our communications staff seeks to bring attention to this work through the media and through direct interaction with policy makers and opinion leaders. Much of our recent work has attempted to demonstrate why radical conservative approaches to important national issues have been counterproductive.

How will your organization impact the public debate in 2008?
Our work is focused on many of the most important issues America will be facing regardless of who becomes president. We are producing reports, papers and issues briefs; holding public events and expert roundtables; offering commentary; and maintaining our seven informational Web sites in order to (1) explain and analyze public issues in plain language, (2) provide facts and opinions about the strengths and weaknesses of different policy strategies, and (3) develop and call attention to distinctive ideas that can work.

What is your 2008 operating budget?
Approximately $5.2 million from Century Foundation resources and grants.

Looking out 2-3 years, how would you like to grow/change your organization?
Over the next several years, we would like to increase our pool of fellows working in specific policy areas, particularly those related to economic issues, immigration and government reform. We also want to do more to support young, progressive scholars through a junior fellows program and other training sessions. To provide these fellows with the greatest possible access and opportunity to weigh in on the public debate over the issues they follow, and to expand that access beyond New York and the Washington beltway, we would hope to increase our communications staff.

What do you need to do that?
We have the plans, the experience, the space and the desire. We need funding.

How will your organization change if progressives win in November? If they lose?
We are committed to helping policy makers, journalists and the public

The Century Foundation produces "sophisticated" policy analysis, and employs "some of the smartest people around."

separate the facts from the hype, and promoting solid, workable ideas in crucial policy debates such as health care reform, education policy, election reform, homeland security and civil liberties. Experience has shown us that a well-funded, well-organized, passionate campaign for or against an issue can greatly influence the debate, no matter who is in charge. So we plan to remain vigilant and active on the issues we care about, no matter who wins in November.

If you had to offer some advice to fellow progressives what would it be?
The Century Foundation will celebrate its 90th anniversary in 2009. The work over those years on behalf of progressive causes has sometimes been lonely. In recent years we have been involved in partnerships and coalitions with like-minded institutions to mount campaigns to promote good policy and battle attempts to institute bad policy. We each brought different strengths and resources to those efforts. Our advice would be to do more to replicate those coordinated efforts, such as the battle over Social Security Reform. At the moment, there is more money available to those promoting a conservative agenda, but there is incredible brain power and creativity among progressives, which can, when pooled, win battles, if not yet the war.

Please list your board of directors and their affiliations.

CITIZENS FOR
TAX JUSTICE

1616 P St NW
#200
Washington, DC 20036

☎ 202-299-1066
🖷 202-299-1065
✂ Bonnie Rubenstein
@ bonnie @ctj.org

🖳 cti.org
⌚ 1979
📊 $200,000*
🔗 501(c)(4)

Robert S. McIntyre
Director

Robert S. McIntyre is director of
Citizens for Tax Justice. CTJ is a
nonpartisan research and advocacy
group that fights for tax fairness—
at the federal, state and local levels.
Widely respected on Capitol Hill
as "the average taxpayer's voice in
Washington," CTJ was ranked at the
top of the *Washington Monthly's* list of
America's "best public interest groups."

*Since he began his career in tax reform
in 1976, Bob has written hundreds
of articles on tax policy issues, in
publications like the Washington
Post, The New York Times, The New
Republic, and academic journals. He
also frequently appears on television*

*and radio programs, and writes
columns and op-eds for various
publications. Bob often advises
government officials on tax policy, both
informally and in written testimony.*

Profiles of Bob have appeared in *The
Wall Street Journal*, *Student Lawyer*,
National Journal, *The National Law
Journal*, *Smart Money*, *The New York
Times* (which called his analytical work
"indispensable"), *The Attleboro Sun*
and *The Hill*.

CTJ's analyses of tax proposals are
cited regularly in the media and by
legislators and candidates in both
parties. For example, in the mid-1980s,
Bob's detailed reports on corporate tax
avoidance are credited with providing
the spark for the bipartisan, loophole-
closing Tax Reform Act of 1986. *The
Washington Post* said that the studies
represented a "key turning point" that
"had the effect of touching a spark to
kindling" (June 29, 1986) and "helped
to raise public ire against corporate
tax evaders" (July 18, 1986). *The Wall*

---

* *CTJ partners with the Institute on Taxation and Economic Policy (ITEP), its 501(c)(3) research and education arm.
ITEP's budget for 2008 is $1,100,000.*

Street Journal (July 18, 1986) said that the studies "helped propel the tax-overhaul effort." CTJ's most recent corporate tax study, *Corporate Income Taxes in the Bush Years*, was published in September 2004.

Tax Notes (Mar. 21, 2001) pointed out that "with government estimators muffled by their political overlords" during the debates over the 2001 Bush tax cuts, CTJ "has filled the void and freely supplied the press as well as members of Congress with distributional analyses" that are "unbiased" and "of extremely high quality."

CTJ, with its 501(c)(3) partner, the Institute on Taxation and Economic Policy, of which Bob is also director, is active in state and local tax debates country-wide as well, and publishes a definitive analysis of state and local taxes called *Who Pays? A Distributional Analysis of the Tax Systems in All 50 States*, in 1996 and 2003 (2nd edition, Jan. 2004)—with a new edition to be published in spring of 2008.

A graduate of the University of Pennsylvania Law School (1975) and Providence College (1970) with an LL.M. from Georgetown University Law Center (1976), Bob is a member of the Massachusetts and D.C. Bars. Bob and his wife Nancy, an artist, have two children.

What does your organization do and how does it do it?
CTJ promotes fair tax policies by providing objective information to lawmakers, advocates and the public. Using a microsimulation tax model we built (with ITEP—see below) and update annually with hundreds of thousands of new tax laws, we simulate the effects of tax laws and proposed tax legislation on Americans at different income levels to determine who benefits or loses from a given policy. From this data, we draw conclusions about which tax policies are a fair deal for Americans and which are not. We present this information and conclusions to lawmakers, to the media and through op-eds and contacts with the press, and to advocates, policy experts and the general public through personal contact, our website and weekly emails.

How will your organization impact the public debate in 2008?
CTJ will write about and produce reports concerning the legislative issues that are likely to be addressed: the federal budget, the Alternative Minimum Tax, corporate tax loopholes and proposals to make permanent the regressive Bush tax cuts. With our proven ability to connect with the media, we anticipate that our findings will get a significant public airing. Many candidates use CTJ data and quote liberally from our material. We will continually make the American public aware of the differences in the candidates' positions on taxes by

"Oh my stars, they are good."

continually talking to, reaching out and educating the media.

What is your 2008 operating budget?

$200,000 (CTJ). CTJ partners with the Institute on Taxation and Economic Policy (ITEP), its 501(c)(3) research and education arm. ITEP's budget for 2008 is $1,100,000.

Looking out 2-3 years, how would you like to grow/change your organization?

A large part of CTJ's (and ITEP in the states) influence is due to the extremely high respect lawmakers and members of the media have developed for the CTJ director over several decades. As these lawmakers and reporters are replaced by a new generation, we want to ensure that CTJ continues to be the source for accurate information about tax policy. CTJ is also grooming a new generation of tax policy experts. Matthew Gardner, ITEP's Executive Director, is highly respected for his work in state tax policy. He has assembled a professional staff of researchers and is looking to add to his staff.

What do you need to do that?

Additional funding! Primarily for additional staff, but also a web overhaul and a major expansion of our email list. Our work is so in demand that it is almost impossible to supply all the requests for analyses (for 50 states, DC and the federal government) with the staff that we have. Just keeping our model updated is a major portion of the work we do.

How will your organization change if progressives win in November? If they lose?

If progressives win, CTJ intends to play a significant role influencing policy and legislation; we will consult with members of Congress and the new administration as they craft tax policy proposals. CTJ can also help generate support for good tax proposals if they are demonstratively fair and adequate for middle- and lower-income people. Through reports, media outreach, public outreach and lobbying activities CTJ is experienced at getting attention for the issues it believes in. Should progressives lose, we will continue to call attention to the unfair impact of the tax cuts that have been enacted in the past several years to help block any efforts to make them permanent.

If you had to offer some advice to fellow progressives what would it be?

Accurate data is of great value to lawmakers who need it to make their case. Progressive proposals have a better chance of being enacted if there is sound data showing their benefits for ordinary Americans. At the same time, our organization along with other progressive organizations need to work harder at reaching out to the public and presenting our ideas in a clear, understandable way, because having the right numbers is not enough all by itself. If it was, the tax policies enacted during the Bush administration would never have happened!

Please list your board of directors and their affiliations.

colorof**change**.org

PO Box 40578
San Francisco, CA 94140

📟 510-903-1809
🖨 415-840-0388
✂ Clarissa Goodlett,
   Outreach Director
@ clarissa@colorofchange.org

💻 colorofchange.org
🔑 September 17, 2005
📊 $473,800
🔗 501 (c)(4) and PAC

James Rucker
Executive Director

James Rucker is the Executive Director of ColorOfChange.org, an online citizens' lobby of nearly 400,000 people dedicated to amplifying the political voice of Black America and forcing politicians to be more responsive to its needs. ColorOfChange.org was created in the aftermath of the failed government response to Hurricane Katrina and has since taken up advocacy and electoral campaigns focused on a variety of issues.

Prior to starting ColorOfChange. org, James served as Director of Grassroots Mobilization for MoveOn.org Political Action and Moveon.org Civic Action, developing and executing fundraising, technology and campaign strategies. Prior to joining MoveOn.org, James worked in various roles in the software industry in Silicon Valley, including founding an enterprise software company in San Francisco, as well as providing management coaching and technology consulting for other start-up ventures. James grew up in Seaside, California and has a BS in Symbolic Systems from Stanford University

What does your organization do and how does it do it?
ColorOfChange.org seeks to amplify and organize the political voice of Black America using the Internet. While the voice and issue-focus of the organization targets a black audience, the goal is to build a multi-racial movement.

ColorOfChange.org's model for engagement is similar to other online organizing efforts such as MoveOn.org and TrueMajority. Through email outreaches, we call upon our members to take collective action to influence legislative and electoral outcomes. One set of tactics is aimed at lobbying, shaming and supporting public officials; another is geared towards influencing public opinion using paid and earned media. Another goal is to increase members' level of political engagement over time. We seek to do this by facilitating the development of their sense of political identity and by providing the basis for building community among our members based on a platform of shared values.

How will your organization imact the public debate in 2008?

The following are a few campaigns that we are tackling in the short term (outside of rapid-response campaigns which are hard to predict):

1. Voter Disenfranchisement/Voter suppression: In this presidential election year, we will raise awareness and run advocacy and lobbying campaigns to support programs and legislation that will combat voter suppression—a problem that disproportionately affects people of color. In both the primaries and the general election, ColorOfChange.org will mount campaigns that ensure Black Americans' votes count and are counted.

2. Gulf Coast Recovery: We will continue to advocate for the fair and equitable rebuilding of the Gulf Coast, with a particular focus on the Gulf Coast Civic Works Project, an initiative to bring 100,000 Katrina survivors home to rebuild.

3. Unequal Justice: In a follow-up to our work in Jena, LA, ColorOfChange.org will continue the push to reform our criminal justice system. Most notably, the organization will campaign for the levelling of sentencing disparities that have led to the over-incarceration of Black men in particular, and support a nation-wide campaign to free the Angola 3, prisoners held in solitary confinement for more than 3 decades for demanding prisoners' rights.

What is your 2008 operating budget?
$473,800

Looking out 2-3 years, how would you like to grow/change your organization?

Despite the unprecedented information proliferation that the Internet has fuelled, there remains a disturbing lack of timely, reliable coverage on issues important to Black Americans and our allies. For that reason, ColorOfChange.org will launch an online information service that educates our members about key political and social issues. To reach more members, and to reach them wherever they are, we are also developing an outreach

James Rucker has built a "powerful model" for reaching the African American community.

program that will make our presence felt offline and nation-wide.

Finally, our sustained campaigns effort will weave discrete calls to action into campaigns that are executed over months and years, not days and weeks. To make this possible ColorOfChange.org will add several new components to our organizing model, in particular "road shows"—multi-stop events with experts, celebrities and multimedia presentations.

What do you need to do that?
The new vision for ColorofChange.org in 2008 requires roughly doubling our operating budget from 2007. It is the right time for us to expand both the scope of our work and its impact; this will require adding new members to the ColorOfChange.org team while strengthening and growing the organization's infrastructure.

How will your organization change if progressives win in November? If they lose?
The central theme of our work at ColorOfChange.org is accountability— holding elected officials accountable to the issues and concerns of our community and working to put leaders in office that are truly committed to progressive values and who meaningfully engage their constituents.

With a larger pool of progressive leaders we can build more relationships and create allies to help us push forward issues that matter to Black Americans and other communities with similar needs. But even with progressive leadership, the push for accountability, while different, remains central. We'll find new ways to challenge our members to create a political climate where progressive officials can move innovative policies, but also challenge them to stay true to the values that earned our support on the campaign trail.

If progressives come up short, our theme remains the same—the push might be harder, but the key is being able to mobilize our members effectively to move leadership— progressive or otherwise.

If you had to offer some advice to fellow progressives what would it be?
The question of racial justice— which guides our work at ColorOfChange.org—is all too often pushed to the margins by the progressive community at large. For the progressive movement to be real and extend to all Americans, this must change, and each of us can play a part. We see part of our work at ColorOfChange.org as being a catalyst to bringing about that change. But our advice—and request—is that individuals and organizations reflect on the questions we raise, collaborate with us or work on their own or with others to bring issues of race and inequity to the center of the conversation.

Please list your board of directors and their affiliations.

James Rucker
ColorOfChange.org, Video the Vote,
Citizen Engagement Laboratory

Van Jones
The Ella Baker Center for Human
Rights, Green For All

CREW | citizens for responsibility and ethics in washington

1400 Eye St NW
Suite 450
Washington, DC 20005

*)) 202-408-5565
202-588-5020
Naomi Seligman Steiner
@ NSeligman@
citizensforethics.org

citizensforethics.org
February 3rd 2003
$3,500,000
501(c)(3)

Melanie Sloan
Executive Director

Melanie Sloan serves as CREW's Executive Director. Prior to starting CREW, she served as an Assistant United States Attorney in the District of Columbia where, from 1998-2003, she successfully tried cases before dozens of judges and juries. Before becoming a prosecutor, Ms. Sloan served as Minority Counsel for the U.S. House of Representatives Judiciary Committee, working for Ranking Member John Conyers (D-MI) and specializing in criminal justice issues.

In 1994, Ms. Sloan served as Counsel for the Crime Subcommittee of the House Judiciary Committee, chaired by then-Representative Charles Schumer (D-NY). There, she drafted portions of the 1994 Crime Bill, including the Violence Against Women Act. In 1993, Ms. Sloan served as Nominations Counsel to the Senate Judiciary Committee, under then-Chairman, Senator Joe Biden (D-DE). Prior to serving in Congress, she was an associate at Howrey and Simon in Washington, DC and at Sonnenschein, Nath and Rosenthal in Los Angeles, California. Ms. Sloan received her B.A. and J.D. from the University of Chicago, has published in the *Yale Law and Policy Review*, *Legal Times*, *The Washington Post*, *The San Francisco Chronicle* and *The San Diego Union-Tribune* and frequently appears on news shows commenting on congressional ethics.

What does your organization do and how does it do it?
Citizens for Responsibility and Ethics in Washington (CREW) is a nonprofit 501(c)(3) organization dedicated to promoting ethics and accountability in government and public life by targeting government officials—regardless of party affiliation—who sacrifice the common good to special interests. CREW advances its mission

using a combination of research, litigation and media outreach. CREW employs the law as a tool to force officials to act ethically and lawfully and to bring unethical conduct to the public's attention.

High impact litigation is at the center of CREW's efforts to expose government corruption. CREW relies on six distinct types of legal actions to perform its work: litigation, Freedom of Information Act requests, ethics complaints, Federal Election Commission complaints, Internal Revenue Service complaints and Department of Justice complaints.

How will your organization impact the public debate in 2008?
In 2008, CREW will continue focusing public attention on the real problem in government: the unethical and often illegal use of power for the financial gain of a few at the expense of the general public. In 2006, as a result of CREW's work, voters overwhelmingly rejected public officials tainted by corruption and scandal. National exit polls following the midterm elections showed that 42% of voters called corruption an extremely important issue in their choices at the polls, ahead of terrorism, the economy and the war in Iraq. Additionally, passing ethics reform legislation was one of the first acts of the new Congress this past January.

What is your 2008 operating budget?
$3.5 million

Looking out 2-3 years, how would you like to grow/change your organization?
As a result of CREW's success and the media attention generated by recent corruption scandals, CREW is ideally positioned to expand its work by substantially increasing the depth and breadth of the organization. CREW will continue to pursue litigation targeting government misconduct, pressing high profile suits and launching new cases. CREW staff will conduct more investigations to produce reports that make government activities more transparent to the public. CREW will continue to increase its pubic exposure and establish collaborative relationships with non-governmental organizations and build relationships with members and committees on Capitol Hill. Its vision is to be the preeminent legal watchdog organization in the country by 2010.

What do you need to do that?
In order to achieve this goal, CREW must have adequate financial resources to pursue greater legal actions and attract top talent, an expanded board of directors, strategic relationships with other non-profits and a significant presence in several states.

CREW is the "powerhouse watchdog" that "single-handedly brought down Tom Delay."

How will your organization change if progressives win in November? If they lose?

CREW will continue to raise public awareness about corruption and mobilize public support for the issue of government reform regardless of election outcomes. Checks and balances are at the heart of our system of government. In the case of one party control, non-governmental groups play an even more important role as they may become the only real check on the party in power. History shows us that those who have power often abuse it. Having a credible, progressive group like CREW on the lookout will work to keep politicians of both parties honest.

If you had to offer some advice to fellow progressives what would it be?

Approach your work knowing that—even alone—you can make a difference. Move forward and play hard despite obstacles and critics. Never pick up your marbles and go home.

Please list your board of directors and their affiliations.

President and Treasurer, Louis M. Mayberg
President, ProFund Advisors LLC; Co-founder, National Capital Companies

Vice President and Secretary, Daniel Berger
Senior Partner, Berger & Montague, Attorneys-at-Law; Contributor, *Yale Law Journal*, Duke and New York University *Law Reviews*, *The Nation* magazine and *The Philadelphia Inquirer*

Assistant Treasurer, Melanie Sloan
Executive Director, CREW

Member, John Luongo
Venture Partner, Opus Capital; Venture Partner, Lightspeed Venture Partners; Former President, CEO and Chairman, Vantive Corporation; Former Senior Vice President, International Division at Oracle

Advisory Board Members

Kathleen Clark
Professor, Washington University School of Law; Former ethics consultant, ABA's Central & Eastern European Law Initiative; Former Federal District Court clerk, Hon. Harold H. Greene; Former counsel, U.S. Senate Judiciary Committee

Whitney North Seymour, Jr.
Former U.S. Attorney, Southern District of New York; Former President, New York State Bar Association; Former Senator, New York State Senate

DAILY KOS

PO Box 3327
Berkeley, CA 94703

📞 510-290-2121
📠 510-981-1418
✂ Will Rockafellow, Business
and Operations Director
@ will@dailykos.com

💻 dailykos.com
🕐 May 2002
📊 peanuts
🔗 LLC (Kos Media LLC)

Markos Moulitsas Zúniga
Founder/Publisher

Markos Moulitsas Zúniga is founder and publisher of Daily Kos, the largest progressive community blog in the United States. Named "the single most successful entrepreneur of the progressive movement" by *NY Times* magazine writer and author Matt Bai, Moulitsas is also co-author of the critically acclaimed book *Crashing the Gate: Netroots, Grassroots and the Rise of People-Powered Politics* and author of the forthcoming *Taking on the System: Rules for Radical Change in the Digital Era*. He's a contributing columnist to *Newsweek Magazine* and a weekly columnist at *The Hill* newspaper. He was named one of the 100 Most Influential Hispanics in the world by *People en Español*,

clocked in at third in *Forbes'* Web Celeb 25 rankings, a *Details* magazine "2008 maverick" and was listed 26th in *PC World's* 2007 list of the "Most Important People on the Web".

Moulitsas was a U.S. Army artilleryman from 1989-1992, and earned two bachelor degrees at Northern Illinois University (1992-96), with majors in Philosophy, Journalism and Political Science and a minor in German. He subsequently earned a J.D. at Boston University School of Law (1996-99).

What does your organization do and how does it do it?
DailyKos is the nexus of the progressive online movement, a community of over 1 million unique ordinary citizens and elected officials congregating to discuss and analyze current affairs,

The "original" political blog. They "set the standard" for progressive blogging.

critique the traditional media, post opinion, organize, strategize, issue calls to action, raise money for progressive candidates and connect with each other. The website encourages progressives from all walks of life to sign up, write original material and comment on the posts of fellow users. Any and all practical steps toward concrete action are encouraged and incubated on the blog, and both long-term progressive infrastructure needs and short-term actions are targeted by the diverse, connected and self-motivated community.

With over 30 million monthly pageviews (and growing), few progressive organizations have been as successful in recent years in helping get specific candidates elected and impacting national media narratives, while fostering the (small "d") democratic bottoms-up popular engagement that is revolutionizing modern-day politics.

How will your organization impact the public debate in 2008?
The same way it has in recent years, by challenging stale traditional media narratives about progressivism, promoting progressive legislation, and by seeking out and promoting unapologetic progressive candidates like Jon Tester in Montana and Jim Webb and Virginia—both candidates we recruited and helped propell to unlikely primary and general election victories.

What is your 2008 operating budget?
Peanuts.

Looking out 2-3 years, how would you like to grow/change your organization?
We will continue to build out affiliate sites based on the enormously successful Daily Kos model, focused on such things as congressional transparency and the environment. We'll work on raising the visibility of our contributing editors, working with them to continue building progressive infrastructure and spread our grassroots message beyond the web to radio, television, magazine articles and books.

Our technology will remain the gold standard in the world of online communities and we expect to lead the progressive charge into the world of convergence—when TV and Internet merge.

What do you need to do that?
Daily Kos has an enviable level of credibility and visibility in both the progressive and mainstream worlds. So the online limiting factor to our growing will be revenues (advertising) and our ability to find strategic investors.

How will your organization change if progressives win in November? If they lose?
We are focused on building a long-term national progressive majority. That focus is little affected by our results this November.

No matter which party is in charge we will insist on transparency, accountability and openness in governmental proceedings. We will continue to fact-check and critique the traditional press and any biased or incomplete coverage of this country's public affairs. We will at every turn encourage ordinary citizens not only to engage, but to take ownership of, their political process by remaining informed, demanding accountability and running for offices themselves. And we will continue to invest in our technology.

If you had to offer some advice to fellow progressives what would it be?
Moulitsas' forthcoming book, *Taking on the System: Rules for Radical Change in the Digital Era* (Sept 2008), is an entire tome of advice to progressives. In short? We live in a time when regular citizens can take charge of their politics without the need of traditional gatekeepers in the political or media world. That includes some of the traditional progressive interests groups, many of which will be rendered irrelevant if they don't adapt to these dramatic changes.

Democracia U.S.A.

☎ 305-573-7329   🖥 democraciausa.org

🖨 305-573-6551   🔑 2004

2915 Biscayne Blvd   Viviana Bianchi   📊 $4,200,000

Suite 210   @ vbianchi@democraciausa.org   501(c)(3) pending*

Miami, Fl 33137

Jorge Mursuli
President and CEO

Born in the province of Sancti Spiritu, Cuba, Jorge Mursuli immigrated with this family to Brooklyn, NY, in 1967. He received his Bachelor of Science degree from the University of Florida.

In 1993 Jorge Mursuli joined SAVE Dade (Safeguarding American Values for Everyone), an organization whose goal, among other things, was to secure the passage of an amendment to the Miami-Dade County Human Rights Ordinance that would include sexual orientation as a category protected by law from discrimination in employment, financing, public accommodation and housing.

In 1997, Jorge took over SAVE Dade as Executive Director; in December 1998, the Miami-Dade County Commission adopted the amendment.

In 2001, Jorge joined PFAW Foundation and PFAW and as the Florida State Director. In September 2002, People For the American Way, together with SAVE Dade, led the fight, and was victorious against a repeal of the sexual orientation clause in Miami-Dade's Human Rights Ordinance. During the 2002 and 2004 elections, he helped organize PFAW Foundation's Election Protection program.

In 2004 PFAW Foundation, in partnership with the Center for Immigrant Democracy, launched Democracia U.S.A. with Jorge as the National Executive Director. In August 2005 Jorge Mursuli was promoted to Vice President of PAFW and PFAW Foundation while maintaining his role as Florida Director of PFAW and PFAW Foundation.

*D-USA became a program of the National Council of La Raza, a 501(c)(3) organization, on March 1, 2008, while awaiting its own 501(c)(3) status in the coming months. After that, D-USA will continue its partnership with NCLR as a loosely affiliated subsidiary.

THE PRACTICAL PROGRESSIVE

In the four years that Jorge has been at the helm of D-USA, the program has grown to be one of the most effective Hispanic civic engagement, voter empowerment and leadership training programs in the nation, moving from its home at PFAW Foundation in 2008 to begin a new partnership with the National Council of La Raza, where the program will become an affiliated corporation of NCLR with Jorge Mursuli as its President and CEO.

Jorge Mursuli served on the Board of the Greater Miami Convention and Visitor's Bureau. He is the former Chair of the Miami-Dade County Community Relations Board Task Force on Police/Community Relations. Currently, he serves on the National Board of the League of Conservation Voters.

What does your organization do and how does it do it?
Democracia U.S.A. (D-USA) is a Hispanic non-partisan, national civic engagement program launched in Florida in 2004. D-USA has grown to be one of the most effective Hispanic civic engagement, voter empowerment and leadership training programs in the nation.

2008 marks a new and exciting period in the development and growth of D-USA. This year Democracia USA has left its home at People For the American Way Foundation (PFAWF) to begin a new partnership with the National Council of La Raza (NCLR), the largest national Hispanic civil rights and advocacy organization in the US. This transition

represents a major step toward increasing Hispanic empowerment and participation in the political and electoral processes of this country. Democracia USA accomplishes its mission through voter empowerment; leadership training; civic engagement and community organizing efforts.

How will your organization impact the public debate in 2008?
By registering over 120,000 new Hispanic voters throughout the country in 2008, Democracia USA will significantly increase the prominence and participation of Hispanics in the political process.

What is your 2008 operating budget?
$4.2M total voter registration and leadership training.

Looking out 2-3 years, how would you like to grow/change your organization?
Democracia USA looks forward to expanding its capacity in an additional three to four states with the goal of continuing to empower the Hispanic community through the civic engagement process.

What do you need to do that?
We need to continue to cultivate our partner organizations on the ground via

Focusing on a "critical" constituency, Democracia is "key to building a sustainable progressive majority."

our Latin American Family Partnerships in existing and new communities where D-USA works, and secure sustainable funding to maintain a significant presence in those communities.

Norman Lear
TV Producer

Maricarmen Aponte
Hispanic Television Network

How will your organization change if progressives win in November? If they lose?

Regardless of the outcome of this year's Presidential election, Democracia USA, a non-partisan civic engagement organization, will continue to educate Hispanic voters of how the electoral process affects the issues that Latinos care about.

If you had to offer some advice to fellow progressives what would it be?

Understand that Latinos are becoming a driving force in American politics. Latinos need to be brought to the table in a significant way for any political agenda to move forward. Those that invest in the development of Hispanic civic engagement, progressives and conservatives alike, will reap the subsequent political benefits.

Please list your board of directors and their affiliations.

Janet Murguía
NCLR

Cecilia Muñoz
NCLR

Jorge Mursuli
Democracia USA

DEMOCRACY ALLIANCE

1800 Massachusetts Ave NW
Suite 5000M
Washington, DC 20008

✖ Alexandra Visher,
Communications Director

@ avisher@
democracyalliance.org

🖳 democracyalliance.org

🔑 January 2005

🗂 Not-for-profit corporation

Kelly Craighead
Managing Director

Kelly Craighead came to the Democracy Alliance with extensive knowledge and experience in politics, media and business. After joining the Alliance team as a consultant in 2004, she was promoted to Vice-President of Partner Services in 2005 and was responsible for recruiting Alliance Partners, managing Partner engagement and aligning millions of dollars in Alliance Partner investments. In January of 2007, Kelly was named Managing Director and is charged with strengthening the Alliance community of donors and organization leaders, all of whom are committed to making our progressive vision of America a reality. Kelly joined the Democracy Alliance after working as a strategic consultant to Media Matters for America during its start-up phase. Prior to that, Kelly worked for Senator Hillary Rodham Clinton, during both her tenure as First Lady and later at her leadership PAC. In the White House, with the rank of Deputy Assistant to the President, Kelly directed all aspects of the First Lady's travels abroad and in the United States as well as managing many special domestic and international initiatives. She and her husband live in Washington, DC.

What does your organization do and how does it do it?
The Alliance is a first-of-its-kind network of progressive donors and movement leaders. The mission of the Democracy Alliance is to strengthen democracy by partnering with, making human and financial investments in and fostering collaboration among progressive leaders and institutions committed to building a sustainable

The DA "changed the strategy" for "winning over the long term."

movement infrastructure that promotes a progressive America. The Alliance recommends that its members invest in a portfolio of carefully selected organizations that are a part of the foundation of a sustainable progressive movement. The Alliance focuses primarily on organizations that advance the progressive agenda through idea generation and development on core issues, train the next generation of progressive leaders, engage and mobilize citizens around a progressive agenda at all levels and use new technologies and approaches to communicate progressive values, policies and messages.

How will your organization impact the public debate in 2008?
By supporting organizations recommended through the collaborative and strategic Alliance investment model, Alliance members support a broad array of progressive organizations that operate at the state and local level, facilitate collaboration, promote progressive ideas and policies, train diverse young leaders to work in progressive organizations, eliminate barriers to voter participation and counter assaults by the Right-wing on progressive values, messengers and messages. A strong democracy is a participatory democracy, and in addition to recommending a portfolio of organizations, the Alliance has catalyzed a collaborative effort to support election administration reform efforts that will help ensure that all votes are counted in 2008, and beyond.

What is your 2008 operating budget?
The Alliance is supported by membership dues, contributions from its members, and operates with a core staff of 15 people.

Looking out 2-3 years, how would you like to grow/change your organization? What do you need to do that?
In the coming months and years we look forward to growing our membership, and thereby increasing the potential funding that can be delivered to organizations through the Alliance's strategic and collaborative funding process. Investing through the Alliance process increases the impact of donor dollars and provides organizations patient capital in the form of multi-year, general operating support that is vital to long-term success. Regular performance monitoring and assessment of organizations in the DA Portfolio offers members valuable information about the return on their investment. In addition, the Alliance works to foster community and facilitate best practice sharing among recommended organizations. Further, membership in the Alliance offers members a unique opportunity to connect with like-minded donors and organizational leaders, and participate in growing an unprecedented community of progressive movement leaders.

How will your organization change if progressives win in November? If they lose?

No matter what happens in November, the Democracy Alliance is committed to a long-term vision of a more progressive America, and believes that a well-organized, well-financed and well-coordinated movement infrastructure is essential for turning this vision into a reality. The Alliance recommends funding organizations that are doing work at the local, state and national level, and that are well positioned to work collaboratively with progressive leaders in the public, non-profit and private sectors.

Please list your board of directors and their affiliations.

Chair, Robert McKay
President, McKay Family Foundation

Vice Chair, Anna Burger
International Secretary-Treasurer, SEIU

Treasurer, Drummond Pike
Founder and CEO, Tides Network

William Budinger
Founding Director,
The Rodel Foundations

Robert H. Dugger
Managing Director, Tudor
Investment Corporation

Al Dwoskin
President and CEO, A.J. Dwoskin
& Associates Inc.

Gail Furman, ACSW, PhD
Assistant Clinical Professor,
New York University

Robert A. Johnson
Partner, Impact Artist Management

Steven Phillips
Founder and President, PowerPAC.org

Charles Rodgers
President, New Community Fund

Deborah Sagner
President, Sagner Family Foundation

Michael Vachon
Soros Fund Management

Rob Stein
Founder, Democracy Alliance

DemocracyForAmerica.com

PO Box 1717
Burlington, VT 05402

☎ 802-651-3200
🖨 802-651-3299
✂ Rachel Moss, Finance Director
@ rmoss@
democracyforamerica.com
✂ Daniel I. Medress, Communications Director
@ dmedress@democracyforamerica.com

💻 democracyforamerica.com
✉ March, 2004
📊 $2,700,000
📊 PAC and 527

**Jim Dean
Chair (above)**

**Arshad Hasan
Executive Director
(not shown)**

Jim Dean

As the chair of Democracy for America (DFA), Jim Dean is committed to carrying on the legacy of his brother, Governor Howard Dean. Jim has been working with DFA since it was founded in March 2004. He serves as the primary spokesman and fundraiser for DFA and has appeared on Meet the Press, Hardball with Chris Matthews, the Thom Hartmann Show, Wisconsin Public Radio, the David Ross Show and many others.

Jim previously worked on Gov. Howard Dean's presidential campaign, beginning in early 2002. Jim has been responsible for a variety of campaign functions including fundraising, political organizing in his home state of Connecticut and supporting several additional DFA state organizations. Jim has always been an active fundraiser for his brother, including Howard Dean's eleven years as Governor of Vermont, and prior four years as Lieutenant Governor. Both Jim and his wife, Virginia, worked full-time on Howard Dean's 1986 race for Lieutenant Governor.

Prior to his brother's presidential campaign, Jim worked in the marketing research business holding various positions, including business development, marketing and sales at both Yankelovich Partners Inc. and Greenfield Online Inc. Jim, his wife and three children live in Fairfield, CT.

Arshad Hasan

Arshad joined Democracy for America

in early 2005 to develop and direct the DFA Training Academy. Before DFA, Arshad worked with MoveOn PAC during the 2004 elections. Prior to this electoral experience, Arshad was an organizer and advocate on environmental issues. He has worked on legislative issue campaigns, corporate accountability campaigns, and grassroots fundraising. In 2006, Arshad worked as the GOTV Director for Jerry McNerney for Congress. Arshad was born and raised in Grand Forks, North Dakota and attended the University of Pennsylvania.

What does your organization do and how does it do it?
Democracy for America (DFA) empowers all Americans to take ownership of our political process to create local and national change. As our nation's largest political action organization, DFA believes in the power of grassroots activism. We focus on building a long-term sustainable progressive movement, by leveraging our community of over 675,000 members. DFA runs a national field program organized into over 800 local groups active in 97% of all congressional districts. The DFA Training Academy prepares tens of thousands of activists, candidates and campaign workers to win campaigns, and supports progressive candidates by providing them with money, media and, most importantly, boots on the ground volunteers.

How will your organization impact the public debate in 2008?
Already in 2008, DFA has led the grassroots efforts to stop retroactive immunity for telecommunications companies who participated in President Bush's program of warrantless wiretapping and to propel Donna Edwards' successful primary challenge to an incumbent Bush-Democrat. DFA's largest impact this year will be our innovative GOTV campaign bringing five million new Democratic voters to the polls. DFA will supply voter information and training that will translate into victory for progressives up and down the ballot.

What is your 2008 operating budget?
$2.7 million

Looking out 2-3 years, how would you like to grow/change your organization?
Over the next 2-3 years, Democracy for America will continue to expand its membership base, train tens of thousands of grassroots activists and leaders, and become our nation's most indispensable progressive action organization.
• Membership: DFA plans to double in size to over 2 million members.

Democracy for America "puts the pressure on the people" and "gets results." Jim Dean "knows what he's doing" and is taking grassroots politics to the "next level."

- Organization: DFA will have over 1,000 local groups organized in 100% of congressional districts.
- Training: DFA will have trained over 50,000 activists, candidates and campaign workers in all 50 states.

What do you need to do that?
Democracy for America will need the resources to expand staff capacity in our field and political departments in order to grow our membership and continue to promote effective grassroots organizing within the progressive movement.

How will your organization change if progressives win in November? If they lose?
Democracy for America knows that the hard work of building a sustainable progressive majority will continue regardless of the outcome of the election in November. If progressives win in November, DFA members will celebrate, and then get right back to this work. Our mission does not end with an election because our goal is not only to elect progressives to all levels of office, but to hold them accountable as well.

If you had to offer some advice to fellow progressives what would it be?
Progressive values like providing health care to all people, a quality education to all children and sensible solutions to the climate crisis are American values. We get lost in labels sometimes, but the issues that motivate progressives are the issues working men and women across the country are concerned about. Join Democracy for America, find a local chapter in your area and start organizing to take our country back at www.democracyforamerica.com.

Please list your board of directors and their affiliations:

Democracy for America is lead by our Chair, Jim Dean and has no official board of directors. From our headquarters in Burlington, VT, our dedicated staff of twelve works hard to activate, connect and train our community and change the direction of the country.

DEMOCRACY
A JOURNAL OF IDEAS

2120 L St NW
Suite 305
Washington, DC 20037

📞 202-263-4382
✳ Andrei Cherny
@ acherny@
democracyjournal.org

🖥 democracyjournal.org
🔑 April 2005
📊 $700,000
🗂 501(c)(3)

Kenneth Baer (l)

Andrei Cherny (r)
Founders and co-editors

Kenneth Baer

Kenneth Baer—a former White House speechwriter, author and analyst—has made his mark in politics, business and academia. As the founder of Baer Communications, he has written for and advised Fortune 500 executives, non-profit leaders, presidential candidates and elected officials at every level of government. During the 2004 election, he was a senior advisor to the Joe Lieberman for President campaign and later advised the Kerry-Edwards campaign on a variety of policy issues.

Before founding Baer Communications in 2001, Baer was Deputy Director of Speechwriting for Gore-Lieberman 2000 and Senior Speechwriter for Vice President Al Gore and wrote on technology and telecommunications issues for FCC Chairman William E. Kennard. Baer brings to his writing this practical experience as well as a deep understanding of American politics, history and culture.

He is the author of *Reinventing Democrats: The Politics of Liberalism from Reagan to Clinton* (2000), has published commentaries in publications such as *Slate*, the *Los Angeles Times* and *The Washington Post*, and has been a political analyst on CNN, MSNBC, Fox News, ABC News, NPR, BBC and CBC. Baer has a doctorate in Politics from Oxford University and graduated from the University of Pennsylvania where he was elected

This is a "must read" for progressives. The progressive debate is "taking place on *Democracy's* pages."

to Phi Beta Kappa. In addition to running Baer Communications, he has taught at Georgetown University and at Johns Hopkins University. During the 2004 election, Baer was an on-line columnist for *The American Prospect*.

Andrei Cherny

Andrei Cherny has been widely recognized as one of his generation's leaders in developing and disseminating a new progressive agenda. He has been called a "superstar" by CNN, "smart, bold and thoughtful" by *The Washington Post's* E.J. Dionne, a "progressive reformer" by *The Washington Monthly* and one of the "more creative thinkers" on the politics of the future by *U.S. News and World Report's* Michael Barone. In 2004, Cherny was a Visiting Fellow at Harvard University's Kennedy School of Government Belfer Center for Science and International Affairs. From February 2003 to April 2004, Cherny served as Director of Speechwriting and Special Advisor on Policy for John Kerry's Presidential campaign. He was a key member of the small team that crafted the message, policy and communications strategies which led to Senator Kerry's upset victory in the presidential primaries.

Cherny is the author of *The Next Deal: The Future of Public Life in the Information Age*, one of the top-selling political books of 2001. *The Next Deal* examined the role technological change has

played in changing perceptions of major institutions over the course of American history and laid out a vision for government and businesses in the 21st Century. He is also the author of *The Candy Bombers: The Untold Story of the Berlin Airlift and America's Finest Hour*, forthcoming in April 2008.

A former Senior Speechwriter and advisor to Vice President Al Gore, Cherny was the youngest White House Speechwriter in American history. In 2000, Cherny was the lead negotiator and chief drafter of the national Democratic Party Platform. In addition to his professional work, Cherny—an officer in the United States Navy, Reserve—is a contributor to a wide range of publications including *The New York Times*, *The Washington Post*, the *Huffington Post* and the *New Republic*. He graduated with honors from Harvard College and received his juris doctorate from University of California Berkeley's Boalt Hall Law School.

What does your organization do and how does it do it?
Democracy: A Journal of Ideas is a quarterly journal of serious progressive thought that seeks to spur new ideas on the big challenges of the 21st Century. *Democracy*—available in print and online—is available for purchase at bookstores and newsstands in every state and has subscribers in over 90 countries. In its first year, it was named "Best New Publication" from a field of 700 magazines by the Independent Press Awards.

Democracy is the progressive analogue to the *Public Interest* and similar journals such as *National Interest*, *Commentary* and *Policy Review*, which are still going strong —and the *American Interest* which conservatives launched in 2005. It brings to light new ideas, stimulates debates about them and pushes forward the process of rebirth and rejuvenation of the progressive movement. *Democracy* focuses on big picture ideas—bigger than even specific policies. It proposes ways of thinking about important issues, eschewing discussion of near-term political developments to concentrate on the long-term trends in American life that will shape the terrain of the future.

How will your organization impact the public debate in 2008?
Democracy has already been having such an impact. Its ideas have found their way into the platforms of every major Democratic presidential candidate. For instance, Senator Hillary Clinton adopted the universal 401(k) plan first unveiled in Gene Sperling's "Rising Tide Economics" (Fall 2007) and the Financial Products Safety Commission first proposed by Elizabeth Warren in the Summer 2007 issue. *The Washington Post's* David Ignatius cited Gene Sperling's article "Rising Tide Economics" from our fall issue as a source for the "next Clintonomics," and the *Politico's* Ben Smith dubbed the piece "probably the most useful read around if you're looking to understand Clintonomics 2.0." Senators Obama and Edwards

have also made proposals straight from the pages of *Democracy*. And our Spring issue, coming in March 2008, will offer a special package of 20 path-breaking ideas that will, without a doubt, help shape the discussion in forming the next progressive agenda.

What is your 2008 operating budget?
$700,000

Looking out 2-3 years, how would you like to grow/change your organization?
Democracy has been able to establish itself as a voice that is central to forming the next progressive vision and agenda. Over the next couple of years our biggest challenge is to continue expanding our reach beyond that of the most plugged-in opinion leaders and to reach even more of the general public.

What do you need to do that?
Some more money, more time and more organizational allies.

How will your organization change if progressives win in November? If they lose?
If progressives win, *Democracy* becomes the place that pushes and prods those in office to think bigger —and offers them ideas on how to do so. If we lose, it will be because in the face of huge political advantages, the agenda offered did not resonate. *Democracy's* work is to fix that.

If you had to offer some advice to fellow progressives what would it be?

Our two big notions are these: 1. Ideas matter—if you don't have a real, concrete vision to offer the American people all the grassroots organizing and media platforms and message massaging in the world will be for naught. 2. We need a radically new set of ideas for an age of globalization, new transnational security threats and a revolutionary moment in American society. The same old won't work – and the ambition of our ideas needs to match the transformational change we're seeing and the courage of progressive leaders who came before us.

Please list your board of directors and their affiliations.

Democracy has an Editorial Committee of senior public intellectuals from the worlds of academia, policy and politics. Current members include:

Louis Caldera
former President of University of New Mexico; former Secretary of the Army

Christopher Edley
Dean of University of California Berkeley Law School; former special counsel to President Clinton

William Galston
Senior Fellow at The Brookings Institution; former White House Deputy Domestic Policy Advisor

Leslie Gelb
President Emeritus of the Council on Foreign Relations; Pulitzer Prize-winning former correspondent for *The New York Times*

Elaine Kamarck
Director of the Visions of Government in the Twenty-First Century Project at Harvard's Kennedy School of Government; former Senior Policy Advisor to Vice President Al Gore

Robert Reich
Professor, University of California Berkeley; former Secretary of Labor

Susan Rice
Senior Fellow, The Brookings Institution; former Assistant Secretary of State

Isabel Sawhill
Senior Fellow at The Brookings Institution, President of the National Campaign to Prevent Teen Pregnancy

Theda Skocpol
Dean of the Graduate School of Arts and Sciences at Harvard University; former President of the American Political Science Association

Anne-Marie Slaughter
Dean of the Woodrow Wilson School of Public and International Affairs at Princeton University

Sean Wilentz
Professor of History at
Princeton University

Democracy also has a Board
of Advisors, which consists of
experienced men and women from
the worlds of business, politics and
community life, includes Robert
Abernethy, John Dyson, Mitch
Kapor, Eric Mindich, Steven Rattner,
Bernard Schwartz, Deane Shatz and
Andrew Stern.

Dēmos

A NETWORK FOR IDEAS & ACTION

	212-633-1405	demos.org
	212-633-2015	2000
220 Fifth Ave	Sophie Rogers-Gessert,	$5,700,000
5th Flr	Director of Development	501(c)(3)
New York, NY 10001	@ rogers-gessert@demos.org	

Miles S. Rapoport
President

Miles Rapoport has served as President since 2001. He began his public interest work as a community organizer, and served as Executive Director of the Connecticut Citizen Action Group. He was elected to the Connecticut legislature in 1984; as a state legislator, he was a leading expert on electoral reform and progressive tax policy and was active in organizing progressive legislators in Connecticut and through Northeast Action. In 1994, he was elected as Secretary of the State of Connecticut, using that office to promote campaign finance reform and expanded voting participation. His articles have appeared in national magazines and newspapers.

What does your organization do and how does it do it?
Démos is a values-based research, policy and advocacy organization dedicated to advancing the principles of an inclusive and vibrant democracy; an economy where prosperity and opportunity are broadly shared; and a more responsive government that can provide for the common good. Based in New York, over the past eight years, in furtherance of these principles, Démos' staff and our 20 Fellows have produced 18 books, nearly 100 reports and briefing papers and thousands of articles, op-eds and interviews. We regularly host the *Démos Forum: Ideas for Change* to create debate and dialogue on key issues, and we serve as a hands-on resource to advocates and policymakers on key issues where we have expertise.

How will your organization impact the public debate in 2008?
We are working closely with media and advocates, and providing factsheets, email alerts, books and articles to candidates to highlight and frame progressive perspectives and

policies. Démos staff and Fellows are regularly called upon to consult on key issues such as election reform and inequality in America. We are also working to mobilize young voters around a progressive economic agenda and working across the country with state leaders to restore a belief in effective government.

What is your 2008 operating budget?
$5.7 million

Looking out 2-3 years, how would you like to grow/change your organization?
Over eight years, Démos has produced a substantial body of work that examines the state of the household economy, our democratic institutions and the role of government. To make a real impact, we must expand our publication and communications efforts; double the number of Fellows we support, and enhance our ability to help young public intellectuals incubate and realize their projects; deepen our relationships with advocacy and grassroots organizations around the country and increase our ability to support their efforts; expand our presence in Washington, DC; and continue to develop collaborative, value-added partnerships with other organizations.

What do you need to do that?
Since our founding, we envisioned creating an institution to rival the leading think tanks on the right—both in scope and impact. We seek to double in size and create a broad-based, vibrant network, including individuals and foundations who are willing to invest in Démos' long-term vision.

How will your organization change if progressives win in November? If they lose?
If progressives win this November, they will need the guidance of organizations like ours more than ever. We will seek to supply ideas and framing to policymakers, and create the space for innovation and new thinking. They will need help in fending off the inevitable pressures to trim sails and play it safe, and instead advance a policy agenda to improve the lives of Americans in concrete, lasting ways. If progressives lose, we will continue the role of combating the ideological thrusts of the conservative establishment while still advancing important evidence, ideas and reforms into the political and public debate.

If you had to offer some advice to fellow progressives what would it be?
Achieving political and social change requires a number of different strategies and even different voices and tones. We should avoid claims to exclusive domain over change strategies; we need ideas and

A "great" place for progressive ideas. Demos is "an important" group.

framing, organizing and lobbying, mobilization and leadership development. We should seek collaboration and collegiality, so that we can be more than the sum of our parts and not less.

Please list your board of directors and their affiliations.

Board Chair, Stephen B. Heintz
President of the Rockefeller Brothers Fund

Ben Binswanger
COO of The Case Foundation

Christine Chen
Executive Director of APIAVote

Amy Hanauer
Executive Director of Policy Matters Ohio

Sara Horowitz
Executive Director of Working Today

Eric Liu
Founder "How We Teach" and author of a book of the same title

Clarissa Martinez de Castro
Director of State/Local Public Policy for The National Council of La Raza

Arnie Miller
Founder of Isaacson Miller

Spencer Overton
Professor at The George Washington University Law School

Wendy Puriefoy
President of Public Education Network

Amelia Warren Tyagi
Co-founder and COO of The Business Talent Group

Ruth Wooden
President of Public Agenda

DRUM MAJOR INSTITUTE FOR PUBLIC POLICY

40 Exchange Pl
Ste 2001
New York, NY 10005

☎ 646-274-5701
🖨 646-274-5699
👥 Andrea Batista Schlesinger
@ abs@drummajorinstitute.org

💻 DrumMajorInstitute.org
DMIBlog.com
TortDeform.com
TheMiddleClass.org
🔑 1999
📊 $1,400,000
🔗 501(c)(3)

Andrea Batista Schlesinger
Executive Director

Since 2002, Andrea Batista Schlesinger has applied her background in public policy, politics and communications to lead the effort to turn the Drum Major Institute into a progressive policy institute with national impact. She has doubled DMI's staff, capacity and budget, making it a leading source for progressive ideas. She has been profiled in publications including *The New York Times*, *The New Yorker* and *Latina* magazine. She has appeared on television shows including CNN's 'Lou Dobbs Tonight' and has been published in publications including *The Nation*, *New York Newsday*, *The Chicago Sun-Times*, *The Mississippi Sun Herald*, *New York Daily News*,

Alternet, Tom Paine.com, *New York Sun*, *Colorlines* magazine, *The Chief-Leader* and *City Limits* magazine. She serves on the Editorial Board of *The Nation*, the New York City Traffic Mitigation Congestion Commission and the boards of the Sadie Nash Leadership Project, WireTap and the Applied Research Center.

What does your organization do and how does it do it?
DMI began during the civil rights movement, and today works to generate ideas in support of the larger movement for social and economic justice. We specialize in getting ideas, research, model policies and even young talent into the hands of those on the frontlines of the progressive movement. Our programming includes

Full of "young and vibrant" progressive minds, DMI is an "innovative" think-tank.

a Fellows program that brings the ideas of grassroots activists and organizers into the media; a *Marketplace of Ideas* series that highlights examples of effective progressive policymaking; research into the middle-class squeeze in the hopes of creating a broader coalition for economic justice; and our recently launched DMI Scholars program, which is creating a pipeline dedicated to guiding talented young people from diverse communities onto a public policy career path. All of DMI's work seeks to impact public policy while also influencing the broader ways in which the public sees issues of social and economic justice.

How will your organization impact the public debate in 2008?
As we have for years, we will put the middle-class squeeze on the national agenda and show how a progressive economic agenda is its answer. We are injecting city issues into the national presidential dialog, showing how the interest of cities and suburbs are the solution to problems from climate change to our fragile economy. And we have offered a platform for how the next president can strengthen our civil justice system.

What is your 2008 operating budget?
1.4 million

Looking out 2-3 years, how would you like to grow/change your organization?
Increase our capacity to do more in-depth original research while developing the rapid response mechanism to concretize our role

as the go-to on how to strengthen and expand America's middle class. Develop our national presence as we collect and present the stories of progressive policies that work through our Marketplace of Ideas speaker series. Fully launch DMI Urban, currently in the gestation stage, a research and communications clearinghouse for those who want to advance a progressive agenda in cities.

What do you need to do that?
We are able to do a lot with a staff of only ten. But to execute the above, we need to strengthen our four core teams—research, communications, strategic relationships and operations—with more talent who come from the worlds we aim to serve: elected office, advocacy and organizing.

How will your organization change if progressives win in November? If they lose?
DMI has long understood that the progressive movement infrastructure is as much about governing as it is about winning. For years we have highlighted, through our *Marketplace of Ideas* series, model policies that are progressive, practical and effective. These policies are a resource to elected officials around the country; we imagine the demand will be even higher for ways to reduce the cost of prescription drugs, rein in the mortgage industry, build affordable housing, etc. And, we are well positioned because we are training the policy staffers who will drive our agenda forward through our DMI Scholars program.

If you had to offer some advice to fellow progressives what would it be?

The conservative right has defined our friends and enemies for too long (unions, lawyers = bad, the free market = good). It's time to reclaim this. We need to make the case that the poor and the middle class have a shared economic interest in a progressive agenda, that a progressive immigration policy is in the best interest of the middle class, that access to the courts and a muscular government prepared to regulate industry is in the best interests of all of us.

Please list your board of directors and their affiliations.

Chairman, William B. Wachtel
Wachtel & Masyr, LLP

Vice Chairman, Rev. James A. Forbes
Healing of the Nations Foundation

Treasurer, Morris Pearl
BlackRock

Secretary, Deborah Sagner
Sagner Family Foundation

John Catsimatidis
Red Apple Group

Bruce Charash
Apple P.I.E. (Partners In Education)

Cecilia Clarke
Sadie Nash Leadership Project

Sandra Cuneo
Cuneo Advocates

Jennifer Cunningham
Knickerbocker SKD

Rosanna M. Durruthy
Aequus Group

Stuart Feldman
Chelsey Capital

Matthew Goldstein
City University of New York

Robert F. Kennedy
Waterkeeper Alliance

Martin Luther King, III
Realizing the Dream

Daniel T. McGowan
HIP Health Plan of New York

Bernard Nussbaum
Wachtell, Lipton, Rosen & Katz

Tom Watson
Changing Our World, Inc.

Randi Weingarten
United Federation of Teachers

Jennefer Witter
The Boreland Group, Inc.

Andrew Young III
Young Solutions

ECONOMIC POLICY INSTITUTE

1333 H St NW
Ste 300 East Tower
Washington, DC 20005

☎ 202-775-8810
🖨 202-775-0819
✂ Noris Weiss Malvey, Director
of Development and Planning
@ noris@epi.org

🖥 epi.org
earncentral.org
🔑 1986
📊 $7,000,000
🔗 501(c)3 and an affiliated
501(c)4 organization, The
Economic Policy Center

Lawrence Mishel
President

Lawrence Mishel came to the Economic Policy Institute in 1987. As EPI's first research director, then as vice president and now president, he has played a significant role in building EPI's research capabilities and reputation. He has researched, written and spoken widely on the economy and economic policy as it affects middle- and low-income families. He is principal author of a major research volume, *The State of Working America* (published every even-numbered year since 1988) which provides a comprehensive overview of the U.S. labor market and living standards.

A nationally recognized economist, Mishel is frequently called on to testify and provide economic briefings to members of Congress and appears regularly as a commentator on the economy in print and broadcast media. Most recently, he wrote a paper outlining a plan to stimulate the economy, which was widely adopted by policy makers in Washington and beyond.

Ph.D. Economics, University of Wisconsin; M.A. Economics, American University; B.S., Pennsylvania State University

What does your organization do and how does it do it?
Our mission is to inform people and empower them to seek solutions that will ensure broadly shared prosperity and opportunity.

EPI's policy experts conduct original economic analyses and commentary, and are active participants in economic and policy debates in policy circles and in the media. EPI disseminates our work through a variety of channels including outreach to the media, policymakers and the general public.

The Economic Analysis and Research Network (EARN) is a national network of state level multi-issue research, policy and advocacy organizations. There are now 55 groups in 40 states; over 90 percent of the nation's population lives in states with EARN groups. The Economic Policy Institute (EPI) acts as the hub of EARN, providing leadership as well as technical and organizational support for the groups as they work to sway public opinion, develop new ideas and promote public policy.

How will your organization impact the public debate in 2008?
EPI is unique within the progressive community because of our focus and extensive expertise on, e.g., macroeconomics, jobs, wages, health, education, globalization, taxes and budget; effectiveness in dissemination and media outreach; network of academic economists; and strong relationships with policymakers and membership/advocacy groups.

We will publish and disseminate timely, relevant research and commentary regarding economic policies and proposals. We will strengthen our already significant media outreach efforts to ensure that progressive economic policy issues are included in national and state debates. EARN groups are effective communicators of national messages in the vernacular of their states, an important asset in 2008.

What is your 2008 operating budget?
Approximately $7 million

Looking out 2-3 years, how would you like to grow/change your organization?
Our mission and values will not change, but we hope to further enhance our communications and outreach capacities. EPI's backbone will always be its research, but we must expand our capacity for policy development and dissemination. This means expanding our capacity to work with in-house and academic experts to incubate and disseminate policy solutions, and expanding our capacity to disseminate and amplify good ideas. EARN staff at EPI plans to work with EARN groups to develop economic narratives for the states, broaden the role of EARN groups as commentators and put EARN group communications and advocacy in a broader context. We will expand EARN groups' capacity for policy advocacy and communications.

EPI has an "extremely well articulated vision" of shared prosperity. This organization is "unrivaled in direction and clarity." They are "thorough" and "indispensable."

What do you need to do that?

Obviously (and likely not unique to us), increased revenues would allow EPI to add staff and commission additional research, which would go a long way toward EPI reaching its longer-term goals. We'd also like to invest in modernizing our internet presence to make full use of the new media toolkit. Also, to communicate effectively with the many, diverse groups within the progressive movement, we need writers and outreach personnel. EARN also needs these things, as well as increased funding.

How will your organization change if progressives win in November? If they lose?

If progressives win, policymakers will be more favorably inclined toward our ideas and proposed policies. We will likely concentrate our efforts on policy development, research that illustrates the benefits of change and cultivating relationships on the Hill. If progressives lose, EPI will marshal its resources and alliances to illustrate the negative impact of any economic policies that would be detrimental to middle-, low-income and poor families.

If you had to offer some advice to fellow progressives what would it be?

1. First and foremost: It's still the economy, stupid.
2. Investing in state organizations builds the progressive movement. Public policies ranging from education, the environment and economic development to an array of social policies are decided primarily at the state level. Many groups working in the states can communicate progressive messages appropriate to the local audience and with the authenticity of being a local messenger.

Please list your board of directors and their affiliations.

Rebecca M. Blank
University of Michigan

Barry Bluestone
Northeastern University

R. Thomas Buffenbarger
International Association of Machinists & Allied Workers (IAMAW)

Larry Cohen
Communications Workers of America (CWA)

Ernesto J. Cortes Jr.
Industrial Areas Foundation

Jeff Faux
Senior Fellow, EPI

Leo W. Gerard
United Steelworkers of America (USWA)

Ron Gettelfinger
United Auto Workers (UAW)

Teresa Ghilarducci
The New School for Social Research

Ernie Green
Lehman Brothers

EMILY'S LIST

1120 Connecticut Ave
NW Ste 1100
Washington, DC 20036

☏ 202-326-1400
🖨 202-326-1415
✂ Lindsay Wolff, Membership
   Services Assistant
@ info@emilyslist.org

🖥 emilyslist.org
🗝 1985
🔗 PAC

Ellen R. Malcolm
President/Founder

As president and founder of EMILY's List, Ellen R. Malcolm has helped level the political playing field for women candidates; given women donors unprecedented influence in electoral politics; brought millions of women voters to the polls; and created a powerful movement dedicated to restoring progressive values to American government.

An acronym for "Early Money Is Like Yeast" (because it "makes the dough rise") EMILY's List is a political network for pro-choice Democratic women candidates that raises money to make women credible contenders, helps women build strong campaigns and mobilizes women voters to go to the polls.

In addition to being the public face and primary fundraiser for EMILY's List, Malcolm in 2003 helped create America Coming Together (ACT), a massive nationwide organization dedicated to empowering and mobilizing voters. Malcolm served as ACT's president in 2003 and 2004, helping to raise over $145 million for a sophisticated and personal voter contact effort in key states. Malcolm was also instrumental in the creation of America Votes, a coalition of progressive groups (including ACT and EMILY's List) that work together to register, educate and mobilize voters.

In a 2004 profile of Malcolm, *The New York Times* described her leadership of EMILY's List and ACT as "a double threat to Republicans." The *Times* quoted Sen. Hillary Rodham Clinton referring to Malcolm as "probably the most influential fundraiser and adviser we've seen."

Malcolm has been active in public service in Washington, DC, for over 30 years. She was an organizer at Common Cause in the early

1970s and later served as press secretary for the National Women's Political Caucus. Malcolm joined the White House staff in 1980 as press secretary for Esther Peterson, President Carter's special assistant for consumer affairs. After completing her masters in business administration at George Washington University, Malcolm founded EMILY's List in 1985.

Malcolm is frequently sought out for comment on campaigns, fundraising and political strategy. She has been featured on "60 Minutes," NBC's "Today" and "CBS This Morning," and in *People* and *Fortune* magazines. Her opinions have been published as guest columns in *The Washington Post*, the *Los Angeles Times*, *The New York Times*, the *Chicago Sun-Times*, *Roll Call* and other newspapers.

The recipient of numerous awards and honors, Malcolm was named one of America's most influential women in 1998 by *Vanity Fair* magazine and, in 1999, one of the 100 Most Important Women in America by *Ladies' Home Journal*.

In 1992, Malcolm was among *Glamour* magazine's Women of the Year, and was also named Most Valuable Player by the American Association of Political Consultants.

What does your organization do and how does it do it?
EMILY's List is the nation's largest political and financial resource for women. We are a network of more than 100,000 citizens across the country dedicated to building a progressive America by electing pro-choice Democratic women to federal, state and local office. EMILY's List recruits and funds viable women candidates; helps them build and run effective campaigns; and mobilizes women voters on behalf of progressive candidates nationwide. We carry out our mission through a variety of programs, including Campaign Services and Training, the Political Opportunity Program (POP), Campaign Corps and WOMEN VOTE!.

Since its founding in 1985, EMILY's List has helped elect 69 women to the U.S. House, 13 to the U.S. Senate and eight governors. EMILY's List has helped elect hundreds of pro-choice Democratic women to federal office, state legislatures, state constitutional offices and other key local offices.

This group continues to be "one of the most important PACs in the nation."

Looking out 2-3 years, how would you like to grow/change your organization?

In accordance with the ten-year plan EMILY's List set forth in 2002, our goals by the year 2012 are to establish an equal and powerful presence of women in federal and state office. We will help Democrats increase their congressional majorities and increase the number of state legislatures under Democratic control. We will work to bring the number of women in the U.S. House and Senate Democratic caucuses and state caucuses to 50 percent, and to dramatically increase the number of pro-choice Democratic women governors.

6930 Carroll Ave
Ste 610
Takoma Park, MD 20912

📞 301-270-4616
🖨 301-270-4133
✂ Ross Margulies
@ RossM@fairvote.org

🖥 fairvote.org
🗓 June 19, 1992
📊 $850,500
🗂 501(c)(3)

Rob Richie
Executive Director

Rob Richie has directed FairVote since 1992. He is co-author of *Every Vote Equal* about establishing a national popular vote for president and *Whose Votes Count* about reforming winner-take-all elections. His writings have appeared in seven additional books and many newspapers and journals. He has been a guest on C-SPAN, NBC News, CNN, FOX, Bloomberg News and MSNBC and has addressed annual conventions of the American Political Science Association, National Association of Counties, National Association of Secretaries of State and National Conference of State Legislatures. A graduate of Haverford College, he is married, with three children.

What does your organization do and how does it do it?
FairVote researches how to reform American elections, distributes our findings to changemakers and selects proposals ready for our own high-profile communication campaigns (like FixThePrimaries.com and IncludeEveryVoter.Org) and ballot measure and state lobbying campaigns. We seek to guarantee universal access to participation, meaningful ballot choices and governments grounded in majority rule and fair representation. Our signature reforms include the national popular vote plan for president, instant runoff voting, universal voter registration and a constitutional right to vote.

Because we measure success with nothing short of changing our nation's most formidable obstacles to

FairVote is "persistent" and "gutsy."

representative democracy, we must be innovative in our thinking, action and coalition-building. Our combination of thinking big but seeking victory explains why we were the group to recognize the promise of the National Popular Vote plan—know it would both defang the Electoral College and demonstrate how any necessary reform can be won with appropriate smarts and resources.

How will your organization impact the public debate in 2008?
This year's historic presidential election will provide powerful reform lessons for future elections. To make the case for how and why to revamp parties' nomination rules and to pass the National Popular Vote plan in states, we will highlight our system's failings with new websites (like the tongue-in-cheek Unpopularvote. com), pointed commentaries, vigorous blogging and changemaker outreach—building on our successes on these issues and others like 17-year-old voting in primaries and 16-year-old voter registration.

What is your 2008 operating budget?
$850,500

Looking out 2-3 years, how would you like to grow/change your organization?
We plan to double our national budget to staff our programs fully, have cross-cutting departments on communications, advocacy and research and fund new outreach tools. We expect to triple our field budget for financing reformers and

lobbyists in the states most ready for victories. We have developed a powerful case for change, viable reform solutions and connections across the pro-democracy community nationally and in states. It's time to build on our impressive track record of local and state wins by enacting the National Popular Vote plan, establishing 16-year-old registration as a norm and winning instant runoff voting in states.

What do you need to do that?
We need money, of course, but also must clearly demonstrate how our organization is ready for this growth and how our nation is ready for major electoral reforms. Internally, we will complete redefinition of our board role and composition and ensure core staffers have appropriate financial support, training and supervision.

How will your organization change if progressives win in November? If they lose?
Progressive victories should mean two things for FairVote: new friends in high places who can support reform, as has been so key for us, and a new climate for state reform and national reform. If progressives lose, federal changes are out, but state reform will be all the more galvanizing to progressives likely to identify electoral rules as barriers to success. Either way, the case for our growth plan will be all the more compelling; the main difference will be greater emphasis on states if progressives lose—and, we suspect, more progressives looking for good jobs with FairVote.

If you had to offer some advice to fellow progressives what would it be?

I would urge them to look beyond the next election. In all seriousness, we are in a struggle for preserving ecological balance and fundamental human rights and dignity. Transformative change is not just desirable, but necessary. These necessary changes won't happen with one electoral success, no matter how sweeping. We must build on successes to institutionalize ongoing opportunities to build the case for change, win that change and sustain it. Doing so will demand being open to new policy ideas, new approaches and new alliances. "Reform" is not enough; we need "transformation."

Please list your board of directors and their affiliations.

Chair, Krist Novoselic
Musician with Nirvana and Flipper, founder of JAMPAC and author of *Grunge and Government*

Vice-Chair, Eddie Hailes
Senior attorney, The Advancement Project and former general counsel, U.S. Civil Rights Commission

Secretary, Cynthia Terrell
Board member, American Friends Service Committee and director, Terrell Family Fund

Treasurer, William Redpath
Certified public accountant, BIA Financial Network

Chair Emeritus, John Anderson
Former U.S. Congressman and 1980 independent presidential candidate

Hendrik Hertzberg
Senior writer, *The New Yorker* and former chief White House speechwriter (Carter administration)

Malia Lazu
Director, The Gathering and former director of the Racial Justice Campaign Fund at Progressive Majority

Pete Martineau
Board member, Californians for Electoral Reform and Consumer Federation of California

Ken Ritchie
CEO, Electoral Reform Society of the United Kingdom

David Wilner
Co-founder and long-time Chief Technical Officer, Wind River Systems

FAITH
IN PUBLIC
LIFE

1101 Vermont Ave NW
9th Flr
Washington, DC 20005

☏ 202-435-0266
🖨 202-435-0261
✄ Jennifer Butler,
   Executive Director
@ jbutler@faithinpubliclife.org

🖳 faithinpubliclife.org
🔑 June 3, 2005
📊 $800,000
🏛 501(c)(3)

Rev. Jennifer Butler
Executive Director

Rev. Jennifer Butler is the Executive Director of Faith in Public Life. An ordained Presbyterian minister, she most recently served as the Presbyterian Church (USA) Representative to the United Nations (UN). During her nine years at the UN, Butler represented the denomination on a range of issues, including women's rights, the AIDS pandemic, genocide in the Sudan and the war in Iraq. When the Christian right shook up a UN proceeding on women's rights in 2000, Butler organized a progressive faith response and became a "go to" source of information on the Christian right's global organizing. Her book *Born Again, The Christian Right Globalized* was published by the Pluto/University of Michigan Press in October 2006. Her research has been featured in a number of publications including *The American Prospect, The Washington Post* and *Mother Jones*.

Butler cut her teeth in organizing as a Peace Corps volunteer working with Mayan villagers to oust a corrupt village chairman and working for anti-poverty coalitions in Trenton, New Jersey. A graduate of Princeton Theological Seminary, she holds a Master of Social Work from Rutgers University and Bachelor of Arts from the College of William and Mary.

What does your organization do and how does it do it?
Faith in Public Life (FPL) is a communications and organizing resource center dedicated to helping faith leaders reclaim the American values debate for justice, compassion and the common good. FPL:
• Consistently places progressive faith voices on national, state and local, print, radio, TV and online outlets.
• Provides a comprehensive menu of tools and services to progressive faith leaders including media strategy,

message development, press event planning and press list creation.

- Shapes existing press narratives through rapid-response deployment of surrogates, umbrella messaging, special events, reports and polling.
- Builds progressive faith infrastructure at the state and national level by providing local and national leaders with tools to increase their organizing capacity online and on the ground, and build broad multi-isse coalitions.
- Mobilizes progressive faith activists through the netroots with our 80,000 member e-advocacy community, FaithfulAmerica.org.
- Forges partnerships and unconventional alliances both locally and nationally.

How will your organization impact the public debate in 2008?
This will be the year of the "common good voter" and the "compassion voter" (concerned about the environment, ending torture, human rights, tolerance, economic equality) rather than the conservative "values voter" concerned only about abortion and gay marriage. FPL's communications and organizing strategy will put faith leaders and their members on the front lines talking about progressive policy and a new moral values agenda for the U.S.

What is your 2008 operating budget?
$800,000

Looking out 2-3 years, how would you like to grow/change your organization?
Since our founding in June 2005 Faith in Public Life has become the "go-to" organization for media and activists. When people visit, they typically say "you are only five people?!" In the coming years we plan to secure funding to bring our organizing and media units to scale. We are building infrastructure in four states—we'd like to start on four more. We earned 600 media hits in 2007 for progressive faith activism; we'd like to increase that to 1500. Faithful America, already the largest interfaith e-advocacy list, should grow from 80,000 to a million members. Through our partnership with Catalist, a progressive data warehouse, we plan to provide list enhancement and civic participation consulting to faith organizations.

What do you need to do that?
FPL is seeking $200,000 in additional funding for 2008 to increase the size of our organizing and media unit and staff our data enhancement program. The Sandler Foundation has generously offered a $200,000 matching grant in 2008, if Faith in Public Life can match it on a 1-for-1 basis. In 2009 we hope to reach a 1.5 million dollar budget.

This group is the "artery" for religion and politics dialogue. Rev. Jennifer Butler is "inspiring" and her wealth of experience is leading the group to "tremendous accomplishments."

How will your organization change if progressives win in November? If they lose?

Our work is for the long haul—rebuilding progressive faith organizing capacity and reaching persuadable faith communities that the Christian right once had in their grasp. Progressives are still struggling toward a unifying message and to enable leadership to be bold. Even if progressives win, will they have the courage to buck the lobbyists and public opinion to make real change? Our job is to enable faith leaders to be prophetic and out in front no matter who is in power.

If you had to offer some advice to fellow progressives what would it be?

We have a once in a lifetime opportunity in the next few years to shift the values debate toward progressive causes. The Christian right is weakened by scandal and the failures of the current administration. Progressive Catholics, mainliners, Muslims and Jews are organizing more effectively thanks to new infrastructure built post 2004 (including FPL). White evangelicals are broadening their agenda and young evangelicals are interested in broadening the values debate to include poverty, climate change and human rights. This is a potential turning point in the struggle for American values that will only happen if foresighted donors come forward to fund this re-emerging sector.

Please list your board of directors and their affiliations.

Chair, Rabbi Rebecca Alpert
Dept. of Religion, Temple University

Nicole Baker Fulgham
VP, Teach for America

Jack Calhoun
author, *Hope Matters*

Rev. Timothy Boggs
Asst. Rector, St. Albans Episcopal Church

Rabbi Steven Jacobs
retired, Kol Tikvah Synagogue

Dr. Nazir Khaja
medical doctor and Chairman of the Board of Islamic Information Services

Dr. Elizabeth Letzler
retired, Citibank VP

Ricken Patel
Founder/CEO, Avaaz.org; Res Publica

Sr. Catherine Pinkerton
NETWORK, A National Catholic Social Justice Lobby

Rev. Meg Riley
Unitarian Universalist Association Director of Advocacy and Witness

Fred Rotondaro
Center for American Progress Fellow

Dr. Susan Thistlethwaite
Pres., Chicago Theological Seminary

Dr. Emilie Townes
Yale Divinity School professor; Pres., American Academy of Religion

freepress

 413.585.1533

 413.585.8904

 Josh Silver

@ jsilver@freepress.net

40 Main St
Ste 301
Florence, MA 01062

freepress.net
savetheinternet.com
stopbigmedia.com
2003
Free Press (c3) $4,500,000;
Free Press Action Fund (c4):
$1,000,000
501(c)(3) and 501(c)(4)[*]

Josh Silver
Executive Director (above)

Robert W. McChesney
Founder/Board Chairman
(not shown)

Josh Silver
Executive Director Josh Silver co-founded Free Press with Robert W. McChesney and John Nichols in 2002. He oversees all programs, campaigns, fundraising and special projects. Josh previously served as campaign manager for the successful statewide ballot initiative for public funding of elections in Arizona and as the director of development for the cultural arm of the Smithsonian Institution in Washington. He has served as the director of an international youth exchange program and as a development and management consultant. Josh publishes frequently on media, campaign finance and other public policy issues. He attended the University of Grenoble, France, and Evergreen State College in Olympia, WA.

Robert W. McChesney
is a professor at the University of Illinois at Urbana-Champaign

Free Press is "effective" as they "fight to preserve the free market and democratic discourse" in the "ever shrinking media landscape."

* Free Press is a 501(c)(3); The Free Press Action Fund, our companion 501(c)(4) organization, was established to expand our range of activities to include lobbying Congress and the White House.

and author or editor of 12 award-winning books, including *Telecommunications, Mass Media and Democracy: The Battle for the Control of U.S. Broadcasting, 1928-1935; Corporate Media and the Threat to Democracy; The Global Media: The New Missionaries of Corporate Capitalism* (with Edward S. Herman); *Our Media, Not Theirs* (with John Nichols); *Rich Media, Poor Democracy: Communication Politics in Dubious Times; The Problem of the Media: U.S. Communication Politics in the Twenty-First Century;* and, most recently, *Tragedy & Farce: How the American Media Sell Wars, Spin Elections and Destroy Democracy* (with John Nichols).

What does your organization do and how does it do it?
Free Press is working to advance policies that promote investigative journalism, diversity of television, radio and newspaper ownership, universal access to fast, affordable, neutral Internet and vibrant public and independent media. We are the public's eyes and ears at the Federal Communications Commission and on Capitol Hill, with 35 staff engaged in policy research, communications, legal filings, grassroots education, online and traditional advocacy (through our c4). We are shining the light of public scrutiny on crucial policy debates to create a media system that serves the American public—not just a few large media conglomerates.

How will your organization impact the public debate in 2008?

Free Press will continue to rebuff efforts by the largest conglomerates to consolidate their power, and make the debate over the future of the Internet the most prominent communications debate of 2008. Thanks to our work, all of the major Democratic presidential candidates declared in 2007 their opposition to consolidation, and their support of an open, neutral Internet. We'll continue to use the elections to spotlight the need for media reform.

What is your 2008 operating budget?
Free Press (c3) $4.5 million; Free Press Action Fund (c4) $1 million

Looking out 2-3 years, how would you like to grow/change your organization?
The gravity and scope of media issues demands that Free Press recruit additional staff in the next three years. They include two more lobbyists, an additional attorney, research assistant, communications assistant, web developer, graphic designer and two more campaign coordinators. We would like to expand our base of 500,000 members to one million in the next three years, and increase our number of paying members from 7,500 to 15,000.

What do you need to do that?
Our c3 budget will increase by $1.5 million over the next three years, and our c4 budget by approximately 15% per year. We will emphasize converting our online membership into paying donors, and of course, we need to continue to hire the most talented staff in the field.

How will your organization change if progressives win in November? If they lose?

If the Democratic Party wins the White House, key federal agencies will be more supportive of our policy agenda. However, history shows that Democrats are prone towards voting with the largest media companies and against the public interest. Free Press cannot take Democratic support for granted, though the shift will enable us to move from a largely defensive position to a proactive agenda. If the Republicans hold the White House, we would continue to use the same successful blocking tactics that we used prior to the 2006 election.

If you had to offer some advice to fellow progressives what would it be?

- Stay out of the policy weeds and make your message simple and easy for regular people to relate to their own lives. While our 200-page white papers and congressional testimony on C-SPAN speaks loudly to one segment of our base, they put the other 99.9% of the population to sleep.
- Wait for teachable moments...and pounce quickly. It is critical to tie your issue to relevant issues as they break. Without the tie-in, your message won't go anywhere.
- If media (and campaign finance reform) are not your first concern, they better be your second. Progressive issues will die a long, slow death if these foundational issues are not addressed.

Please list your board of directors and their affiliations.

Founder/Board Chairman, Robert W. McChesney
Professor, University of Illinois at Urbana-Champaign; author

Olga M. Davidson
Visiting Associate Professor, Middle Eastern Studies Program, Wellesley College; Board Chair, Ilex Foundation

Susan Douglas
Director, Ph.D. Program in Mass Communication, University of Michigan; author

James Counts Early
Director of Cultural Heritage Policy, Smithsonian Center for Folklife and Cultural Heritage.

Kim Gandy
President, National Organization for Women (NOW)

Van Jones
civil rights lawyer and environmental activist; co-founder and executive director of the Ella Baker Center for Human Rights

Lawrence Lessig
Professor of Law, Stanford Law School; founder of the school's Center for Internet and Society

John Nichols
Washington correspondent, *The Nation*; Editorial page Editor, *The Capital Times*, Madison, WI

THE GATHERING

328 8th Ave
#304
New York, NY 10001

☎ 212 691-2563
🖷 212-691-2553
✂ Malia Lazu
@ malia@
thegatheringforjustice.org

🖳 thegatheringforjustice.org
☛ August 29, 2005
📊 $560,000
🖧 Project of Tides Center,
a 501c3 organization

Malia Lazu
Executive Director

Malia is currently the Executive Director of Harry Belafonte's, The Gathering, an intergenerational intercultural organization working to reintroduce nonviolence to our communities to stop child incarceration.

Formerly Progressive Majority's Director of The Racial Justice Campaign (RJC), Malia and her team identifies, trained and elected progressive candidates of color at the state and local level. Under Malia's leadership, RJC has expanded to include; The People of Color PAC Coalition and The Racial Justice League, a collection of some of the greatest minds of our time charged with reshaping public conversation and pubic policy around racial justice in The Untied Sates and the world. In 2006 RJC had a 78% win rate with 33 candidates in 5 states.

Before joining the Progressive Majority, Malia's vast experience included serving as National Field Director for The Institute for Policy Study's Cities for Progress Program, for Democracy Action Project and campaign manager for several state and local races.

A graduate of Boston's Emerson College, Malia was the founding Executive Director of Mass VOTE, a statewide non-partisan coalition of community and faith-based organizations and neighborhood associations recognized by the Massachusetts State Senate and House for increasing voter turn out in Boston.

Malia was named one of *Source* magazine's "Power 30" in 2007 and "Activist of the Year" by MTV. Her work has been featured in print, radio and television. Malia was also listed in *Boston* magazine as one of the most powerful minorities in Boston. Malia also currently sits on the boards of The League of Pissed Off Voters, The Ruckus Society and Oil Change. Malia is also co-author of *How to Get Stupid White Men Out of Office* and was a participant in the Showtime Original Series, American Candidate where she mounted a presidential campaign and finished second in the national call-in vote.

What does your organization do and how does it do it?
The mission of The Gathering for Justice is to build an intergenerational movement, rooted in history, cultures and nonviolent direct action. Our purpose is to heal communities, build collective strength and generate an environment of hope and opportunity. The Gathering creates a coordinated space to 1) fortify relationships between grassroots organizations regionally, 2) Create and support local policy campaigns around child incarceration and 3) Train community leaders in the practical application of nonviolence. Central to the mission of The Gathering is to awaken and strengthen the moral conscience of this country, to the growing catastrophe of childhood incarceration.

The Gathering accomplishes these actions through:
1) Provide a 2 day intensive on the practical application of nonviolence in all 11 regions.
2) Organize 2 national meetings a year for model and strategy exchange nationwide.
3) On going monthly meetings in

11 regions to execute local policy campaigns.

How will your organization impact the public debate in 2008?
Our children have become the symbol of violence; The Gathering will impact the public debate in 2008 by introducing young people from the streets to the public debate and supporting their platform on how they want to organize themselves from their dark future of increasing confinement at younger and younger ages. Allow them to redefine themselves beyond the narrow definition of the growing violence in our young people.

What is your 2008 operating budget?
$560,000

Looking out 2-3 years, how would you like to grow/change your organization?
The Gathering Executive Committee is working to create a decentralized structure that will allow the organization to support the work locally and allow the debate to come from the bottom up. In 2-3 years the organization hopes to have full time organizers supporting the local policy campaign work in all

The Gathering is "addressing a serious problem" in our society. They are "strengthening empowerment" through peace and justice.

11 regions and a solid analysis of what consistent nonviolence organizing in the 21st Century looks like.

What do you need to do that?
In order to do that The Gathering needs to continue to identify resources to hire and train our young leaders on the ground to continue to organize in our regions. The Gathering needs to create a technical expression of The Gathering to allow for user driven coordination through out the country.

How will your organization change if progressives win in November? If they lose?
Progressives winning in November is only the first step in regaining our equilibrium as a country, The Gathering does not foresee its work changing regardless of who wins in November. Our work is critical to supporting democracy, by creating critical citizens and empowered peoples who understand how to raise the level of civic tension to demand change.

If you had to offer some advice to fellow progressives what would it be?
We as progressives must not waver in our commitment to radical change in order to claim a victory. We must be vigilant in remaining on the side of right and fighting with the invisible people of our country rather than fighting for them in small rooms for small victories. This strategy takes longer to achieve change but we must understand that the public is critical to increasing our gains significantly.

Trust our young people, give them the tools and they will build their house. They may not do it your way, but that's what is great about being progressive, we are into diversity.

Please list your board of directors and their affiliations.

Executive Committee (The Gathering Advisory Board)

The Gathering for Justice is a project of the Tides Center. Our Advisory Committee includes the leadership of:

Ivanhoe Donaldson
The Feldman Group

Omo Moses
Young People's Project

Nane Alejandrez
Barrios Unidos

Amelia Kirby
Appalshop

Juan Pacheco
Barrios Unidos

Carmen Perez
Probation Office of Santa Cruz, CA

Curtis Jones
City Councilor, Erie, PA

Anasa Troutman
Highlander Center

Oren Lyons
Onondaga Indian Nation

Father M. Pfleger
St. Sabina Church

Sylvia Stone
Innovative Approach

James Bell
Burns Institute

Haatim Gyenyame
Simba Circle

Gus Newport
Vanguard Foundation

GILL ACTION

2215 Market St
Denver, CO 80205

601 13th St NW, 730N
Washington, DC 20005

📟 303-285-3000 (Denver)
🖨 202-347-0703 (DC)
✂ 303-292-2155 (Denver)
    202-347-5902 (DC)
✂ Bill Smith
@ bsmith@gillaction.org

🖥 gillaction.org
🔑 2005
📊 501 (c)(4)

Patrick Guerriero
Executive Director

Guerriero has been an unwavering bi-partisan voice on behalf of all lesbian, gay, bisexual, and transgender (LGBT) Americans helping secure victories for hate crimes legislation, the Employment Non-Discrimination Act, HIV/AIDS funding and marriage equality. He was named executive director of Gill Action in 2006. From 2002 to 2006, Guerriero served as President of the Liberty Education Forum and Log Cabin Republicans leading both organizations through periods of unprecedented growth while successfully helping orchestrate opposition of the Federal Marriage Amendment. From 1993 to 2001,

Guerriero won five consecutive elections: serving three terms as a state representative and two terms as mayor of Melrose, Massachusetts. As mayor, Guerriero supported landmark state education reforms and was recognized by the U.S. Conference of Mayors for his civility initiative. Under his leadership, the city built its first new schools in more than 30 years. In 2002, he became the nation's first openly gay candidate for lieutenant governor.

What does your organization do and how does it do it?
Gill Action works to secure equal rights for all Americans regardless of sexual orientation and gender expression, emphasizing partnerships with allied organizations in order to create lasting and effective political change at the state level. Gill Action provides resources to individuals and organizations working to advance equality, to encourage civic engagement and to invest in strong leadership. Gill Action

values bipartisanship and seeks out partnerships with organizations that engage people on both sides of the aisle.

How will your organization impact the public debate in 2008?
Gill Action will be working with its partners through the political process to attain legislation at the state level that positively impacts LGBT people and their families. Additionally, Gill Action will be working to engage other progressive allies and organizations to ensure that LGBT rights are among the issues included in the narrative of the broader progressive movement.

Looking out 2-3 years, how would you like to grow/change your organization?
Our two-year goals are to achieve meaningful legislative victories for LGBT people currently denied rights and protections. We will remain nimble in order to effectively achieve these victories and respond to changes in the political climate. Gill Action will also continue to expand our relationships with progressive allies, working together to achieve common goals.

What do you need to do that?
We need to continue engaging people in a conversation about equality. This dialogue must happen in a bipartisan way, involving a broad spectrum of progressive organizations.

How will your organization change if progressives win in November? If they lose?
Our dedication to working for political and legislative victories for LGBT citizens will remain steadfast regardless of who takes office.

If you had to offer some advice to fellow progressives what would it be?
Remember our allies and friends as we work for progress, because only by working together can real change take place.

Demand real results, not just symbolic victories from our elected officials.

Do not discount our perceived enemies—they have the potential to become allies.

Please list your board of directors and their affiliations.

Founder and Chairman
Tim Gill
Retired, Quark, Inc.

David Dechman
Summit Rock Advisors

Urvashi Vaid
Arcus Foundation

Gill Action is "incredibly strategic."

The Brookings Institution
1775 Massachusetts Ave
Washington, DC 20037

☎ 202-797-4360
🖨 202-741-6515
✂ Karen Anderson,
   Communications Director
@ kanderson@brookings.edu

🖥 hamiltonproject.org
🔑 April 5, 2006 (official launch)
📊 $2,500,000
🔗 Part of the Brookings Institution,
   a 501(c) (3) organization

Jason Furman
Director

Jason Furman is a Senior Fellow at the Brookings Institution and Director the Hamilton Project, an initiative aimed at developing policy solutions to promote shared growth and opportunity. He has conducted research and policy work in a wide range of economic policy areas, including fiscal policy, tax policy, health economics, Social Security and monetary policy. In 2005, CQ named him one of the five Social Security analysts who "exert more influence over the Social Security debate than any other individuals outside government." Furman has worked in a several public policy positions including Special Assistant to the President for Economic Policy in the Clinton Administration, Staff Economist at the Council of Economic

Advisers and a Senior Director at the National Economic Council. He has written numerous papers and articles on economic issues and testified frequently before Congress. Furman received his Ph.D. in economics from Harvard University.

What does your organization do and how does it do it?
The Hamilton Project produces research and policy proposals on how to create a growing economy that benefits more Americans. Working with outside experts, the Hamilton Project has released a series of "Discussion Papers" on a broad variety of topics, ranging from universal health insurance to tax reform to climate change. While these papers do not reflect a specific position taken by The Hamilton Project on a given issue, they are meant to help guide the public debate by looking at issues through a pragmatic, analytical lens. The Hamilton Project also produces broad "Strategy Papers" which help frame the debate on a given issue. Each paper release is accompanied

by a public forum on that issue to help further inform the discussion. The Hamilton Project also hosts informative, timely discussions on key current events, such as the financial market turmoil and fiscal stimulus.

How will your organization impact the public debate in 2008?
The Hamilton Project will continue to promote the idea that long-term prosperity is best achieved by making economic growth broad-based, by enhancing individual economic security, and by embracing a role for effective government in making needed public investments. More specifically, using our ability to convene experts and influential stakeholders on targeted issues, and by producing pragmatic, analytical policy proposals on those issues, The Hamilton Project will help inform the public debate on issues dominating the 2008 agenda and provide new ideas for moving our domestic agenda forward.

What is your 2008 operating budget?
Roughly $2.5 million

Looking out 2-3 years, how would you like to grow/change your organization?
With US elections looming in 2008 and 2010 at the federal, state and local levels, and changes taking place within the international community, the policy priorities for our domestic agenda will undoubtedly change in the coming years. The Hamilton Project will seek new sources of expertise as we strive to produce research and public dialogue on

timely and relevant topics on key policy issues in an understandable and analytically sound manner.

What do you need to do that?
Our organization will continue its tradition of broad outreach to policy leaders across the political spectrum, both to share our policy ideas and to stay informed of key policy priorities. In addition, we will find new and creative ways to tap into new areas of expertise—from academics and practioners around the country—as we tackle new policy challenges relevant to our unfolding agenda.

How will your organization change if progressives win in November? If they lose?
The Hamilton Project will continue to do the same work, including releasing discussion papers with specific, implementable policy proposals and strategy papers that develop a broad vision no matter what happens in November or beyond. The Hamilton Project is hoping that its ideas on, for example, market-based solutions to climate change or the uninsured have broad appeal. We will stand ready to

This organization is "intellectual" and "pragmatic." "Fueling the progressive policy debate," the Hamilton Project is "top notch."

serve as a resource on these policies through the work we have produced on these and other priority areas of focus.

If you had to offer some advice to fellow progressives what would it be?
The Hamilton Project functions best when it helps develop specific, implementable policy ideas or provides specific analysis, commentary and economic strategies around existing policy areas. This may be a concept that works successfully for other groups as well.

Please list your board of directors and their affiliations.

Hamilton Project Advisory Council Members:

George A. Akerlof
Koshland Professor of Economics, University of California, Berkeley
2001 Nobel Laureate in Economics

Roger C. Altman
Chairman, Evercore Partners

Howard P. Berkowitz
Managing Director, BlackRock; Chief Executive Officer, BlackRock HPB Management

Alan S. Blinder
Gordon S. Rentschler Memorial Professor of Economics, Princeton University

Timothy C. Collins
Senior Managing Director and Chief Executive Officer, Ripplewood Holdings, LLC

Robert E. Cumby
Professor of Economics, School of Foreign Service, Georgetown University

Peter A. Diamond
Institute Professor, Massachusetts Institute of Technology

John Doerr
Partner, Kleiner Perkins Caufield & Byers

Christopher Edley, Jr.
Dean and Professor, Boalt School of Law, University of California, Berkeley

Blair W. Effron
Partner, Centerview Partners, LLC

Judy Feder
Dean and Professor, Georgetown Public Policy Institute

Harold Ford
Vice Chairman, Merrill Lynch

Mark T. Gallogly
Managing Principal, Centerbridge Partners

Michael D. Granoff
Chief Executive Officer, Pomona Capital

Glenn H. Hutchins
Founder and Managing Director, Silver Lake

James A. Johnson
Vice Chairman, Perseus, LLC

Nancy Killefer
Senior Director, McKinsey & Co.

Jacob J. Lew
Managing Director and Chief
Operating Officer, Citigroup Global
Wealth Management

Eric Mindich
Chief Executive Officer,
Eton Park Capital Management

Suzane Nora Johnson
Senior Director and Former
Vice Chairman, The Goldman Sachs
Group, Inc.

Richard Perry
Chief Executive Officer, Perry Capital

Steven Rattner
Managing Principal,
Quadrangle Group, LLC

Robert Reischauer
President, Urban Institute

Alice M. Rivlin
Senior Fellow, The Brookings
Institution; Director of the Brookings
Washington Research Program

Cecilia E. Rouse
Professor of Economics and Public
Affairs, Princeton University

Robert E. Rubin
Director and Chairman of the
Executive Committee, Citigroup Inc.

Ralph L. Schlosstein

Gene Sperling
Senior Fellow for Economic Policy,
Center for American Progress

Thomas F. Steyer
Senior Managing Partner,
Farallon Capital Management

Lawrence H. Summers
Charles W. Eliot University Professor,
Harvard University

Laura D'Andrea Tyson
Professor, Haas School of Business,
University of California, Berkeley

William A. von Mueffling
President and CIO,
Cantillon Capital Management, LLC

Daniel B. Zwirn
Managing Partner, D.B. Zwirn & Co.

THE HUFFINGTON POST

TOP NEWS AND OPINION

560 Broadway
New York, NY 10012

☎ 212-245-7844

✉ Mario Ruiz,
VP, Media Relations,
646-274-2439

@ mario@huffingtonpost.com

🖥 huffingtonpost.com

🔑 May 9, 2005

🖧 News and opinion site

Arianna Huffington
Co-Founder/Editor-in-Chief

Arianna Huffington is the co-founder and editor-in-chief of The Huffington Post, a nationally syndicated columnist, and author of eleven books. She is also co-host of "Left, Right & Center," public radio's popular political roundtable program.

In May 2005, she launched The Huffington Post, a news and blog site that has quickly become one of the most widely-read, linked to and frequently-cited media brands on the Internet.

In 2006, she was named to the Time 100, *Time* magazine's list of the world's 100 most influential people.

Originally from Greece, she moved to England when she was 16 and graduated from Cambridge University with an M.A. in economics. At 21, she became president of the famed debating society, the Cambridge Union.

What does your organization do and how does it do it?
The Huffington Post is a leading news and opinion site that has become a singular go-to place online for smart news, blogs and original content. The site has 11 million unique users a month and is the fourth most-linked-to blog on the Internet. HuffPost provides a platform for prominent opinion-makers, including politicians, advocates, academics, policy makers and boldface names. Bloggers include Jon Soltz, Gary Hart, Sen. Russ Feingold, Wesley Clark, Mia Farrow, Sen. Edward Kennedy, Paul Rieckhoff, Barbara Ehrenreich, Nancy Keenan, Cristina Page, Andy Stern, John Sweeney, Sen. Bernie Sanders and Laurie David.

How will your organization impact the public debate in 2008?
HuffPost will continue to present news and opinion too often overlooked by mainstream media. From the Iraq war and American politics to the environment and the economy, HuffPost will offer an alternative to conventional wisdom and the common "on the one hand and on the other" approach to news.

Looking out 2-3 years, how would you like to grow/change your organization?
The site will continue to add bloggers—many of whom will be progressive—and grow its news-gathering capabilities. HuffPost will also have a larger audience offering an increasingly influential platform for its bloggers.

A "must read" for progressives. "Bright" and "smart." Arianna Huffington "really hit the nail on the head."

HUMAN RIGHTS CAMPAIGN

1640 Rhode Island Ave NW
Washington, DC 20036

☏ 800-777-4723
🖨 202-347-5323
✂ Anastasia Khoo
@ Anastasia.Khoo@hrc.org

🖥 hrc.org
🔑 1980
📊 $41,300,000
🏛 HRC operates a 501(c)(3), 501(c)(4), non-federal 527 as well as federal and state PACs

Joe Solmonese
President

As president of the Human Rights Campaign, Joe Solmonese has demonstrated that he has the political, strategic and communications skills to make the organization a powerhouse both in Washington and around the country. Under his leadership, the *National Journal* has rated the organization the second most successful interest group in all of Washington during the 2006 election.

Before coming to HRC, Joe was chief executive officer of EMILY's List, overseeing one of the nation's most successful efforts to elect progressive women in every part of the United States. Joe brings that experience to HRC and is leveraging his experience to make the organization a national model of effective advocacy. Heading up an organization with more than 700,000 members and supporters, as well as an annual budget of more than $30 million, Joe understands that the fight for equality is a people-powered movement that is only as strong as the troops "on the ground." That is why he implemented an unprecedented field and political operation in the last two years.

Whether adding expertise and resources to HRC's Workplace, Family and Coming Out Projects, appearing on CNN or in *The New York Times*, or hosting his weekly XM radio show, "The Agenda with Joe Solmonese," Joe is committed to educational work that changes public opinion and ultimately moves our country forward.

A native of Attleboro, Mass., Joe is 42 and lives in Washington, DC. He graduated from Boston University in 1987 with a Bachelor of Science degree in communications.

As president of the Human Rights Campaign, Joe Solmonese has demonstrated that he has the political, strategic and communications skills to make the organization a powerhouse both in Washington and around the country.

What does your organization do and how does it do it?

The Human Rights Campaign (HRC) is America's largest civil rights organization working for gay, lesbian, bisexual and transgender equality. By educating Americans, working with corporations and lawmakers, supporting fair-minded candidates and ensuring that everyone can be safe, out and open in their homes, communities and at work, we are working toward a vision of a fair and equal country. HRC works to secure equal rights for GLBT individuals and families at the federal and state levels by lobbying elected officials, mobilizing grassroots supporters, educating Americans, investing strategically to elect fair-minded officials and partnering with other GLBT organizations.

How will your organization impact the public debate in 2008?

HRC will continue to be active this year in the 2008 elections, endorsing candidates and mobilizing pro-equality voters to be involved in the campaigns of candidates who support GLBT civil rights.

What is your 2008 operating budget?

$41.3 million

Looking out 2-3 years, how would you like to grow/change your organization?

HRC plans to continue expanding its programs beyond federal legislation, addressing the issues that affect the daily lives of GLBT people. These include workplace equality, healthcare, family life and religion and faith. HRC also intends to grow fundraising efforts, increase membership size and commitment, and recruit, cultivate and engage a diverse group of volunteers and staff.

What do you need to do that?

HRC will be focusing on expanding the fight for GLBT civil rights by appealing to a greater segment of the population. We are at a critical moment in the struggle for equal rights for the GLBT community. It is imperative that we continue to expand our base supporters beyond simply the gay, lesbian, bisexual and transgender community by bringing more straight allies into the fold.

How will your organization change if progressives win in November? If they lose?

If progressives win in November, HRC will have more allies in state legislatures, Congress and possibly the White House. This will translate

HRC is a "powerhouse" that "gets results."

into signing into law important pieces of federal legislation including expanding hate crimes coverage and workplace protections for members of the GLBT community. If progressives lose, we stand to see our community, once again, used as a political wedge issue and the erosion of rights for the GLBT community.

Please list your board of directors and their affiliations.
We have an extensive board, please visit hrc.org for the full list.

◖◗ human rights *first*

333 7th Ave
13th Flr
New York, NY 10001

📞 212-845-5200
🖨 212-845-5299
📠 Catherine Carpentieri
@ carpentieric@
humanrightsfirst.org

💻 humanrightsfirst.org
🔑 1978
📊 $10,378,000
🔌 501(c)(3)

Michael Posner
President (above)

Maureen Byrnes
Executive Director (not shown)

Michael Posner
Michael Posner, President of Human Rights First, has been at the forefront of the international human rights movement for nearly 30 years. He joined Human Rights First in 1978. As its Executive Director he helped the organization earn a reputation for leadership in the areas of refugee protection, advancing a rights-based approach to national security, challenging crimes against humanity and combating discrimination. He is a frequent public commentator on these and other issues, and he has testified dozens of times before the U.S. Congress. In January 2006,

Michael stepped down as Executive Director to become the President of Human Rights First. As President he is focused on public outreach, writing and public advocacy to advance the organization's core mission.

Since its founding in 1978, Human Rights First has supported and partnered with frontline rights activists around the world—in places like Guatemala, Russia, Northern Ireland, Egypt, Zimbabwe and Indonesia. Human Rights First runs the largest program providing volunteer legal representation to asylum seekers in the U.S., representing more than 1,000 clients from more than 80 countries. In 1980, Michael played a key role in proposing and campaigning for the first U.S. law providing for political asylum, which became part of the Refugee Act of 1980.

"Incredible." This group "changed the conversation on torture." HRF "delivers."

Human Rights First has long fought to strengthen systems of accountability in countries where human rights violations occur, especially for the worst human rights crimes like genocide, other crimes against humanity and torture. Michael proposed, drafted and campaigned for the Torture Victim Protection Act (TVPA), a U.S. federal statute passed in 1992 that was designed to give victims of the most serious human rights crimes anywhere in the world a remedy in U.S. courts.

In 1998, he led the Human Rights First delegation to the Rome conference at which the statute of the International Criminal Court (ICC) was adopted. The ICC is the first international tribunal to prosecute violations for genocide, crimes against humanity and war crimes.

He has also been a prominent voice in support of fair, decent and humane working conditions in factories throughout the global supply chain. He helped found the Fair Labor Association (FLA), an organization that brings together corporations, local leaders, universities and NGOs to promote corporate accountability for working conditions in the apparel and athletic footwear industries. He sits on the FLA's Board.

In 2004, Human Rights First launched its End Torture Now Campaign, a public education and advocacy effort that challenges coercive interrogation practices by US agencies in Iraq, Afghanistan and elsewhere. Human Rights First has organized a group of retired admirals and generals to speak out publicly on this issue.

He lectured at Yale Law School from 1981 to 1984, and has been a visiting lecturer at Columbia University Law School since 1984. A member of the California Bar and the Illinois Bar, he received his J.D. from the University of California, Berkeley Law School (Boalt Hall) in 1975 and a B.A. with distinction and honors in History from the University of Michigan in 1972.

Maureen Byrnes

Maureen Byrnes is the Executive Director of Human Rights First. She joined in 2006. As Executive Director, Maureen is responsible for providing institutional leadership and overall management of the organization's programs, staff and resources.

Before joining Human Rights First, Maureen served at The Pew Charitable Trusts in Philadelphia as Director of Policy Initiatives and the Health and Human Services (HHS) program. Under her leadership, the Trusts' HHS program established a strong reputation for its ability to identify and seize opportunities to help solve tough policy problems. Its approach focused on engaging experts, exploring divergent views and building broad consensus for change. While at the Trusts, Maureen redesigned the organization's health and human services program and was responsible for a wide range of highly successful policy initiatives, including helping to rebuild the nation's public health infrastructure, reforming the nation's foster care system and addressing challenging science and technology issues.

Before going to The Pew Charitable Trusts, Maureen worked in Washington, DC for 15 years. She served as Executive Director of the National Commission on AIDS, a 15-member commission established by law to make recommendations to both the President and the Congress on how the country should address the many challenges associated with the HIV epidemic. As Executive Director, Maureen was responsible for the publication of all commission reports, designed and coordinated a series of commission site visits around the country to a wide range of venues and cities and she represented the commission in the press.

Maureen served on Capitol Hill as both majority and minority staff director for the Subcommittee on Labor, Health and Human Services, Education and Related Agencies of the United States Senate Committee on Appropriations and she served as vice president of the Association of American Universities, where she worked with the presidents and chancellors of more than 60 leading public and private research-intensive universities on a wide variety of federal research policy issues.

Maureen graduated magna cum laude from LeMoyne College in Syracuse, New York and holds

a master's degree in Public Administration from the University of North Carolina at Chapel Hill.

What does your organization do and how does it do it?
Human Rights First believes that building respect for human rights and the rule of law will help ensure the dignity to which every individual is entitled and will stem tyranny, extremism, intolerance and violence.

Human Rights First protects people at risk: refugees who flee persecution, victims of crimes against humanity or other mass human rights violations, victims of discrimination, those whose rights are eroded in the name of national security, and human rights advocates who are targeted for defending the rights of others. These groups are often the first victims of societal instability and breakdown; their treatment is a harbinger of wider-scale repression. Human Rights First works to prevent violations against these groups and to seek justice and accountability for violations against them.

Human Rights First is practical and effective. We advocate for change at the highest levels of national and international policymaking. We seek justice through the courts. We raise awareness and understanding through the media. We build coalitions among those with divergent views. And we mobilize people to act.

How will your organization impact the public debate in 2008?

HRF is influencing the debate on the U.S.'s interrogation practices and policies by making it clear that ending torture is an integral component of strong national security policies. We will continue to work with retired military leaders to educate presidential candidates and other public figures about the need for legal bans on torture; activate a grassroots constituency to ensure that the next president ends the use of torture; and generate a public debate on the role of popular culture in its portrayal of official cruelty.

What is your 2008 operating budget?

$10,378,000.

Looking out 2-3 years, how would you like to grow/change your organization?

Human Right's First's work is influential with policymakers, but not sufficiently visible to a larger public audience. Effective policy change and the will of the public are often inextricably linked. Over the next several years, HRF will work to build a more robust and well-defined public advocacy focus to its work. In tandem, we will seek to expand our base of supporters, as both activists working with us to achieve specific human rights goals and financial investors ensuring our capacity to engage in effective human rights advocacy.

What do you need to do that?

We are continuing to bring diverse skills into our program staff—including content expertise, campaigning, public communications and constituency building experience. We are building a more robust communications capacity using both traditional media and new media. And we will conduct broader fundraising and outreach efforts to engage more people in our work and organization.

How will your organization change if progressives win in November? If they lose?

Whichever party wins the presidential election in 2008, HRF will continue to pursue its core mission. We will continue to employ an integrated approach to the issues on which we work, an approach that includes coalition building, insider advocacy, litigation, research and reporting, public constituency building and strategic communications to solve human rights problems around the world. HRF will respond to new opportunities that may arise on the legislative agenda, in particular, and concerning U.S. policy, based on a change in Administration and/or control of Congress.

If you had to offer some advice to fellow progressives what would it be?

In the next year this country has an opportunity to revise policies relating to human rights and national security. In preparing for a new administration in Washington, we should develop a practical, principled, result-oriented plan that both corrects the most egregious policies, but also paves the way for the U.S. to regain our global leadership on human rights issues.

Please list your board of directors and their affiliations.

M. Bernard Aidinoff
Sullivan & Cromwell LLP

Mark Angelson
MidOcean Partners

Tom A. Bernstein
Chelsea Piers Management, Inc

Raymond Brown
Greenbaum, Rowe, Smith & Davis LLP

Lynda Clarizio
Platform-A

Craig Cogut
Pegasus Capital Advisors, L.P.

Donald Francis Donovan
Debevoise & Plimpton LLP

A. Whitney Ellsworth
Publishing Consultant

Kenneth R. Feinberg
The Feinberg Group LLP

Gail Furman
Psychologist

Leslie Gimbel
Bernard F. and Alva B. Gimbel
Foundation

R. Scott Greathead
Wiggin & Dana LLP

Myrna K. Greenberg
City Lights Youth Theater

Louis Henkin
Columbia University School of Law

John D. Hutson
Franklin Pierce Law Center

Robert D. Joffe
Cravath Swaine & Moore LLP

Lewis B. Kaden
Citigroup, Inc.

Kerry Kennedy
RFK Memorial Center for Human Rights

Harold Hongju Koh
Yale Law School

Philip A. Lacovara

Mayer Brown

Jo Backer Laird

Robert Todd Lang
Weil, Gotshal & Manges LLP

Michael K. Rozen
The Feinberg Group, LLP

Barbara A. Schatz
Columbia University School of Law

George A. Vradenburg
Vradenburg Foundation

Sigourney Weaver
Actor

William D. Zabel
Schulte, Roth & Zabel LLP

LAWYERS' COMMITTEE FOR
CIVIL RIGHTS
U N D E R   L A W

☎ 202-662-8600   🖥 lawyerscommittee.org

🖨 202-783-0857   🔑 June 21, 1963

1401 New York Ave NW   ✖ Tim Wierzbicki, Chief   📊 $7,212,550

Ste 400   Development Officer   🔲 501(c)(3)

Washington, DC 20005   @ twierzbicki@lawyerscommittee.org

     ✖ Stacie Miller, Director

     of Communications

     @ smiller@lawyerscommitte.org

Barbara R. Arnwine
Executive Director

A graduate of Scripps College in Claremont, California, Ms. Arnwine received her law degree from Duke University School of Law. Prior to her employment with the national office of the Lawyers' Committee, Ms. Arnwine was the Executive Director of the Lawyers' Committee for Civil Rights Under Law of the Boston Bar.

She has become renowned for her work on passage of the landmark Civil Rights Act of 1991. Throughout the 1991 campaign, the technical assistance of the Lawyers' Committee for Civil Rights was critical to passage of the Act.

In April 1994, Ms. Arnwine visited South Africa as a member of the advance team of the Lawyers' Committee's South Africa Electoral Observers Delegation.

In 1995, Ms. Arnwine served as the National Convenor of the National Conference on African American Women and the law held in Washington, DC, attended by over 1,000 persons. As a result of the conference, Ms. Arnwine led a delegation to the NGO Forum and Fourth World Conference on Women in Beijing. Her efforts there contributed to a United Nations Platform for Action that provides protection for women who confront multiple forms of discrimination.

In 2000, Ms. Arnwine convened the third national conference of African American Women in the Law in Washington, DC. Some 250 participants in fifteen workshops provided input into the preparation of a Report and Action Agenda for advocacy before the UN General Assembly Special Session on Women.

In 2001, Ms. Arnwine represented African descendants from the Americas in helping draft provisions of the program for action of the UN World Conference Against Racism, Racial Discrimination, Xenophobia and related Intolerance in Durban, South Africa. She also organized a Lawyers' Committee delegation to participate in the NGO Forum at the WCAR.

In 2002, Ms. Arnwine received the Charlotte E. Ray Award from the Greater Washington Area Chapter, Women Lawyers Division of the National Bar Association.

In 2004, Ms. Arnwine was a prominent leader of the nonpartisan Election Protection Coalition and helped to organize 8,000 lawyers throughout the nation to staff the 1-866 OUR VOTE National Hotline, serve as poll monitors and mobile field attorneys in over 28 states. In addition, Ms. Arnwine has been a frequent public speaker in the national media on the issue of electoral barriers and needed federal and state reforms.

Ms. Arnwine has been quoted and featured in numerous media articles about civil rights and her personal accomplishments. She was profiled in the June 2003 issue of *MORE* magazine in an article entitled: "We Are Family" regarding her accomplishments and those of her sister. In addition, Ms. Arnwine has been the recipient of many awards from national, regional and local civil rights organizations, most significantly, the National Bar Association's Equal Justice Award, the highest honor bestowed by that organization. Ms. Arnwine is also a frequent speaker on radio and television.

What does your organization do and how does it do it?
Formed in 1963 at the request of President John F. Kennedy, the Lawyers' Committee for Civil Rights Under Law marshals the pro bono resources of the private bar to obtain equal opportunity for minorities, by addressing factors that contribute to racial justice and economic opportunity. Using legal action to secure equal justice, the Lawyers' Committee:
- Deploys volunteer attorneys to protect individual rights to vote, at polling sites across the country and through the (866) OUR-VOTE hotline;
- Brings legal action to ensure justice and equal application of the law in housing, employment and community development;
- Protects the environmental health of minority communities by challenging large scale construction in environmentally sensitive areas or decisions to locate schools on

This group is a "fighter" that has "achieved a great deal."

contaminated sites that endanger community health; and

- Strives to guarantee that all American students receive equal educational opportunities in public schools and institutions of higher learning, especially with regard to school integration, The No Child Left Behind Act, parental involvement and financial adequacy.
- Seeks innovative use of the law to broaden inclusion of racial minorities in all sectors of American society.

How will your organization impact the public debate in 2008?

Now celebrating our 45th anniversary, the Lawyers' Committee has a long history of influencing public discourse on civil rights issues. In 2008, our work will include:

- Hosting a Civil Rights Symposium, examining the civil rights challenges of the past and how they shape our strategy for ensuring equal justice moving forward;
- Recruiting 10,000 volunteers to work directly with voters across the nation whose rights to vote are challenged on election day, in order to amplify minority voices in the voting booth; and
- Convening a Commission on the 40th Anniversary of the Fair Housing Act, to examine the effectiveness of the Act and make recommendations for ensuring strong and stable communities anchored by safe and affordable housing.

What is your 2008 operating budget?
$7,212,550

Looking out 2-3 years, how would you like to grow/change your organization?

In accordance with our strategic plan, during the next 2-3 years, the Lawyers' Committee will bolster our traditional litigation activities with an increased focus on public policy and public education, expand our networks of volunteer attorneys for non-litigation civil rights work, strengthen partnerships with organizations who share common goals and leverage the principles encompassed in international civil rights treaties into our domestic work.

What do you need to do that?

The Lawyers' Committee needs expanded outreach to attorneys willing to engage in pro bono civil rights work. We need financial support, especially from outside the legal community. We will encourage the funding community to increase their commitment to civil rights programs and ask them for support in accessing new funding sources.

How will your organization change if progressives win in November? If they lose?

As a non-partisan organization, the Lawyers' Committee will continue the fight for equal justice, regardless of who wins in November. But if progressives win, the change in our organization will be dramatic and our opportunities will be greatly expanded. We will lead the fight for stronger enforcement of civil rights laws and for legislation to address emerging civil rights issues. Public education on the urgency of the continuing struggle for civil rights will be paramount. During the transition to the new administration, we will prepare position papers to keep civil rights at the forefront of the agenda.

If you had to offer some advice to fellow progressives what would it be?
Continue to work together collaboratively and creatively toward our shared goal of equal justice. Together we are stronger!

Please list your board of directors and their affiliations.

Victoria Bjorklund, Esq.
Simpson Thacher & Bartlett, LLP

David J. Bodney, Esq.
Steptoe & Johnson LLP

John W. Borkowski, Esq.
Hogan & Hartson L.L.P.

Kim M. Boyle, Esq.
Phelps Dunbar LLP

Patricia A. Brannan, Esq.
Hogan & Hartson, L.L.P.

Harry B. Bremond, Esq.
Wilson, Sonsini, Goodrich & Rosati

Steven H. Brose, Esq.
Steptoe & Johnson LLP

William H. Brown, Esq.
Schnader, Harrison, Segal & Lewis LLP

Brooks R. Burdette, Esq.
Schulte Roth & Zabel LLP

Michael Cardozo
Corporation Counsel City Of New York

Douglass W. Cassel, Esq.
Notre Dame Law School

Michael H. Chanin, Esq.
Powell Goldstein LLP

Nicholas T. Christakos, Esq.
Sutherland, Asbill & Brennan LLP

Fay Clayton, Esq.
Robinson Curley & Clayton, P.C.

Jay Cohen, Esq.
Paul, Weiss, Rifkind, Wharton & Garrison LLP

Michael A. Cooper, Esq.
Sullivan & Cromwell LLP

Edward Correia, Esq.
Latham & Watkins

Nora C. Cregan, Esq.
Bingham McCutchen LLP

Thomas F. Cullen , Jr., Esq.
Jones Day

Drew S. Days, Esq.
Yale Law School

James T. Danaher, Esq.
Danaher & Klynn

Johnita P. Due, Esq.
Turner Broadcasting System

Jack W. Londen, Esq.
Morrison & Foerster

Lawrence S. Lustberg
Gibbons, DelDeo, Doland, Griffinger
& Vecchione, PC

Christopher L. Mann, Esq.
Sullivan & Cromwell LLP

Colleen McIntosh
Medco Health Solutions, Inc.

John E. McKeever, Esq.
DLA Piper Rudnick Gary Cary US LLP

Neil McKittrick
Goulston & Storrs

Kenneth E. McNeil, Esq.
Susman Godfrey L.L.P.

D. Stuart Meiklejohn, Esq.
Sullivan & Cromwell

Ronald S. Miller, Esq.
Miller, Shakman & Hamilton
& Beem LLP

Charles R. Morgan, Esq.
On Site—E-Discovery

Robert A. Murphy, Esq.
Casner & Edwards LLP

Frederick M. Nicholas, Esq.
The Hapsmith Company

John Payton, Esq.
Wilmer Hale

Bradley S. Phillips, Esq.
Munger, Tolles & Olson LLP

Bettina B. Plevan, Esq.
Proskauer Rose, LLP

Stephen J. Pollak, Esq.
Goodwin Procter LLP

Sheldon Raab, Esq.
Fried, Frank, Harris, Shriver
& Jacobson LLP

Paul W. Rebein, Esq.
Shook, Hardy & Bacon L.L.P.

Norman Redlich, Esq.
Wachtell, Lipton, Rosen & Katz

Michael J. Remington, Esq.
Drinker Biddle & Reath LLP

Prof. William L. Robinson
David A. Clarke School of Law

Sidney S. Rosdeitcher, Esq.
Paul, Weiss, Rifkind, Wharton
& Garrison LLP

Lowell E. Sachnoff, Esq.
Sachnoff & Weaver, Ltd.

Paul C. Saunders, Esq.
Cravath, Swaine & Moore LLP

John F. Savarese, Esq.
Wachtell, Lipton, Rosen & Katz

Richard T. Seymour, Esq.
Law Office of Richard T. Seymour,
P.L.L.C.

Valerie Shea
Gordon Hargrove & James, P.A.

Robert C. Sheehan, Esq.
Skadden, Arps, Slate, Meagher & Flom
LLP

Jane C. Sherburne, Esq.
Citigroup, Inc.

Michael S. Shuster, Esq.
Kasowitz, Benson, Torres & Friedman
LLP

Richard H. Silberberg, Esq.
Dorsey & Whitney LLP

Jeffrey A. Simes, Esq.
Goodwin Procter, LLP

Marsha E. Simms, Esq.
Weil, Gotshal & Manges LLP

Robert E. Sims, Esq.
Latham & Watkins

John S. Skilton, Esq.
Heller Ehrman LLP

Rodney E. Slater, Esq.
Patton Boggs LLP

Eleanor H. Smith, Esq.
Zuckerman Spaeder LLP

Grace E. Speights, Esq.
Morgan Lewis & Bockius

John B. Strasburger, Esq.
Weil, Gotshal & Manges LLP

Michael Traynor, Esq.
Cooley Godward, LLP

Suzanne Turner, Esq.
Dechert LLP

Michael W. Tyler, Esq.
Kilpatrick Stockton LLP

Donald B. Verrilli, Jr., Esq.
Jenner & Block, LLC

Kenneth M. Vittor, Esq.
The McGraw-Hill Companies

Herbert M. Wachtell, Esq.
Wachtell, Lipton, Rosen & Katz

Sylvia H. Walbolt, Esq.
Carlton Fields

Charles E. Wall, Esq.
Altria Group

Robert N. Weiner, Esq.
Arnold & Porter

Melvyn I. Weiss, Esq.
Milberg Weiss Bershad Hynes
& Lerach LLP

Karen Hastie Williams, Esq.
Crowell & Moring

Thomas S. Williamson, Jr., Esq.
Covington & Burling LLP

LC LEADERSHIP CONFERENCE
CR ON CIVIL RIGHTS
LC Education
CR Fund

1629 K St NW
10th Flr
Washington, DC 20006

📞 202-466-3315
🖨 202-785-3859
Mistique Cano
@ cano@civilrights.org

🖥 civilrights.org
🔑 LCCR, 1950; LCCREF, 1969
📊 LCCR, $1,200,000;
LCCREF, $6,000,000
🔀 LCCR, 501(c)(4);
LCCREF, 501(C)(3)

Wade Henderson,
President/CEO, LCCR (l)

Karen Lawson,
President/CEO, LCCREF (r)

Wade J. Henderson

Wade Henderson is the president and CEO of the Leadership Conference on Civil Rights (LCCR); and counselor to the Leadership Conference on Civil Rights Education Fund (LCCREF). The LCCR is the nation's premier civil and human rights coalition. Mr. Henderson is also the Joseph L. Rauh, Jr., Professor of Public Interest Law at the David A. Clarke School of Law, University of the District of Columbia.

Mr. Henderson is well known for his expertise on a wide range of civil rights, civil liberties and human rights issues. He works principally in the areas of civil rights enforcement; voting rights; public education reform; fair housing policy; immigration policy reform; media and telecommunications policy; economic and political empowerment for people of color, women, persons with disabilities and the poor. Under his leadership, the LCCR has become one of the nation's most effective defenders of federal affirmative action policy and one of the strongest advocates for passage of the Hate Crimes Prevention Act.

Since taking the helm of the LCCR in June 1996, Mr. Henderson has worked diligently to address

LCCR is "the coordinator" of civil rights lobbying. Their work is "about our country's essentials."

emerging policy issues of concern to the civil rights community and to strengthen the effectiveness of the coalition. Mr. Henderson is actively involved with the newly reconstituted National Quality Forum Board of Directors that seeks to improve healthcare quality through performance measurement and public reporting; and the FDIC Advisory Committee on Economic Inclusion, which was created in 2006 to provide the FDIC with advice and recommendations on important initiatives focused on expanding access to banking services by underserved populations. He also leads an effort to pass the Employee Free Choice Act (EFCA), legislation to revive the right of workers to organize unions.

Prior to his role with the Leadership Conference, Mr. Henderson was the Washington Bureau director of the National Association for the Advancement of Colored People (NAACP). In that capacity, he directed the government affairs and national legislative program of the NAACP.

Wade Henderson was previously the associate director of the Washington national office of the American Civil Liberties Union (ACLU), where he began his career as a legislative counsel and advocate on a wide range of civil rights and civil liberties issues. Mr. Henderson also served as executive director of the Council on Legal Education Opportunity (CLEO).

Mr. Henderson is a graduate of Howard University and the Rutgers University School of Law. He is a member of the Bar in the District of Columbia, New Jersey and the United States Supreme Court. As a tireless civil rights leader and advocate, Mr. Henderson has received countless awards and honors. He holds an honorary Doctorate in Law from Queens College School of Law, City University of New York.

He is the author of numerous articles on civil rights and public policy issues.

Karen McGill Lawson
Karen McGill Lawson currently serves as LCCREF president and CEO and deputy director for educational operations for LCCR. During her lifetime she says she has "really seen this country transform," and is glad to know "that her granddaughter will never have to experience the segregation that she witnessed as a little girl back in Martin, West Virginia."

Karen McGill Lawson was born in Martin, West Virginia, where she experienced segregation as a child and still has vivid memories of having to sit in the balcony area of movie theaters. She soon noticed that the effects of segregation were not confined to the south alone once her family moved to Philadelphia, PA, where she saw the disparity in resources among predominately White and Black schools. As a young woman, she was influenced by the civil rights movement of the 1950s and 1960s, the assassination of President John F. Kennedy, and Lyndon B. Johnson's war on poverty.

Motivated by a desire to go into public service and "change the system," Ms. Lawson pursued her B.A. and M.A. degrees, both in sociology, from Penn State and Notre Dame, respectively, a decision she calls, "a natural choice for me." During the 1970s and early 1980s, Ms. Lawson served at the United States Commission on Civil Rights (USCCR), then chaired by Arthur Flemming, a committed advocate for civil rights. During her tenure at USCCR, Ms. Lawson was the education monitor, where she was responsible for coordinating fact finding missions at nationwide hearings on the progress of desegregation efforts within the nation's public schools, and helped produce status reports on federal regulations, and budgetary spending, including "With All Deliberate Speed 1954 - ??" She left USCCR during the Reagan administration, after seeing conservatives diminish the power and independence of the Commission's civil rights enforcement duties.

Ms. Lawson came to Leadership Conference on Civil Rights (LCCR) in 1985 when the organization had only four people on staff. At that time, the Leadership Conference on Civil Rights Education Fund (LCCREF), LCCR's sister organization, was no more than an organization on paper. Ms. Lawson quickly created the Civil Rights Monitor, a quarterly publication that reports on civil rights issues pending before the three branches of government, and became a fierce fundraiser. With the generous support of the Ford Foundation, and under Ms. Lawson's guidance, LCCREF produced educational materials for teachers and children on diversity in American life. Ms. Lawson is co-author of *Talking to Our Children About Racism, Prejudice and Diversity; Building One Nation, A Study Of What Is Being Done Today in Schools, Neighbors and the Workplace*; and *All Together Now!*; and is a contributing editor of *Voting Rights in America: Continuing the Quest for Full Participation*, a collection of essays on voting rights, which includes an essay by President Bill Clinton.

What does your organization do and how does it do it?
LCCR coordinates the national lobbying campaigns for a civil rights coalition of nearly 200 organizations, the largest and most diverse in the nation. LCCREF, the public education and research arm of the coalition, conducts research, holds briefings on the Hill and in the states, and develops message strategies for its various campaigns.

How will your organization impact the public debate in 2008?
This year, we have a campaign to educate our constituencies that

the digital television transition will happen in 2009. Part of that campaign is an aggressive communications strategy to inject our message into the national coverage of the issue.

What is your 2008 operating budget?
LCCR - $1,200,000
LCCREF - $6,000,000

Looking out 2-3 years, how would you like to grow/change your organization?
On both the legislative side (LCCR) and the education and research side (LCCREF), meaningful growth will rely on education, communications and branding, addressing audiences that include organizations on the national level and individuals at the grassroots level throughout the United States. Enactment and enforcement of sound federal policy regarding civil rights is reliant on comprehensive education among groups and individuals in order to properly inform the debate.

What do you need to do that?
Lawmakers and opinion shapers need to be part of a dialogue that is conducted in Washington and throughout local communities across the nation. The key to success is coalition, which is at the heart of the Leadership Conference mission.

How will your organization change if progressives win in November? If they lose?
We expect that if progressives

win big this year, that many of our strategies will become more offensive, less defensive, which will allow us to move some important bills that have been stalled over the last couple of years.

If you had to offer some advice to fellow progressives what would it be?
We work under the firm conviction that it is only through uniting our voices in coalition that we will be heard and have a greater overall impact on society.

Please list your board of directors and their affiliations.

LCCREF Board of Directors

Chair, William L. Taylor
Civil Rights and Children's Rights Attorney

Vice-Chair, Muriel Morisey
Professor of Law, Temple University School of Law

Treasurer, Carolyn Osolinik
Partner, Mayer, Brown, Rowe & Maw

Secretary, William L. Robinson
Professor of Law, David A. Clarke School of Law, University of the District of Columbia

Mary Frances Berry
Geraldine R. Segal Professor of American Thought and Professor of History, University of Pennsylvania

Cheryl Mills
Counselor for Operations,
New York University

John Podesta
President and CEO, Center for
American Progress

Marilyn Sneiderman
Director of Field Mobilization,
AFL-CIO

Frank H. Wu
Dean, Wayne State University
Law School

LCCR Executive Committee

Chairperson, Dorothy I. Height
National Council of Negro Women

**Vice Chairpersons,
Judith Lichtman**
National Partnership for
Women and Families

**Compliance/Enforcement
Committee Chairperson,
Karen K. Narasaki**
Asian American Justice Center

William Taylor
Citizens' Commission on Civil Rights

Secretary, William D. Novelli
AARP

Treasurer, Gerald W. McEntee
AFSCME

**American Association of People
with Disabilities**

**American Association of
University Women**

AFL-CIO

American Civil Liberties Union

**American Federation of
Teachers, AFL-CIO**

**American-Arab Anti-
Discrimination Committee**

Human Rights Campaign

**International Union, UAW
Japanese American Citizens
League**

**Lawyers' Committee for
Civil Rights Under Law**

League of Women Voters

**Mexican American Legal
Defense & Educational Fund**

NAACP

**NAACP Legal Defense
& Educational Fund, Inc**

**National Congress
of American Indians**

National Council of Churches

National Council of La Raza

National Education Association

National Fair Housing Alliance

National Organization for Women

National Partnership for
Women and Families

National Urban League

National Women's Law Center

People for the American Way

Religious Action Center
of Reform Judaism

Service Employees
International Union

THE LEAGUE OF CONSERVATION VOTERS

1920 L St NW
Ste 800
Washington, DC 20036
202-785-8683

202-835-0491
David Sandretti,
Communications Director
@ david_sandretti@lcv.org

lcv.org
1970
$9,000,000
LCV, 501(c)(4); LCV
Action Fund, PAC;
and an affiliated 527

Gene Karpinski
President

Gene Karpinski joined LCV and LCV Education Fund as president in April 2006, after serving for many years as a member of the LCV and LCVEF boards of directors and the LCV Political Committee. Prior to joining LCV and the LCV Education Fund, Gene worked for 21 years as the executive director of the U.S. Public Interest Research Group (US PIRG), the national lobbying office for state PIRGs across the country, where he led many national environmental issue campaigns. Before his tenure at US PIRG, he was the field director for People for the American Way and Congress Watch, and executive director of the Colorado PIRG. He has served on the boards of Earth Share, the Partnership Project, the Beldon Fund, and the National Association for Public Interest Law. Gene is a graduate of Brown University and Georgetown University Law Center.

What does your organization do and how does it do it?
LCV, the nation's independent voice for the environment, engages in public education, lobbying and accountability to turn environmental values into national priorities. LCV has made global warming and America's energy future a central focus of its activities in Congress and the 2008 election cycle.

We know that policies affecting our environment are directly tied to the outcome of elections. In 2006, we put a pro-environment majority in charge of Congress for the first time in 12 years.

As a direct result, we were able to pass an energy bill that raised fuel efficiency

The LCV is a "very effective model."

standards for automobiles for the first time in a generation.

Through our National Environmental Scorecard and Presidential Voter Guide, we inform the public about official positions on important environmental legislation and issues.

In 2006, we defeated 9 of the 13 worst anti-environment lawmakers on our Dirty Dozen list. As a matter of fact, Dirty Dozen politicians we defeated had a combined average lifetime score of just 8% in our 2007 Scorecard; they were replaced by legislators with an average score of 88%.

We also educate the public, build coalitions, promote grassroots power and train the next generation of environmental leaders.

How will your organization impact the public debate in 2008?
The League of Conservation Voters intends to drive clean energy and global warming to the forefront of public debate. Since we need 60 votes in the US Senate to break filibusters, we will focus on key Senate races to bring effective energy legislation to the president. In the presidential and congressional races, we will emphasize the importance of swing voters who, polls show are concerned about these issues with respect to our national security, economy, jobs, consumers and the health of the Planet. LCV will work in conjunction with other related groups that are a part of a "war room" strategy on

national and state-level politics.

What is your 2008 operating budget?
$9.6 million.

Looking out 2-3 years, how would you like to grow/change your organization?
Our overarching goal is to create a system in which the national LCV's and the state leagues' capacity, strength and self-sufficiency are continually enhanced to the benefit of their own missions and the shared goals of the league movement as a whole. In future years, we will focus on doubling the number of environmental champions elected to office, activists mobilized and dollars raised, as well as pass significant pro-environment legislation at all levels of government

What do you need to do that?
Additional resources will allow us to implement our proven strategy in more key states. We will also be able to increase the capacity of our state league partners and to mobilize a greater number of e-activists and to turn them into on-the-ground activists. Closer collaboration with other progressive organizations will allow us to focus our resources most effectively to maximize our impact on key races, thereby increasing the environmental leadership at the federal and state level.

How will your organization change if progressives win in November? If they lose?
If the progressives win in November, we can do more work inside the Beltway and provide protection of legislators

who make global warming a priority with support from the White House. We can also play a larger role in states where we are not already active, play a key role in administrative appointments, and other transition strategies. If the progressives lose, we will fight to overcome filibusters in the Senate and on the details of global warming policy such as nuclear power and so-called clean coal. Our focus will shift to building grassroots advocacy.

If you had to offer some advice to fellow progressives what would it be?
We feel that each organization in the progressive community needs to focus on its specific strengths while working collaboratively. Our list program, which we have run for more than ten years, is testimony to this. LCV has a tested plan, a strategy to implement it and the partnerships to be effective in key states. It is crucial that progressive organizations trust in each other that each will execute its plan successfully.

Please list your board of directors and their affiliations.

Chair, Bill Roberts
Beldon Fund

John H. Adams
Trustee, Natural Resources Defense Council

Marcia Aronoff
Environmental Defense

Paul Austin
Conservation Minnesota &
Conservation Minnesota Voter Center

Brent Blackwelder (Honorary)
Friends of the Earth

Sherwood Boehlert
Accord Group

Carol Browner
The Albright Group, LLC

Marcia Bystryn
New York League of
Conservation Voters

Everett (Brownie) Carson
Natural Resources Council of Maine

Carrie Clark
Conservation Council of North Carolina

Donna F. Edwards
Arca Foundation (on leave of absence)

George T. Frampton, Jr.
Boies, Shiller & Flexner

Wade Greene (Honorary)
Rockefeller Family and Associates

Lisa Guthrie
Virginia League of Conservation Voters

John (Jay) A. Harris
Changing Horizons Fund

Rampa R. Hormel
Global Environment Project Institute

John Hunting (Honorary)
Beldon Fund

Tom Kiernan
National Parks Conservation
Association

William H. Meadows III
The Wilderness Society

Jorge Mursuli
People for the American Way

Scott A. Natha
The Baupost Group

John D. Podesta
Center for American Progress

Jonathan Poisner
Oregon League of Conservation Voters

Lana Pollack
Michigan Environmental Council

Larry Rockefeller
American Conservation Association

**Theodore Roosevelt, IV
(Honorary Chair)**
Lehman Brothers

Donald K. Ross
Rockefeller Family & Associates

Rodger O. Schlickeisen
Defenders of Wildlife

Peggy Shepard
West Harlem Environmental
Action WE ACT

Susan Smartt
California League of
Conservation Voters

Linda B. Uihlein
Brico Fund LLC

THE LEAGUE OF YOUR VOTERS

45 Main St

Ste 628

Brooklyn, NY 11201

☎ 718-305-4245

🖨 718-522-4840

✂ Heather Box

@ heather@theleague.com

🖥 theleague.com

🔑 2003

📊 $2,200,000 (501 c3, 501 c4, and PAC combined)

📁 501 c3, 501 c4, and PAC

Robert 'Biko' Baker
Executive Director (above)

Rob 'Biko' Baker

Rob 'Biko' Baker is Executive Director of The League of Young Voters, an organization created to empower young people to be players and winners in the political game nationwide. Biko has been with the League since its inception, first as an innovative organizer with Milwaukee's "Campaign Against Violence" and later as national Organizing and Training Director. Biko is a nationally-recognized hip hop organizer, journalist and scholar. Biko also served as the Deputy Publicity Coordinator and Young Voter Organizer for the Brown and Black Presidential Forum (a nationally televised presidential debate which aired on MSNBC). Biko is a Ph.D. candidate at UCLA, a frequent contributor to

The Source and serves on Wiretap's editorial board.

What does your organization do and how does it do it?
The League supports young people to build power to make changes in their communities, with an emphasis on youth from low-income communities, communities of color and non-college youth. Our core program invests deeply in disenfranchised communities around the country to build the trust, provide the tools and offer the education needed to make young people viable players in the civic process.

Our long-term strategy is to build an inspired, engaged and effective culture and community around youth participation. We run year-round, youth-driven field and issue based campaigns that are building the power needed to

The League is "energetic" and a "great way to reach young people".

significantly impact local, state and federal policy and elections nationwide.

Here's how we do it:

1. Engage young people who have been shut out of the political process.
2. Train them to be sophisticated organizers in their own communities.
3. Build multi-racial, multi-issue alliances.
4. Run issue campaigns on the local, state and national level.
5. Register, educate and turn out young voters.
6. Support progressive candidates, and hold them accountable once they're in office.

How will your organization impact the public debate in 2008?
By engaging, training and turning out young voters across the country we are bringing youth issues into the public debate. We have seen issues like access to education, healthcare, climate change and ending the war become central parts of the discourse. But we are still working vigilantly to bring some of the most critical youth issues we work on locally to the forefront of the national debate like: prison reform, economic justice, LGBT equality, immigrant rights, violence prevention, gun control and election administration.

What is your 2008 operating budget?
Our combined c3, c4 and PAC budget is $2.2 million.

Looking out 2-3 years, how would you like to grow/change your organization?

For us, it's not really about the 2-3 year plan it's about the 30-40 year plan. Fundamental change will not happen over night and we're committed to the long-term work it will take to actualize our vision of a progressive governing majority and an engaged youth electorate. We have incubated major local affiliate organizations with 3-4 paid staff on the ground in three states: Pennsylvania, Maine and Wisconsin and have several smaller projects in key states around the country. We plan to replicate our proven models and expand state by state using a strategy based on sustainable and incremental growth.

What do you need to do that?
We need loyal, long-term support. We believe that our permanent campaign approach is key to building the trust, skills and power necessary to not only increase young voter turnout in the short term, but to leverage long-term change and form a generation of engaged and active young leaders. This requires our donors and allies to stand with us whether or not it's an election year.

How will your organization change if progressives win in November? If they lose?
We will certainly celebrate the much needed shift in the political debate when progressives win this November. But no matter who is in office we will continue to do the deep local work of engaging young people to make the changes needed in their communities.

If you had to offer some advice to fellow progressives what would it be?

Work on local issues. We all know that changing the powers in Washington is not going to solve all the problems in our country. It is important that we take action locally on progressive issues and hold elected officials accountable. Year-round work on the local level is how to build the power needed to make the fundamental changes we'd like to see in our country.

Please list your board of directors and their affiliations.

Esther Morales
Independent Political Consultant

Maria Bacha
Community Organizer

Jeff Chang
Journalist; author, *Can't Stop Won't Stop*

Ryan Friedrichs
Michigan Voice Director,
Center for Civic Participation

Grant Garrison
Independent Consultant

Kris Lotlikar
Director of Business Development,
Renewable Choice Energy

Adam Smith
Executive Director, Mail-In
Voting Project

Tracy Sturdivant
Independent Political Consultant

Adam Smith
Consultant, Astro Data Services

Malia Lazu
Independent Political Consultant

MEDIA**MATTERS**
F O R   A M E R I C A

📞 202-756-4100

🖨 202-756-4101

👥 Jenny Hoffman, Strategic
Communications Associate

@ jhoffman@mediamatters.org

💻 mediamatters.org

🔑 May 3, 2004

🏛 501(c)(3)

1625 Massachusetts Ave NW
Ste 300
Washington, DC 20036

David Brock
President/CEO

David Brock is the author of four political books, including *The Republican Noise Machine: Right-Wing Media and How It Corrupts Democracy*. His preceding book, *Blinded by the Right: The Conscience of an Ex-Conservative*, was a 2002 *New York Times* best-selling political memoir in which he chronicled his years as a conservative media insider. Brock was the recipient of the New Democrat Network's first award for political entrepreneurship. He currently serves on the board of The Progressive Legislative Action Network, an organization created to support progressive state legislators. He is the President and CEO of Media Matters for America.

What does your organization do and how does it do it?
Media Matters for America is a Web-based, not-for-profit, 501(c)(3) progressive research and information center dedicated to comprehensively monitoring, analyzing and correcting conservative misinformation in the U.S. media.

Launched in May 2004, Media Matters for America put in place, for the first time, the means to systematically monitor a cross section of print, broadcast, cable, radio and Internet media outlets for conservative misinformation—news or commentary that is not accurate, reliable or credible and that forwards the conservative agenda—every day, in real time.

Using the website www.mediamatters.org as the principal vehicle for disseminating research and information, Media Matters posts rapid-response items as well as longer research and analytic reports documenting conservative misinformation throughout the media. Additionally, Media Matters works daily to notify activists, journalists, pundits and the public about instances of misinformation, providing them with the resources to rebut false claims and to take direct action against offending media institutions.

How will your organization impact the public debate in 2008?
Media Matters has been at the forefront of challenging the media's reliance on unfair stereotypes of progressives and myths and falsehoods about progressive viewpoints and initiatives. Our organization has the research and rapid communications capabilities to effectively counter assaults on the progressive brand launched by the right-wing media and amplified by the mainstream media. Media Matters combats these attacks with fact-based rebuttals and calls for the inclusion of more progressive voices in the public debate.

Looking out 2-3 years, how would you like to grow/change your organization?
Already having established Media Matters as the preeminent progressive media research and information center, our goal moving forward is to increase the effectiveness and impact of our research and action campaigns. We plan to intensify our outreach efforts in order to continue to educate and invest progressives in the importance of media criticism in effectively combating misinformation and calling for the most accurate and complete news coverage everyday. In order

to promote the highest level of journalistic integrity, we aim to expand the scope of our media criticism beyond the national media as well.

What do you need to do that?
As we continue to expand the scope of our efforts, Media Matters will also increase the capabilities and resources of all of our departments, including the areas of research, editorial and strategic communications.

How will your organization change if progressives win in November? If they lose?
Since our inception, Media Matters has focused on our mission to document and correct misinformation in the media, as well as to educate the public about this issue. As a comprehensive media watchdog and research institute, our objectives remain the same no matter what the outcome of the November elections is. We will continue to document instances of distortions and errors in media coverage and provide news consumers with the tools and information to contact offending

Media Matters provides an "unbeatable critique" of the "distortions of the mainstream press." This group is the "new world of communications" and is "tremendously helpful." One contributor "can't even imagine not having it."

media outlets directly and advocate for honest journalism.

If you had to offer some advice to fellow progressives what would it be?
It is essential that every progressive take a sophisticated and aggressive, hands-on approach to the media and the coverage of important issues. At the end of the day, conservatives will use every tool at their disposal to shape media coverage to their advantage, unless progressives demand fair and accurate coverage. No matter what issue you are primarily concerned about, the media is more important and influential in shaping the political landscape than it has ever been before. Media criticism should be considered an integral tool for every progressive.

www.MN2020.org

	📟 651-917-1026	🖥 mn2020.org
	🖨 651-917-0765	🗝 June 26, 2007
2324 University Ave W	✂ John Van Hecke	📊 $500,000
Ste 204	@ john.vanhecke@mn2020.org	📇 501(c)(3)
Saint Paul, MN 55114		

Matt Entenza
Founder/Board Chair

Matt Entenza is a graduate of southern Minnesota's Worthington Senior High School. A scholarship student, Matt started at Augustana College then transferred to Macalester College. After graduating, Matt studied law at England's Oxford University and taught high school. Returning to the Twin Cities, he received his J.D. with honors from the University of Minnesota Law School.

After law school, Matt clerked for U.S. District Judge Harry McLaughlin. Next, as an Assistant Attorney General, in the Charities Division, Matt successfully prosecuted scamming telemarketers, fraudulent adoption agencies and even a deceitful minister stealing money meant for children's health care. While at the Attorney General's office Matt also was an Assistant Professor at St. Mary's University, teaching law.

Matt joined the Hennepin County Attorney's office, continuing his watchdog activities as an Assistant County Attorney, prosecuting white-collar crime. While there, Matt assembled a strike force to catch a swindling car salesman who was stealing thousands of dollars from the public. He took legal action against a company illegally dumping toxins into wetlands that fed into the public's drinking water.

Matt represented Minnesota State House of Representatives District 64A from 1995-2007. As a State Representative, Matt continued his role as a public watchdog, strengthening laws regarding child support, child protections, DWI, white-collar crime

Minnesota's local "progressive engine." This organization is "exemplary."

prosecution, nonprofit disclosure and fighting for property tax relief. He was chief author of the "Do Not Call" bill, protecting families' privacy. He has been a leader in education, fighting for better nutritional programs in our schools and exposing fraudulent practices by a few charter school administrators, saving thousands of dollars for Minnesotans.

Matt was elected House Democratic Leader by his colleagues, serving from 2002-2006. DFL Leader in the State House. He did not seek re-election but ran for Attorney General. During his tenure, he served on the K-12 Finance, Education Policy and Commerce Committees and is widely recognized for his hard work and tireless focus on consumer and family protections.

Matt founded Minnesota 2020; a progressive, non-partisan think tank in June of 2007. He serves as the group's Board Chair.

Matt is also a Senior Fellow at the Institute for Law and Politics at the University of Minnesota Law School.

Matt and his wife, Lois Quam, have been married for 23 years. They have three children, Ben (18) and twins Will and Steve (16).

What does your organization do and how does it do it?
Minnesota 2020 is Minnesota's newest non-profit progressive think tank and advocacy-based new media organization. We're moving Minnesota's public policy by focusing on what really matters: education, healthcare, transportation and economic development.

Accountability and responsibility–in management, project execution, and strategic choice–are our guiding touchstones. We link academic and traditional foundation research with change-ready communities, seeking nonpartisan application and tangible, demonstrable solutions. We have already been favorably published on over 114 Minnesota newspapers and have been covered in every major TV market.

How will your organization impact the public debate in 2008?
Minnesota 2020 delivers smart, accurate policy research with rigorous mission discipline, creating and disseminating smart, effective progressive messaging through a new media platform. We are framing Minnesota's public policy debate. Through our communications strategy, we've compelled legislative and executive branch policy change.

What is your 2008 operating budget?
$500,000

Looking out 2-3 years, how would you like to grow/change your organization?
As Minnesota 2020 has become Minnesota's progressive messaging development center, we've embraced our new media flexibility to expand our reader reach and our impact on traditional media. We look forward to developing and launching a

visual narrative capacity to our communications mission.

What do you need to do that?
Several additional skilled visual and new media professionals and the funding to support their work.

How will your organization change if progressives win in November? If they lose?
Regardless of the electoral outcome, we will continue focusing on what really matters to Minnesotans: education, healthcare, transportation and economic development.

If you had to offer some advice to fellow progressives what would it be?
A strong mission, smart people, an articulated values core and an aggressive communications strategy are essential to progressive success.

Please list your board of directors and their affiliations.

Matt Entenza
Founder/Board Chair,
Minnesota 2020

Tom Welna
Executive Director, The High Winds Fund of Macalester College

Mary Rosenthal
Service Employees International Union

MomsRising.org

c/o Donna Rea
12011 Bel-Red Rd
Ste 100
Bellevue, WA 98005

 206-226-4126
Kristin Rowe-Finkbeiner
@ kristin@momsrising.org

momsrising.org
May 2006
$500,000
501(c)4, with a significant 501(c) program, sponsored by the Western States Center.

Joan Blades
President

Kristin Rowe-Finkbeiner
Executive Director

Joan Blades

MomsRising.org President, Joan Blades is also co-founder and board member of MoveOn.org, which has an online membership of over 3 million. On Mother's Day 2006 she co-founded MomsRising.org with Kristin Rowe-Finkbeiner to tap the power of online grassroots organizing for mothers and families in the U.S.A. She is also the co-author of *The Motherhood Manifesto* which won the Ernesta Drinker Ballard Book Prize in 2007, and a member of the Reuniting America advisory board. Last century she co-founded Berkeley Systems best known for the flying toaster screen saver "After Dark," taught mediation at Golden Gate Law School, practiced mediation and wrote *Mediate Your Divorce*, published by Prentice Hall. She is a past member of the California and Alaska bar associations. Joan was also selected as *Ms.* magazine 2003 Woman of the Year, as well as for the Hollander Award for Women in Leadership, as well as other awards. Ms. Blades is an artist, with collages published on both greeting cards and software packaging. She enjoys creating fused glass jewelry, is a nature lover, Sunday soccer player and being a mother.

Kristin Rowe-Finkbeiner

MomsRising.org Executive Director, Kristin Rowe-Finkbeiner, is also co-founder of the organization. With MomsRising co-founder and President, Joan Blades, Rowe-Finkbeiner is also the co-author of *The Motherhood Manifesto*, which won the Ernesta Drinker Ballard Book Prize. Rowe-Finkbeiner also wrote the award-winning book *The F-Word: Feminism in Jeopardy*. In 2006, she was given an Excellence in Journalism award by the Society of Professional Journalists for her magazine writing. Rowe-Finkbeiner's writing also appears in several other books. Rowe-Finkbeiner has also been deeply involved in cutting edge politics and policy analysis for over a decade. Prior to MomsRising.org, she worked as a consultant in the field of political strategy and policy analysis for many non-profit clients. Previous to working as a consultant, during her tenure as Political and Field Director of the Washington Conservation Voters, the political arm of the environmental movement in Washington State, she created a model statewide program to elect, endorse and support environmentally responsible candidates. Rowe-Finkbeiner was recently selected as a Prime Movers Fellow by the Hunt Alternatives Fund, and was also given the 2008 Good in Government Award from the Washington State League of Women Voters. She currently serves on the board of the Economic Opportunity Institute. Rowe-Finkbeiner lives in Washington State with her husband, two children, dog and hamster.

What does your organization do and how does it do it?
Started in May of 2006, MomsRising.org is working to bring millions of people together who share a common concern about the need to build a more truly family-friendly America. MomsRising uses the power of online strategies, coordinated with grassroots on-the-ground activities, aligned organization collaboration and dynamic media outreach, to educate the public about problems facing American families which impede women's economic security, and to propose common-sense solutions through increased citizen engagement. We provide the public with opportunities to amplify their voices, strengthen their participation in our democracy and to bring about positive change.

Our over 130,000 (and growing) members include women of all ages—from grandmothers to new, young mothers. They are stay-at-home moms and working mothers, from rural and urban communities and represent a range of socio economic backgrounds and the diversity of American families. In addition, more than 90 national and state organizations have signed on to be aligned with our work. They represent some of our nation's strongest women's and mothers' organizations, family and child advocacy groups, unions, healthcare organizations and faith groups.

MomsRising is working to reframe many long sought progressive policy changes through the lens of motherhood as a way for people to hear them anew. Using this framing, we are drawing in people that who have not been civically engaged, as well as people from across the political spectrum. Organizing mothers is a powerful strategy for bringing about

Focused on "what matters." The "MoveOn for families."

progressive policy changes to reduce the number of families living in poverty, decreasing the gender wage gap and for increasing voter engagement and voter turnout.

How will your organization impact the public debate in 2008?
Mothers pack a political punch for both elections and advocacy. Women make up 54% of the total electorate, and 82% American women are mothers by the time they are 44 years old. Today, there are 80.5 million mothers in our country, and 10.4 million of these are single mothers living with children younger than 18 years old. Motherhood is a unifying framework that crosses socioeconomic, cultural and political lines. MomsRising is bringing in, and placing the voices of women, mothers, at the center of our national political dialogue.

To impact the public debate, MomsRising is active at the national and state levels educating people about the need for a more truly family-friendly nation, as well as actively advocating for those changes. In addition, MomsRising is launching a MomsVote '08 program to register and turn out more mothers to vote, primarily through a peer-to-peer platform.

Looking out 2-3 years, how would you like to grow/change your organization?
MomsRising's unique combination of online and on-the-ground activism, paired with strong media appeal and positive, effective messaging around motherhood and its systemic economic challenges for women and families, is engaging an increasing number of women in the American democratic process. In the next 2-3 years we'd like to see the number of people involved tripled, and the number of family-friendly policies passed—like paid family leave and healthcare policies—significantly increased. Since our founding in 2006, MomsRising members have already generated over 1 million online actions on issues they care about. In addition, they've helped pass Paid Family Leave in Washington State, Paid Sick Days in DC, advance healthcare reform and are near passage of other policies in additional states. That's in our first 18 months—just imagine what we can do to advance the cause of women's civic engagement and economic equality in the years to come.

What do you need to do that?
The primary need of MomsRising. org at this time, like that of many organizations, is to increase our funding base. MomsRising is essentially a pilot project which shows success in membership growth, media coverage, citizen online and on-the-ground engagement and passage of policies which support families. In order to take the next steps, and to grow into our full potential, MomsRising needs increased resources to keep up with the opportunities and passion of our rapidly growing membership.

How will your organization change if progressives win in November? If they lose?

Whether or not progressives win in November 2008, the work of MomsRising is needed to push forward family-friendly policies which are the norm in the rest of the world, but have too long been lacking in America. MomsRising is working on policy changes on the M-O-T-H-E-R-S issue platform (see www.MomsRising.org for the platform) as part of a greater push for overall cultural change and women's economic equality. Studies show that countries with family-friendly policies and programs in place, like those in the MomsRising M-O-T-H-E-R-S platform, don't have the same degree of maternal wage gaps as we do here (Women without children make 90 cents to a man's dollar, mothers make 73 cents, and single moms make the least at about 60 cents to a man's dollar). Passing family-friendly policies will help narrow the wage gaps, and bring women and families out of poverty. Solving these issues is going to take the support of leaders across the political spectrum, and leaders are better able to make important changes when they know large groups of citizens back them, so MomsRising will be engaged after November regardless of who wins.

If you had to offer some advice to fellow progressives what would it be?

Well, this advice is as much a reminder to ourselves as advice for others, but here goes: Make listening to members an organizational priority, save time in each day to rapidly respond to emerging issues; and also take time to dance, play soccer and smell the roses because change doesn't usually happen overnight and most of us are in this for the long haul.

MoveOn.ORG
POLITICAL ACTION ®

PO Box 9218
Berkeley, CA 94707

 510-524-3492
 360-397-2645
 Carrie Olson, Chief
Operating Officer
 carrie@moveon.org

 moveon.org
 September 1998
 $20,000,000
PAC

Eli Pariser
Executive Director (above)

Wes Boyd
President/Co-founder (not shown)

Wes Boyd
Mr. Boyd is a software industry veteran, having founded a leading entertainment software company, Berkeley Systems. Prior to his work in consumer software, Mr. Boyd authored software for blind and visually impaired users allowing full access to computers with a graphical user interface.

What does your organization do and how does it do it?
MoveOn brings real Americans back into the political process. With over 3.2 million members across America—from carpenters to stay-at-home moms to business leaders—we work together to realize the progressive promise of our country. MoveOn is a service—a way for busy but concerned citizens to find their political voice in a system dominated by big money and big media.

Our campaigns integrate great volunteers, great PR work and ads paid for by our members, to highlight issues we care about. For more information about our successes, go to www.moveon.org/about.html.

How will your organization impact the public debate in 2008?
As a political action committee, entirely funded with hard-money contributions under $5,000, MoveOn will help mobilize millions of progressives to get out the word in this election year—focusing on key issues like the Iraq war, health care and renewable energy. Unlike 501c3 and c4 organizations, MoveOn can powerfully connect the dots—from the hot issues of the day to directly supporting specific candidates. In 2008, MoveOn will run the largest volunteer-based vote turnout

operation, outside of the candidate campaigns—mobilizing tens of thousands of volunteers.

What is your 2008 operating budget?
$20 million.

Looking out 2-3 years, how would you like to grow/change your organization?
Participation is our core mission. Our fondest hopes are that a progressive wave is coming to America and that we may see a day when all Americans will be ready to drop their cynicism and passivity and work to build a new kind of civic life. No matter who is president in 2008, a deep and broad progressive movement will be crucial to anything good happening in Washington. Without such a movement, the structural impediments are too great. We see MoveOn as a catalyst for this change, and our members as models for this new civic life. We will continue to innovate in using technology—email, web-based tools, mobile phones and social networks—to build the network and connections this movement will be based on.

What do you need to do that?
We need to support our members in building successes. We need individuals to make a significant commitment of their resources but also of their time and talents, as MoveOn members.

How will your organization change if progressives win in November? If they lose?
We all hope to be moving into an era when the progressive movement can be on offense rather than defense. If Democrats win in November, we will be one step closer to that day. But even a Democratic president will be absolutely hamstrung, until there is a vibrant progressive movement behind him or her.

If you had to offer some advice to fellow progressives what would it be?
Don't focus on the candidates. We won't be saved by any single man or woman. We have to do the work, building the systems and infrastructure and vision. We have to talk to our neighbors and friends and get them on board. We need to focus on the issues and on building a bright future, not on the latest candidate gossip and horserace rumors. Turn off the news and lets get to work. Together.

Please list your board of directors and their affiliations.

Wes Boyd
President, MoveOn

Doug Carlston
Software Industry Entrepreneur

Carrie Olson
Chief Operating Officer, MoveOn

You "can't get better" than MoveOn. They "invented" the use of the internet for community organizing and "made it look easy."

NARAL
Pro-Choice America

1156 15th St NW
Ste 700
Washington, DC 20005

☎ 202-973-3000 (main line)
📠 202-973-2027
✂ Stephanie Kushner, Vice
   President of Development
@ 202-973-3027

💻 naral.org
🔑 1969
📊 $18,499,000 (total for
   501(c)(3), 501(c)(4), PAC)
🔗 501(c)(3), 501(c)(4), PAC*

Nancy Keenan
President

Nancy Keenan began her tenure as president of NARAL Pro-Choice America in December 2004. Committed to working on behalf of America's pro-choice majority, Nancy took the reigns of the organization pledging to protect and defend the American values of freedom and privacy.

A successful elected official in her native state of Montana, Nancy applied her experiences as a candidate in overseeing NARAL Pro-Choice America's political program in the 2006 midterm elections, which helped fuel the gain of 23 pro-choice seats in the U.S. House and three in the U.S. Senate. The organization also worked with state-based leaders to defeat three anti-choice ballot measures, including the repeal of an abortion ban in South Dakota that was designed as a direct threat to Roe v. Wade.

In its 2006 post-election analysis, *National Journal* listed NARAL Pro-Choice America as one of the top five major political organizations and as a leader among groups that "mobilized their grassroots and got voters to the polls in the most competitive races." Seventy-five percent of NARAL Pro-Choice America's endorsed candidates won their races.

Under Nancy's leadership, NARAL Pro-Choice America launched Prevention First, a values-based initiative encouraging lawmakers to focus on commonsense ways to prevent unintended pregnancies and reduce the need for abortion. In February

---

* NARALPro-Choice America's work is divided among three organizations: NARAL Pro-Choice America, Inc., a 501(c)(4) non-profit organization; NARAL Pro-Choice America PAC, a political action committee; and NARAL Pro-Choice America Foundation, a 501(c)(3)charitable organization founded in 1977

2005, Nancy issued a challenge to President Bush and his allies who oppose abortion to stop attacking a woman's right to choose and join the organization in supporting efforts to prevent unintended pregnancies through medically accurate sex education, birth control, including the "morning-after" pill, and improved family-planning services.

Nancy's work to reshape the debate on reproductive rights and protect women's access to safe, legal abortion has gained her significant attention. *Washingtonian* magazine named her one of the top 100 most powerful women in Washington, DC. *The Detroit News* described her as both "forthright and politically savvy," noting that she, among other pro-choice leaders, is responsible for "honing a message about American values of personal responsibility, freedom and privacy" defined as "a new stance and a realistic one."

The American Prospect described Nancy's approach to the debate on choice as "a cunning strategy" that allows "pro-choice advocates to define the terms of the debate." Nationally syndicated columnist Ellen Goodman wrote that "after years of playing defense, NARAL has gone on the offense."

Before coming to NARAL Pro-Choice America, Nancy served as a Montana state legislator and State Superintendent of Public Instruction and ran a strong campaign for the U.S. House of Representatives in 2000.

Nancy's commitment to public service was shaped early in life as one of five children born into an Irish-Catholic family in Anaconda, Montana, a small copper smelter town in the western part of this "red" state. Nancy earned a bachelor's degree in elementary education from Montana State University and a master's degree in education administration from the University of Montana. Before seeking elected office, Nancy taught children with disabilities in her hometown.

Nancy Keenan is a leading commentator on reproductive health issues. Her list of appearances includes NBC Nightly News, The Today Show, The Brit Hume Report on FOX, CNN and NPR. She is also routinely quoted in *The New York Times*, *The Washington Post*, *Newsweek* and other major national and regional publications.

What does your organization do and how does it do it?
NARAL Pro-Choice America is the nation's leading advocate for privacy and a woman's right to choose. With more than one million members and activists and 30,000 on-the-ground volunteers, NARAL Pro-Choice America protects the pro-choice

NARAL is "central" and "exhaustive" and "critical." They "know exactly what they're doing."

values of freedom and privacy in the following ways:

- Electing pro-choice candidates through voter contact and education, research and polling, and direct PAC contributions.
- Mobilizing and educating pro-choice Americans using traditional and innovative online methods.
- Lobbying Congress to improve women's access to reproductive-health care and stop anti-choice restrictions on reproductive freedom and privacy.
- Providing up-to-the-minute information about state bills, the enactment of new laws and decisions handed down by state and federal courts related to reproductive rights.
- Working with 23 state affiliates, a California chapter and an Illinois Choice Action Team to advance pro-choice legislation in the states, elect pro-choice candidates and educate and engage the public on choice issues.

How will your organization impact the public debate in 2008?
Building on our 2006 electoral successes, we will persuade pro-choice Independent and Republican women to cross party lines and vote for a pro-choice congressional and presidential candidate. No other progressive organization, or issue outside of choice, moves these voters. Our "MCFL" tax status allows us to advocate for the explicit defeat or support of any federal candidate right up to Election Day and permits individuals to contribute

unlimited amounts to our c4.

What is your 2008 operating budget?
NARAL Pro-Choice America and NARAL Pro-Choice America PAC: $11,854,000;
NARAL Pro-Choice America Foundation: $6,645,000;
Combined c4, PAC and c3 operating budgets: $18,499,000

Looking out 2-3 years, how would you like to grow/change your organization?
We have a five-year plan that maps out an aggressive, strategic vision to advance our pro-choice values. On the electoral front, we could expand and enhance our lists of identified pro-choice voters in key battleground states. That's the best way to secure electoral gains, especially in the fast-growing Southwest region of the country. We also could further utilize new technology to communicate with these identified voters in non-election years and help cultivate a younger and more diverse activist base to support both our electoral- and policy-related efforts at the state and federal levels.

What do you need to do that?
The 2008 elections present an opportunity to achieve electoral successes. We could spend $348,800 per congressional district to reach between 40,000–60,000 households with persuadable mail, calls and door-to-door staff at a cost of $8 per voter.

We also need at least $2 million to assist as many as five state affiliates that could face anti-choice ballot measures in 2008.

How will your organization change if progressives win in November? If they lose?

The gains in Congress and in the states in 2006 illustrate how electoral successes can help us advance some pro-choice measures and stop attacks that happen when anti-choice politicians are in control.

One election cannot change everything. A pro-choice president in the White House or pro-choice legislative leadership doesn't guarantee action since anti-choice members still outnumber pro-choice members in Congress. In addition, anti-choice groups will continue to use the states to spur legislative challenges and ballot measures. They are emboldened by the addition of Bush appointees to the Supreme Court and lower courts who are hostile to Roe v. Wade.

If you had to offer some advice to fellow progressives what would it be?

We are fortunate to work with progressive partners on a range of issues that affect women's health and privacy. We value this partnership and understand that it's critical for collective progressive wins in the future.

We would advise progressives to think long-term about the best ways to build and sustain a progressive infrastructure. We need consistent messaging, and growing base of activists. We can get there with funding for specific projects with measurable goals. We must think long term and resist efforts to recreate the wheel, rather than improving the structure we already have.

Please list your board of directors and their affiliations.

NARAL Pro-Choice America Board

Chair, Maria T. Vullo
Partner, Paul, Weiss, Rifkind, Wharton & Garrison LLP, New York, NY

Vice-Chair, Janet Denlinger
President, Matrix Biology Institute, Fort Lee, NJ

Secretary, Elizabeth Hager
Legislator and Executive Director, United Way of Merrimack, Concord, NH

Treasurer, Vivian Shimoyama
President, Breakthru Unlimited, Los Angeles, CA

Volunteer, Coni Batlle
Tempe, AZ

Of Counsel, Chris Bell
Patton Boggs LLP; Former U.S. Representative, Houston, TX

Linda Binder
Consultant, Binder & Sickles Consultants LLC; Former State Legislator, Lake Havasu, AZ

Sachin Chheda
Partner, Nation Consulting, Milwaukee, WI

Nation.

33 Irving Pl
8th Flr
New York, NY 10003

☎ 212-209-5400
🖨 212-982-9000
✂ Ben Wyskida
@ ben@thenation.com

🖥 thenation.com
🔑 1865
📊 $12,000,000
🖧 The Nation Company, LP

Katrina vanden Heuvel
Editor/Publisher

Katrina vanden Heuvel is Editor and
Publisher of *The Nation*. Katrina has
been *The Nation's* editor since 1995
and publisher since 2005. She is the
co-editor of *Taking Back America–
And Taking Down The Radical Right*
and, most recently, editor of *The
Dictionary of Republicanisms*. She is
a frequent commentator on American
and international politics on MSNBC,
CNN and PBS. Her articles have
appeared in The Washington Post,
the *Los Angeles Times*, *The New
York Times* and *The Boston Globe*.
Her web column, "Editor's Cut," is
posted at thenation.com. She has
received awards for public service
from numerous groups including The
Liberty Hill Foundation, The New York
Civil Liberties Union and the Asian
American Legal Defense and Education
Fund. She serves on the boards of The
Institute for Policy Studies, The Institute
for America's Future and the Franklin
and Eleanor Roosevelt Institute.

**What does your organization do
and how does it do it?**
The Nation is America's oldest
weekly news magazine and the
most widely read journal of political
thought. The mission of *The Nation*
and of thenation.com is to serve
as a critical, independent voice
in American journalism. We offer
reporting and analysis of breaking
news, politics, social issues and the
arts. *The Nation* is often considered
"the flagship" of the left: we spark
debate on critical issues to the
progressive community and offer
a platform for independent, small
"d" ideas. The magazine, with over
200,000 subscribers, and the website,
with nearly 1 million visitors a month,
are complemented by a range of
related projects including video and
radio platforms, community forums
and events and a robust "Nation
Associates" donor program.

How will your organization impact the public debate in 2008?

The Nation is planning extensive coverage of the critical 2008 election with a focus on policies, grassroots and netroots movements and solutions–not just the horse race. We will continue to provide a platform for progressives to debate the big issues this year, and will also focus on critical local elections and grassroots campaigns that are making a difference. We want to broaden and deepen the debate in this country.

As always, *The Nation* will also impact the debate with hard-hitting investigative reporting. In 2007 our reporting had a dramatic impact on issues like benefits for veterans and the use of military contractors in Iraq. In 2008 we expect Nation investigative reporting to have an equally bold impact.

What is your 2008 operating budget?
$12 million.

Looking out 2-3 years, how would you like to grow/change your organization?

Over the next 2-3 years, *The Nation* will continue to take advantage of the changing media landscape. Through an expanded online presence, including the use of video and social networking, *The Nation* will look to grow our new media footprint. Most importantly, though, *The Nation* will continue to challenge a downsized politics of excluded alternatives by providing bold, in-depth reporting and analysis. As mainstream newsrooms continue to struggle, we believe this reporting will be more relevant than ever.

What do you need to do that?
Continued financial support–through traditional and online outreach–from our subscribers and donors, and strong partnerships with other progressive institutions.

How will your organization change if progressives win in November? If they lose?

Win or lose, *The Nation* will continue to push our politics (and the Democratic Party in particular) in a small "d" democratic and progressive direction. If progressives win, *The Nation* assumes an important role of seeking accountability and proposing bolder policies and ideas for the country. If progressives lose, *The Nation* will continue to hold the right accountable, and will be a forum for debate on what progressives can and should do next.

The Nation is "a firecracker" read. They give journalists an opportunity to "break free" from mainstream media, writing "fascinating" and "compelling" pieces on the real world.

If you had to offer some advice to fellow progressives what would it be?

It's time to build! Let's take our politics of passion and principle, our values, our ideas and our energy and drive our issues into the political debate, into our movements and into the electoral arena. After 8 years of a disastrous and extremist rule, let's restore America to its democratic promise. We can no longer play defense in the battle of ideas. The stakes are too high. We must make the debate between our vision of the future versus theirs. It is time for conviction, not caution. It is time to dare to imagine.

Please list your board of directors and their affiliations.

We do not have a Board of Directors. Our Editorial Board is listed on our masthead.

The Nation Institute

———— DEDICATED TO A FREE AND INDEPENDENT PRESS ————

Nation Books
Journalism Fellowship Program
The Investigative Fund

116 East 16th St

8th flr

New York, NY 10003

📞 212-822-0250

🖨 212-253-5356

✂ Taya Kitman,

Development Director

@ taya@nationinstitute.org

💻 nationinstitute.org

nationinstitute.org/ifunds/

nationbooks.org

🔑 1966

📊 approx $3,200,000

🔗 501(c)3

Hamilton Fish
President

Hamilton Fish has served as president of The Institute since 1996. He was appointed President of the Public Concern Foundation, publishers of *The Washington Spectator,* in 1992; before then he was managing director of Human Rights Watch and publisher of *The Nation* magazine. He was a producer of two Marcel Ophuls documentaries, including the Academy Award-winning Hotel Terminus, and serves on the boards of several non-profit public interest organizations.

What does your organization do and how does it do it?
The Nation Institute promotes free speech and an expanded public discourse, with special emphasis on strengthening the independent press in the face of increasing corporate control over American media. The Institute is home to Nation Books, where Editor Carl Bromley and his team publish titles on the social and cultural forces that shape our lives today, including, recently, the national bestseller *Blackwater* by Jeremy Scahill. The Institute administers the Journalism Fellowship Program, which supports up-and-coming journalists (Deepa Fernandes, Max Blumenthal, Ari Berman) as well as established writers (Chris Hedges, Katha Pollitt, Jonathan Schell, Jeremy Scahill, Naomi Klein, Gary Younge, Eric Alterman, Pamela Newkirk), who

The Nation "challenges the status quo" and "questions" the current state of affairs "relentlessly."

inject progressive reporting and analysis into both mainstream and alternative media outlets. The Institute sponsors TomDispatch.com, a widely read website and list serve offering progressive political commentary. It is home to three major awards programs, each designed to recognize courageous progressive voices. And it is home to The Investigative Fund, led by director Joe Conason (columnist for Salon.com and *The New York Observer*, and author of *It Can Happen Here: Authoritarian Peril in the Age of Bush*) and investigative editor Esther Kaplan (radio and print journalist, author of *With God on Their Side*). Investigative Fund stories have earned national awards (IRE, Polk), sparked Congressional investigations and federal legislation, gained coverage on the major networks and led to the resignation of at least one top Bush official who contributed to the illegal treatment of Guantánamo detainees.

What is your 2008 operating budget?
Approximately $3.2 million

Looking out 2-3 years, how would you like to grow/change your organization?
Our primary near term goal is to expand the impact of our content. We need to increase the number of writing fellowships we offer, and to award more grants for investigative reporting. There is a real need for us to provide more institutional backup for reporters, from legal assistance on FOIA requests to research assistance to mentoring of young reporters. We need to strengthen our capacity to inject the information in

our books and articles into the broader culture, and to magnify the impact of our content on the political and public policy discourse.

What do you need to do that?
We have embarked on the second phase of our Operating and Endowment Campaign, in search of the next $10 million we will need for fellowships and writing grants and book research; we will use the funding to develop a dedicated promotion department team to push our stories, books and authors out to the mainstream press and the public sector; and we will continue to expand our presence on the web, adding content to our site and adapting newly developed techniques for building online community and the wider distribution of information.

How will your organization change if progressives win in November? If they lose?
Without a doubt, a significant expansion of Democratic majorities in November would encourage us to focus more on the legislative process, with the idea that our reporters' muckraking reporting and political analysis could gain more traction on Capitol Hill. But most of our core concerns, such as environmental degradation and the challenges of environmental protection; the growing divide between rich and poor; affordable, publicly funded health care; the decline of labor unions; the assaults on the rights of women, people of color and gays and lesbians; and America's imperial engagement with the world,

will persist regardless of who wins in November. In addition, the legacy of the Bush administration will remain with us for many years, particularly its privatization of public assets and decision-making, decimation of our tax base, deregulation of Wall Street and our efforts to expose these depredations and spark corrective action will continue.

If you had to offer some advice to fellow progressives what would it be?
Our main advice would be for progressives not to trim their sails. Progressives should learn a lesson from the right and work to move this country's political center, rather than accommodate it. A Democratic majority in Congress was elected in 2006 to stop the war and deal with working Americans' economic desperation, but quickly abandoned its mandate. It will require a combination of unsparing investigative journalism, tough-minded political analysis from journalists and think tanks and bold grassroots activism to force progressive agenda items back onto center stage.

Please list your board of directors and their affiliations.

Ellen Chesler
Hunter College, City University of New York

Ron Daniels
Institute of the Black World

Adrian DeWind
Paul, Weiss, Rifkind, Wharton & Garrison

Howard Dodson
The Schomberg Center for Research in Black Culture

Nancy Dunlap
Jon S. Corzine Foundation

Hamilton Fish
The Nation Institute

Paula Giddings
Smith College

Stephen Gillers
New York University School of Law

Danny Goldberg
Gold Village Entertainment

Steven Haft
Haft Entertainment

David Jones
Community Service Society

Doug Kreeger
Entrepreneur

Jeff Levy-Hinte
Antidote International Films; Jeht Foundation

Victor Navasky
The Nation

Tim Robbins
Havoc Films

NATIONAL CONGRESS OF BLACK WOMEN

📞 202-678-6788   🖥 npcbw.org

🖨 202-678-7080   🗝 August 1984

✂ Dr. E. Faye Williams, Esq.   🔗 501(c)(3)

@ efayed@aol.com

1224 W St SE
Washington, DC 20020

**Dr. E. Faye Williams, Esq.
National Chair**

What does your organization do and how does it do it?
We are a women's organization that works for the benefit of the Black family in all aspects: Economic, Educational, Health, Political, Spiritual, etc. We honor the high achievements of Black women. We introduce young children to various professions, assist them with passing standardized tests, teach them conflict resolution and motivate them to be involved in community service. We work through our volunteer membership.

How will your organization impact the public debate in 2008?
NCBW membership includes Presidential cabinet members, Presidential appointees, elected officials, doctors, lawyers, entrepreneurs, religious leaders, educators and community activists. NCBW will participate in public discussions of issues that have an impact on our members. We will participate in voter registration and Get-Out-The-Vote activities in several states. Our National Chair, National Board Members and our Local members will serve as keynote speakers at numerous events in several key cities across the country to outline the interests of our organization in an effort to gain support for them. We will host candidate forums to provide a platform for candidates seeking our support to outline their positions on issues and hear our concerns about them.

The NCBW is an "amazing endeavor." They are about "acting" and "doing."

Looking out 2-3 years, how would you like to grow/change your organization?

Included in our 5 year long range goals, we have plans to develop workforce housing for single mothers. We are planning a memorial to Sojourner Truth who will become the first Black woman to have a memorial erected in her honor in the United States Capitol. We plan to add a new group called "Young Ambassadors" to teach young people diplomatic skills. We also have plans for organizing a separate Political Action Committee, so that we can begin to do candidate endorsements.

What do you need to do that?

We have to raise more funds in order to implement the projects, and we need to work toward consistent annual funding so that we know in advance approximately what our resources will be for the ensuing year. This would allow us to do more advance planning.

How will your organization change if progressives win in November? If they lose?

We have been able to work collaboratively with whatever party is in office; however, historically, when Progressives are in leadership roles, greater resources have been available for our programs; thus, we have been able to do more good for more people and provide greater access to education and economic stability for underserved populations.

If you had to offer some advice to fellow progressives what would it be?

Progressives should empower those around us to work together and identify those who have common goals as we have without regard to partisan politics. We'd like to see more collaboration so that we can accomplish more with our resources pooled rather than having a lot of small programs that duplicate our work.

Please list your board of directors and their affiliations.

National Chair, Dr. E. Faye Williams, Esq.

1st Vice Chair, Trish Morris Yamba
Entrepreneur

2nd Vice Chair, Gladys Evans
Retired Business Owner

3rd Vice Chair, Nicole Duncan
Graduate Student

Corresponding Secretary, Ophelia Averitt
Entrepreneur

Corresponding Secretary, Bernice J. Oden
Retired Federal Government Employee

Treasurer, Dr. Jacquelyn Jordan
Dean (School of Nursing)

Board, Glinda Anderson
Minister

NATIONAL COUNCIL OF LA RAZA

Raul Yzaguirre Building
1126 16th St NW
Washington, DC 22036

☎ 202-785-1670
🖨 202-776-1792
@ comments@nclr.org

🖥 nclr.org
⚷ 1968
📊 $30,000,000
🔗 403(b)

Janet Murguía
President and CEO

Janet Murguía has emerged as a key figure among the next generation of leaders in the Latino community. Since January 1, 2005, she has served as the President and Chief Executive Officer of the National Council of La Raza (NCLR), the largest national Hispanic civil rights and advocacy organization in the U.S.

Murguía began her career in Washington, DC as legislative counsel to former Kansas Congressman Jim Slattery, serving for seven years. She then worked at the White House from 1994 to 2000, ultimately serving as deputy assistant to President Clinton, providing strategic and legislative advice to the president on key issues. She served as deputy director of legislative affairs, managing the legislative staff and acting as a senior White House liaison to Congress.

She then served as deputy campaign manager and director of constituency outreach for the Gore/Lieberman presidential campaign. In that role, she was the primary liaison between former Vice President Gore and national constituency groups. She also served as a spokesperson for the campaign, working with radio, print and TV media outlets.

In 2001, Murguía joined the University of Kansas (KU) as Executive Vice Chancellor for University Relations, overseeing KU's internal and external relations with the public, including governmental and public affairs. She coordinated the university's strategic planning and marketing efforts at the four KU campuses with those of the Alumni Association, the Athletics Corporation and the Endowment Association.

Murguía is currently a Board member of the Independent Sector, a coalition of leading nonprofits, foundations and corporations committed to connecting, informing and advocating on behalf of the nonprofit and philanthropic community. She is also a member of the Merrill Lynch Diversity & Inclusion Council and is an executive committee member of the Leadership Conference on Civil Rights. In addition, Murguía sits on the Board of the Hispanic Association on Corporate Responsibility and the National Hispanic Leadership Agenda.

In 2007, Murguía was featured in *Newsweek's* Third Annual Women and Leadership issue; was named to *Poder* magazine's "The Poderosos 100," *Latino Leaders* magazine's "101 Top Leaders of the Hispanic Community," and *Hispanic* magazine's "Powerful Latinos 2007"; and was the first Hispanic to give the keynote speech at the annual Dr. Martin Luther King, Jr. Unity Breakfast in Birmingham, Alabama. In 2006, Murguía was named to *Washingtonian* magazine's "100 Most Powerful Women in Washington," *The NonProfit Times'* "Power and Influence Top 50" leaders, and *People En Español's* "100 Most Influential Hispanics 2006." *Hispanic Business* magazine named Murguía as a finalist for its 2005 "Woman of the Year Award," and in 2004, *Hispanic* magazine chose her for its annual list of "100 Top Latinas" and *Hispanic Business* magazine selected her as one of the "100 Most Influential Hispanics."

Janet Murguía grew up in Kansas City, Kansas. She received three degrees from KU: a B.S. degree in journalism (1982), a B.A. degree in Spanish (1982), and a J.D. degree (1985) from the School of Law.

What does your organization do and how does it do it?
The National Council of La Raza (NCLR) – the largest national Hispanic civil rights and advocacy organization in the United States – works to improve opportunities for Hispanic Americans. Through its network of nearly 300 affiliated community-based organizations (CBOs), NCLR reaches millions of Hispanics each year in 41 states, Puerto Rico and the District of Columbia. To achieve its mission, NCLR conducts applied research, policy analysis and advocacy, providing a Latino perspective in five key areas—assets/investments, civil rights/immigration, education, employment and economic status and health. In addition, it provides capacity-building assistance to its Affiliates who work at the state and local level to advance opportunities for individuals and families.

Founded in 1968, NCLR is a private, nonprofit, nonpartisan, tax-exempt organization headquartered in Washington, DC. NCLR serves all Hispanic subgroups in all regions of the

The NCLR is "key" to the Latino community.

country and has operations in Atlanta, Chicago, Los Angeles, New York, Phoenix, Sacramento, San Antonio and San Juan, Puerto Rico.

How will your organization impact the public debate in 2008?
In addition to our traditional work of providing policy expertise on the issues that most affect Latinos (education, health care, jobs and the economy, civil rights, housing, among others) NCLR is actively engaged in challenging the presence of hate groups and extremists in the immigration debate (see www.WeCanStoptheHate.org. This debate is having a major impact on mobilizing the Latino vote, another area in which NCLR is deeply engaged.

What is your 2008 operating budget?
$30 million

Looking out 2-3 years, how would you like to grow/change your organization?
NCLR is currently implementing a strategic plan that is focused on reframing and strengthening its relationships with its nearly 300 affiliates, community-based organizations around the country who provide services to and act as advocates for Latinos. Among our goals for the next several years is to strengthen this network of organizations and leaders with an eye toward building advocacy capacity within the community.

NCLR is also interested in strengthening the presence of Latino voices among the netroots,

and progressive blogosphere and encouraging constructive dialogue about the issues that matter to Latinos and the way this important community can better connect to others with complementary goals.

What do you need to do that?
NCLR is building resources and staff that are focused on our affiliates, and building new ways of working together, particularly on advocacy. In addition, we're working to build relationships with allies in the progressive movement and among new media to increase the presence and visibility of Latinos and our issues.

How will your organization change if progressives win in November? If they lose?
NCLR's broad goals are unlikely to change, regardless of the outcome of the elections. But our avenues for achieving them will be very much affected by the extent to which policy makers are sensitive to the issues that affect Latinos and willing to engage the community in moving forward. Regardless of who is elected, we will be looking for allies to advance the goals of opportunity and justice for all Americans.

If you had to offer some advice to fellow progressives what would it be?
Building a true partnership among Latinos and progressives will take investment where there are opportunities for moving an agenda forward, and where there is building to do before people can fully link

arms on an agenda. There are a range of issues that make Latinos natural partners in the progressive movement, and a range of issues where education and dialogue still need to take place. Some in the conservative movement have reached the same conclusion about Latinos, and are attempting to engage in a dialogue. Progressives and Latinos need to engage with each other with vigor and energy in order to move forward together as partners on a broader social justice agenda.

Please list your board of directors and their affiliations.

2007-2008 Executive Committee

Chair, Mónica Lozano
Publisher & CEO, *La Opinión*
Los Angeles, CA

**First Vice Chair,
Andrea Bazán-Manson**
President, Triangle Community
Foundation Research,
Triangle Park, NC

**Second Vice Chair/Secretary,
Daniel Ortega**
Partner, Roush, McCracken, Guerrero,
Miller & Ortega, Phoenix, AZ

Treasurer, Dorene Dominguez
Chairman, Vanir Construction
Management, Inc., Sacramento, CA

Janet Murguía
President and CEO, National Council of
La Raza, Washington, DC

Salvador Balcorta
Executive Director, Centro de Salud
Familiar La Fe, El Paso, TX

Elba Montalvo
Executive Director, Committee for
Hispanic Children and Families, Inc.
New York, NY

Herminio Martinez
Executive Director, Bronx Institute,
Lehman College, Bronx, NY

Maria Pesqueira
Executive Director, Mujeres Latinas en
Acción, Chicago, IL

Hon. Arturo Valenzuela
Director, Center for Latin American
Studies Georgetown University,
Washington, DC

General Membership

Tom Castro
President and CEO, Border Media
Partners, Houston, TX

Patricia Fennell
Executive Director, Latino
Community Development Agency,
Oklahoma City, OK

Maria S. Gomez
President/CEO, Mary's Center for
Maternal & Child Care, Washington, DC

Lupe Martinez
United Migrant Opportunity Services,
Milwaukee, WI

Maricela Monterrubio Gallegos
Galt, CA

Hon. Rafael Ortega
County Commissioner, Dist. 5
Ramsey County Board Office.
St. Paul, MN

Jorge Plasencia
Chairman and CEO, República
Miami, FL

Robin Read
President & CEO, National Foundation
for Women Legislators, Inc.
Washington, DC

Hon. Felipe Reinoso
State Representative, Bridgeport, CT

Arturo S. Rodriguez
President, United Farm Workers of
America, Keene, CA

Juan Romagoza, MD
Executive Director, La Clínica del
Pueblo, Washington, DC

Isabel Rubio
Executive Director, Hispanic Interest
Coalition of Alabama, Birmingham, AL

Angela Sanbrano
Executive Director, Central American
Resource Center, Los Angeles, CA

Dr. Juan Sanchez
Southwest Key Program, Inc.,
Austin, TX

Lionel Sosa
Sosa Consultation & Design,
Floresville, TX

Jim Padilla
Sarasota, FL

Isabel Valdés
President, Isabel Valdés Consulting,
Palo Alto, CA

Anselmo Villarreal
Executive Director, La Casa de
Esperanza, Waukesha, WI

National Security Network

1225 Eye St NW
Ste 307
Washington, DC 20005

 202-289-5999

202-682-6140

Moira Whelan, Director of
Strategy and Communications

@ mwhelan@nsnetwork.org

nsnetwork.org

June 2006

$1,400,000

501(c)(4) with an affiliated
501(c)(3), the National Security
Initiative

Rand Beers
Founder and President (above)

Heather Hurlburt
Executive Director (not shown)

Rand Beers
Rand Beers is the President and
Founder of the National Security
Network. Previously, he served as
the National Security adviser to the
Kerry-Edwards 2004 campaign. Mr.
Beers spent 35 years as a senior
civil servant. After serving as a
Marine officer and rifle company
commander in Vietnam, he entered
the Foreign Service in 1971 and the
Civil Service in 1983. From 1988-98,
Mr. Beers served on the National
Security Council Staff at the White
House as Director for Counter-
terrorism and Counter-narcotics,
Director for Peacekeeping and Senior
Director for Intelligence Programs.

From 1998-2003 he was Assistant
Secretary of State for International
Narcotics and Law Enforcement
Affairs. In 2002-03 he was Special
Assistant to the President and Senior
Director for Combating Terrorism at
the National Security Council. Beers
earned a BA from Dartmouth College
and an MA from the University of
Michigan.

**What does your organization do
and how does it do it?**
NSN provides progressive national
security infrastructure, connecting
decision-makers and opinion leaders
with the best foreign policy options.
We offer our partners–Congressional
and campaign leadership, advocacy
groups, the media–substantive policy
and messaging advice, build bridges

**"The who's who of
progressive foreign
policy." They work
"on a shoe-string" and
are a "critical piece of
infrastructure."**

and lead outreach to give progressives an effective voice on national security.

Policy development: we convene experts and advocates to develop innovative policy proposals and synthesize the best existing work, then provide it to candidates, elected officials and activists in forms that they can use.

"War Room:" we promote progressive messages and push back on right-wing distortion by booking speakers and surrogates, organizing media conference calls and doing press releases, fact-checks and rapid reaction in both old and new media.

Candidate 'Help Line:' we brief candidates, elected officials and advocates on national security issues, with basic foreign policy primers and a 24/7 response service, putting candidates in touch with top national security experts.

How will your organization impact the public debate in 2008?
NSN will ensure that the national security debate rises above lowest-common-denominator negative politics to encompass a positive progressive vision for the US role in the world. We will ensure that the debate has two sides, by pushing back on conservatives who try to prevent progressive views from being heard or taken seriously; critiquing the national security policies of the current administration; and using messengers

and messages that resonate with opinion leaders and the public.

What is your 2008 operating budget?
$1.4 million

Looking out 2-3 years, how would you like to grow/change your organization?
NSN's progressive national security infrastructure initiatives should become permanent. That should include:
• Elected officials turn to us to meet outside support and research needs for governing;
• The policy community is confident that we are a permanent progressive pipeline for getting the best new ideas to decision-makers;
• NSN grows into facilitating the bridge-building conversations that need to take place among progressives on the hardest questions of policy and strategy, so that we can govern effectively and grow as a movement.
• Candidates count on us every two years.

What do you need to do that?
NSN needs partners who are committed to building progressive policy infrastructure for governing; a steady progressive focus on foreign policy whether in or out of government, on or off the front page; and the resources to build a core organization that functions as strongly in off-years as in election years.

How will your organization change if progressives win in November? If they lose?
If progressives win in November,

we will have the opportunity and challenge of governing effectively–and if progressives break with the past and win on security, we will be positioned to change the debate for good. We will need to build bridges between experts and political leaders, policy wonks and grassroots advocates, Beltway insiders and local leaders to help show policy coherence, resolve the toughest dilemmas and demonstrate real change.

If progressives lose the security debate and the election, we will share the responsibility of understanding what failed and developing a national security narrative that better communicates with voters.

If you had to offer some advice to fellow progressives what would it be?
NSN wants every progressive to feel as comfortable talking about national security as about domestic politics, to see and to draw for others the connections between our choices at home and our policies overseas. Progressives should embrace debates on foreign policy rather than shying away from them–the public is looking for change in how the US relates to the world and is eager for a positive vision that better reflects core American (and progressive) values.

Please list your board of directors and their affiliations.

Rand Beers
President and Founder,
National Security Network

Michael Froman
Managing Director, Citigroup
Alternative Investments

Gordon Goldstein
Senior Vice President for Global
Affairs, D.B. Zwirn & Co

Gayle Smith
Senior Fellow, Center for American
Progress

Doug Wilson
co-founder and President, The
Leaders Project; Senior Consultant,
Penn Schoen and Berland

Lee Wolosky
Partner, Boies Schiller Flexner LLP

new ideas fund

1225 Eye St NW
Ste 307
Washington, DC 20005

📠 202-289-5999

📠 202-682-6140

✂ Patrick Barry,
   Program Manager

@ Pbarry@newideasfund.org

🖥 newideasfund.org

🔑 June 2006

📊 $400,000

🗄 501(c)(3) organization, with
   fiscal sponsorship from the
   National Security Initiative,
   also a 501 (c)(3)

**Patrick Barry
Program Manager**

Pat Barry is the Program Manager for the New Ideas Fund. Pat comes to the NIF from Haverford College, where he earned a BA in History, with a concentration in nationalism and political violence. In addition to his position with the New Ideas Fund, Pat also serves as a Research Associate for the National Security Network. A member of the Young Professionals in Foreign Policy, he is a native of Baltimore, MD.

What does your organization do and how does it do it?
Guy Saperstein, Daniel Berger and David DesJardins founded the New Ideas Fund to address a progressive thought deficit in national security and foreign policy. In this area, progressives suffer from a lack of a coherent world view within which to understand rapid global changes. We sorely need new ideas to rectify this problem.

To that end, the New Ideas Fund provides grants to promising scholars to establish a foundation for a progressive thought infrastructure in national security and foreign policy. We are one of the few organizations to directly fund the development of innovative, progressive ideas in this field.

Producing influential scholarship requires that we draw thinkers to the Fund from across the foreign policy community. To that end, we deploy both broad and targeted outreach strategies to get an array of proposals from established, but also

A "sharp" new group. An excellent "talent spotter."

non-traditional, sources of thought generation.

Once we have identified talented individuals with ideas that would not otherwise receive their due attention, we furnish those thinkers with small grants ranging from $5,000 to $25,000 to conduct writing and research, expanding on their thinking in a written product, similar to a white-paper style report. In exceptional cases, larger grants may be considered.

Finally, we will assist our authors as they promote their projects in a variety of mediums, both conventional and unconventional, ranging from periodical, compendiums and books to the blogsphere.

How will your organization impact the public debate in 2008?
2008 will be a critical year for progressives to create a space in which their ideas will flourish. While the Fund will not focus on the elections specifically, our financial support for scholarship that addresses future policy challenges to the United States will help to ensure that any gains made by progressives in 2008 will be durable. This is crucial in the area of national security and foreign policy. For success here to be anything but ephemeral, Americans will need to view progressives as the primary source for compelling visions for how the United States can relate to the world. If given the opportunity to lead the nation in 2008, progressives will need ideas that can reach beyond the myopic focus on Iraq to address, among other things, challenges like terrorism, poverty and environmental upheaval. We are helping to lead this effort.

What is your 2008 operating budget?
$400,000

Looking out 2-3 years, how would you like to grow/change your organization?
The New Ideas Fund is laying the foundation for the production and dissemination of progressive foreign policy and national security policies and providing citizens with the opportunity to learn from innovative, and sometimes unknown, thinkers. Over the next two years, the NIF will aggregate the published concepts and refine the means of dissemination, creating a virtual progressive "Brookings" without the brick infrastructure, becoming a nimble and effective platform attracting creative policy thinkers and an audience of receptive policy implementers.

What do you need to do that?
We can succeed with the help of benefactors who understand that for progressives to be ascendant, they need to present scholarship that clearly and forcefully articulates their vision for America's interaction with the world. Equally as crucial, will be advocates who can take these ideas once they have been put into written form, and disseminate them in a way that maximizes their impact.

How will your organization change if progressives win in November? If they lose?

Success in November, especially if there is a clear mandate for a progressive national security and foreign policy vision, will allow us the chance to bring our visions to Americans in a tangible way. But, the opportunity alone is not enough. For progressives to be influential in any meaningful sense, we will need to be ready to pluck the best ideas, provide support for their development, and present them in a way that people recognize. It is not enough to govern. We must govern well, and to do that we will need ideas that are not only bold, but developed and tested.

Failure in November will not change the imperative for new ideas. If a progressive message on security and foreign policy does not resonate in a way consistent with our values, then we, as progressives, must find and support approaches that do, so that when we next face an opportunity, we will be prepared to embrace it.

If you had to offer some advice to fellow progressives what would it be?

Years of political privation have sometimes caused progressives to be overly tactical, cautiously articulating their ideas whenever conservatives offer them an opening to do so. For Americans to turn to progressives for guidance on national security and foreign policy issues, they must offer alternative approaches that are sound in detail, but more importantly, ambitious in scope.

Please list your board of directors and their affiliations.

New Ideas Fund Founders

Guy Saperstein
Saperstein Family Foundation

David DesJardins
Private Philanthropist

Daniel Berger
Berger & Montague, P.C.

Planned Parenthood®
Federation of America, Inc.

434 West 33rd St
New York, NY 10001

☎ 212-541-7800
🖨 212-245-1845
✂ Rachel Goodman
@ rachel.goodman@ppfa.org

💻 plannedparenthood.org
plannedparenthoodvotes.org
🔑 October 16, 1916
⚏ 501(c)(3), 501(c)(4),
PAC, 527*

Cecile Richards
President

Cecile Richards is president of Planned Parenthood Federation of America (PPFA) and the Planned Parenthood Action Fund, the advocacy and political arm of PPFA. She is a nationally recognized progressive leader and fierce advocate for reproductive health and rights. Since coming to Planned Parenthood in February 2006, Ms. Richards has led the organizations to many significant achievements, including their success in ensuring FDA approval of over-the-counter status for emergency contraception, the launch of a nationwide campaign to provide

comprehensive, medically accurate sex education for all young people in America and the Action Fund's success in helping pick up 23 pro-choice seats in the U.S. Congress (four pro-choice senators and 19 pro-choice representatives) as well as elect four new pro-choice governors.

Before joining Planned Parenthood, Ms. Richards served as deputy chief of staff for Democratic Leader Nancy Pelosi and played a key role in her election as the Democratic leader of the House of Representatives.

Ms. Richards has a long history of organizing in support of reproductive freedom and social justice. In 2004, she founded and served as president of America Votes, a coalition of 42 national membership-based organizations, that works to maximize voter registration, education and mobilization efforts at the grassroots

*Planned Parenthood Federation of America: 501(c)(3); Planned Parenthood Action Fund (the advocacy and political arm of Planned Parenthood Federation of America): 501(c)(4); Planned Parenthood Federal PAC: separate segregated fund of Planned Parenthood Action Fund, 527

level. She also established the Texas Freedom Network, a grassroots organization that has grown to include more than 28,000 clergy and community leaders, to advance a mainstream agenda of religious freedom and individual liberties across the state.

The daughter of former Texas Governor Ann Richards, Ms. Richards was raised in a family committed to social justice and public service. She worked side by side with her mother on her very first campaign—the successful election to the state legislature of Sarah Weddington, the lawyer who successfully argued the landmark 1973 U.S. Supreme Court case *Roe v. Wade*, which legalized abortion nationwide.

What does your organization do and how does it do it?

PPFA is the nation's leading reproductive health and rights organization with an affiliate network that covers all 50 states, and operates 860 health centers that provide the highest quality reproductive health care and medically accurate, comprehensive sexuality education to women, men and young adults. One in four women will visit a Planned Parenthood health center in her lifetime, and we provide care and education to more than five million people worldwide. For more than 90 years, Planned Parenthood has done more than any other organization in the United States to improve women's health and safety, prevent unintended pregnancies and advance the right and ability of individuals and families to make responsible health care decisions.

The Planned Parenthood Action Fund, the advocacy and political arm of PPFA, works at the local, state and federal levels to advance and protect reproductive health and reproductive rights for all women and men. The Action Fund engages in educational and electoral activity, including legislative advocacy, voter education and grassroots organizing.

How will your organization impact the public debate in 2008?

Through its One Million Strong Campaign, the Planned Parenthood Action Fund will mobilize more than one million activists, supporters and donors with the goal of electing and supporting pro-choice, pro-family planning candidates at all levels of elected office. PPFA's 2008 goals include making affordable birth control available to all the women who need it, putting an end to failed abstinence-only programs in our schools and expanding publicly supported family planning.

Looking out 2-3 years, how would you like to grow/change your organization?

PPFA will leverage strength through our

Planned Parenthood is "central and crucial;" "a rock."

affiliated structure to expand Planned Parenthood health centers to reach all Americans, and to be an authoritative and passionate advocate for our clients and society, and at the forefront of developing the next generation of leaders of the sexual and reproductive health and social justice movement.

What do you need to do that?
We need to mobilize our more than four million supporters to fight for our goals of comprehensive health care reform, including access to sexual health care, and through our Planned Parenthood Action Fund, work for the election of progressive leadership on a statewide and federal level.

How will your organization change if progressives win in November? If they lose?
For the last eight years, PPFA has fought against ultraconservative initiatives to block access to basic health care, including many anti-choice ballot measures. With progressive government leadership, PPFA will work to refocus the public dialogue on positive preventive policies that address the real health priorities of individuals and families. We will continue to advocate for legislation that strengthens American's access to health care, working to pass laws and policies that support women's health. When family planning funding is secure, Planned Parenthood health centers will be better able to provide prevention services—medically accurate sex education and affordable, accessible health care—while, at the same time, working to ensure access to safe, legal abortion services.

If you had to offer some advice to fellow progressives what would it be?
Effective partnerships are critical. We must work to build effective collaborations across the progressive spectrum to accomplish our shared goals, and seek out the varied expertise of one another to achieve a better America for all.

Please list your board of directors and their affiliations.

Planned Parenthood Federation of America Board:

Kenetta Bailey

Harry Carter

Rev. Mark Bigelow

Ellen Chesler

Tracey L. Brown

Lida L. Coleman

Teree Caldwell-Johnson

Annette Cumming

Debra Carnahan

Amanda Dealey

Deborah De Witt

PROGRESSNOW

1536 Wynkoop St
Ste 4A
Denver, CO 80202

📞 303-991-1900
🖨 303-991-1902
Michael Huttner
@ Michael@progressnow.org
Bobby Clark
@ Bobby@progressnow.org

🖥 progressnow.org
🔑 progressnowaction.org
📊 $2,800,000
September, 2003
501(c)(3), 501(c)(4)

Bobby Clark
PEC Co-Director and ProgressNow
Executive Director (l)

Michael Huttner
PEC Co-Director and ProgressNow
Deputy Director (r)

Michael Huttner

As a private political consultant Mr. Huttner helped spearhead Colorado's legislative efforts in 2004. He is an adjunct professor at the University of Denver College of Law where he teaches Legislation and Lobbying. Mr. Huttner worked as Policy Advisor to Governor Roy Romer and before returning to Denver he clerked at the White House for the Office of the Counsel to the President. Mr. Huttner earned his law degree from the University of California, Hastings College of Law and his Bachelor of Arts from Brown University and studied civil rights at Howard University. He was chosen by *The Denver Business Journal* as one of the "Forty under 40" Leaders of Denver and by Denver's *5280* magazine as the "Top Up-and-Comer to Keep Your Eye On."

Bobby Clark

Bobby Clark led the development of ProgressNow's innovative and nationally-recognized Internet tools and strategies. Bobby manages all of ProgressNow's day-to-day operations. As one of the earliest members on Howard Dean's presidential campaign staff, he pioneered use of the Internet for online fundraising, outreach and grassroots engagement. He developed the campaign's first official website and put in place the system used to raise more than $25 million online and grow an email network of more than 750,000 people in just one year. Bobby received his J.D. from Vanderbilt Law School in 1991 and a B.A. from the University of Oklahoma in 1988, where he was honored as the Outstanding Senior Man.

What does your organization do and how does it do it?
ProgressNow is a recognized national leader in the use of new media and the internet to advance a progressive agenda at the state and local level. We do this by using cutting edge technology to educate the public and encourage civic participation about critical community issues. We have affiliate organizations in California, Colorado, Florida, Ohio, Michigan, Minnesota, New Mexico, Washington and Wisconsin.

We work through:
1. State and Local Online Civic Action Network: Nothing motivates citizens to action more than an issue with immediate local impact. By engaging people online around state and local issues year-round, ProgressNow is building a power base of networked citizens who are making change happen. By focusing on issues that cross party lines, we're reaching beyond "the choir" to engage new voters for progressive causes and candidates.
2. 24/7 Hard Hitting Press and New Media: When citizens take action, they make news. With the help of our active network members, we take action to generate press on

issues of importance at the state and local level. Combined with the creative use of new media, including YouTube, we change the public dialogue and promote progressive ideas.

3. Voter Outreach: We activate our network members in cutting-edge voter-to-voter outreach using the Internet to increase capacity for getting out the vote. The ProgressNow model earned The 2007 Golden Dot Award for the best online GOTV efforts by the Institute for Politics, Democracy and the Internet.

How will your organization impact the public debate in 2008?
As we lay the groundwork for the 2008 election cycle we hope to accomplish the following things:
• Outreach to underrepresented communities including Latinos, Youth, LGBT and single women: We want to engage these communities around local issues to lower the entry point into civic engagement. While registering these communities to vote is an important step in encouraging civic engagement, the most important first step is getting these people engaged around a local issue of

ProgressNow is "on the pulse" of communities across America. A "powerful model," we "need them in 50 states."

which they are passionate. This then leads them to an action and hopefully a changed outcome as a result of that action. Once this connection between action and outcome is established, individuals begin to connect the importance of their vote with a desired outcome. As a result, more unlikely voters who register to vote will turn out on Election Day.

- Localized Voter Registration and Early Voting: With communities mobilized around local issues, we will work with our partner organizations to coordinate voter registration drives and expand our absentee and early vote ballot chases.
- New Media Technologies: We will test text messaging technologies, expand our online video capabilities and use social networking sites to mobilize people around issues and create ongoing connections.
- YouTube as GOTV tool: We recently received a grant from the Arca Foundation to expand our multimedia and new media technologies. With these funds we will provide YouTube trainings for instate groups, individuals and our ProgressNow affiliates in other states. We hope to have dozens of people create content to capture the "macaca" moments of 2008.
- Bilingual Online Voter Guides: Create a widely distributed bilingual voter guide to help voters understand the issues on and make progressive choices when they vote.

What is your 2008 operating budget?
$2.8 million

Looking out 2-3 years, how would you like to grow/change your organization?

The long-term goal of ProgressNow is to find progressive solutions to critical community problems, challenge right-wing misinformation and hold our leaders accountable. As we look forward to the next three years, we hope to continue to play a critical role in driving public opinion and increasing civic engagement throughout each of our affiliate states. Increased civic participation and a greater awareness of the role ProgressNow plays in Colorado and the 8 other affiliate states will cultivate and push progressive issues and responses at the local level. The direction of our country is ultimately a choice of individuals and our job is to inform and engage people to choices that will continue to move our country forward.

What do you need to do that?

We will need continued financial resources to be a leader in new media technologies, to test new technologies and to expand into other states. Our goal is to be in 25 states by 2012. Ambitious yes, and we have a proven track record—we've already launched in 8 states, 9 including Colorado.

How will your organization change if progressives win in November? If they lose?

While progressive victories will impact each of our states positively, the need to create and maintain a strong progressive infrastructure will not change with victories in November. There is still a lot of work to be done—

from creating proactive progressive policies to holding conservative misinformation accountable to fighting for local initiatives and against bad public policies. Because ProgressNow works primarily at the state and local level, we will continue to work on community issues to move each of our affiliate states forward.

If you had to offer some advice to fellow progressives what would it be?

Tip O'Neil said it best: "All politics is local." People connect with the issues they care about in their communities. So remember, if you are advocating or fighting for an issue, make it relevant to people's lives, and when you want them to take action, keep it simple and make it easy.

Please list your board of directors and their affiliations.

Wes Boyd
Founder of MoveOn

Rob McKay
Chair of the Democracy Alliance

Doug Phelps
Founder and Chair of the PIRGs

Jared Polis
Progressive Philanthropist

Deborah Rappaport
President of the Rappaport Family Foundation

Bill Roberts
Executive Director of the Beldon Fund

Jeff Rusnak
Partner M&R Strategies, Advisor to Rachel Pritzker

Adam Solomon
DA Partner, Chair of the Progressive Book Club

Anne Summers
Executive Director of the Brico Fund

Ted Trimpa (Chair)
Partner Brownstein Hyatt & Farber & Advisor to Tim Gill

Joe Zimlich
Chief Executive Officer of Bohemian Companies

PROGRESSIVE
BOOK CLUB®

641 6th Ave
4th Floor
New York, NY 10011

212-871-8215
212-871-8103
Vivian Cacia
vcacia@
progressivebookclub.com

progressivebookclub.com
LLC

Elizabeth Wagley
President/Executive Director

Elizabeth Wagley brings more than a decade of experience in leadership, management and business development to the PBC. With a strong background in fundraising and communications, she has applied her entrepreneurial and creative skills to a broad variety of humanitarian, media and political organizations.

What does your organization do and how does it do it?
Progressive Book Club will find–and promote–the books that can change our nation by harnessing the power of the Internet to create an important new platform for progressive ideas. Part bookseller, part social networking website and part online magazine, Progressive Book Club is a vibrant forum that has transformed the traditional book club model. Today people's interests are as varied as they are vast–from the world environment, to global poverty, the economy, health care, religion and war–and amid the noise it is increasingly difficult to hear the ideas that will influence the nation's direction in the 21st Century. The prominent authors, journalists, activists and other opinion leaders on the book club's editorial board will enable our members to discover the stimulating, important and inspiring books that can shape our future for the better. Progressive Book Club is also committed to supporting the broader community, by creating a new income stream for progressive organizations and media through sales of our books.

How will your organization impact the public debate in 2008?
We will showcase key political and policy ideas and help voters dig deeper into the issues–from climate change to economic insecurity to the war on terror–that are shaping this election.

Looking out 2-3 years, how would you like to grow/change your organization?

We are seeking to achieve membership levels far higher than those ever reached by the Conservative Book Club during its 40 years of existence. We want to show that the center left can use the market to effectively showcase our ideas and expand our audience. Within three years, we would like to help restore balance to the national debate.

What do you need to do that?

We need strong partnerships with progressive organizations across the spectrum of issues and identities on the left that will build our membership while connecting and integrating our audience around important ideas. We also need to establish a strong presence in the mainstream and independent media and on the Internet.

How will your organization change if progressives win in November? If they lose?

Depending on who wins in November, we may emphasize different ideas and themes.

If you had to offer some advice to fellow progressives what would it be?

Be more open and willing to work together. Join in broad coalitions to promote and demand change, since even a Democratic administration will require a lot of pressure from below to achieve progressive goals. Spend your money in ways that promote the businesses and organizations that support the movement.

Please list your board of directors and their affiliations.

Deb Callahan
President, North Star Strategy

Roger Cooper
Publisher, Vanguard Press

Peter Joseph
Managing Director,
Palladium Equity Partners

Derek Kirkland
Managing Director, Morgan Stanley

Seth Radwell
President, E-Scholastic

Rob Stein, Founder
The Democracy Alliance

The PBC will soon be "Oprah's Book Club for progressives."

PROGRESSIVE MAJORITY

1825 K St NW
Ste 450
Washington, DC 20006

☏ 202-408-8603
🖨 202-429-0755
✳ Gloria A. Totten
@ gtotten@
progressivemajority.org

🖥 progressivemajority.org
📅 December 21, 1999
📊 $5,500,000
🔗 527

Gloria A. Totten
President

Gloria A. Totten is the President of Progressive Majority, a national multi-issue organization dedicated to recruiting and electing progressive champions at the state and local levels. Gloria was appointed to build Progressive Majority in 2001. There, she identified an urgent need for progressives to have their own "farm team" of progressive candidates and developed what is now the most comprehensive national progressive candidate recruitment program in the country. Under Gloria's leadership, Progressive Majority has established permanent state offices in Arizona, California, Colorado, Minnesota, Ohio, Pennsylvania and Washington. At Progressive Majority, Gloria also established the Racial Justice Campaign, a program to prioritize the recruitment and election of candidates of color as part of a plan to establish racial parity in government at all levels. Gloria served as Political Director for NARAL from 1996-2001, Executive Director for Maryland NARAL from 1993-1996 and, prior to that, worked as a political and community organizer for many campaigns and organizations in her home state of Minnesota. Gloria serves on the boards of directors for Advocates for Youth, Gadflyer.com and True Majority ACTION PAC. She is the President of the Ballot Initiative Strategy Center and an Advisory Committee Member for the Women's Information Network and the Drum Major Institute Scholars Program. Gloria was named a "Rising Star" in 2002 by *Campaigns & Elections* magazine and was awarded the "Progressive Champion Award" by Campaign for America's Future and the "Progressive Leadership Award" by Midwest Academy in 2006.

What does your organization do and how does it do it?
Progressive Majority recruits authentic progressives to run for state and local offices, shapes their campaigns, coaches them to be competitive candidates–and gets them elected.

Specifically, Progressive Majority is the candidate recruitment operation for the progressive movement and the only national organization dedicated to this work. The hallmark of our program is the extensive individual coaching we provide to the candidates we recruit, including:

- One-on-one political coaching and training;
- Preparation of campaign plans, budgets and fundraising plans;
- One-on-one message and communications training;
- Small group trainings;
- Training manuals;
- Direct contributions and fundraising;
- Assistance hiring staff and recruiting volunteers; and
- Help securing the endorsements of allied organizations.

Progressive Majority has demonstrated stunning success. As of January 2008, 55% of our candidates have won their elections and their victories have helped capture control of four state legislatures, 28 local governments and three statewide offices.

How will your organization impact the public debate in 2008?
Progressive Majority already has 205 candidates recruited and ready to run in 2008. These candidates will run on a strong progressive agenda focused on economic issues, including jobs and the economy, the need to do more for the middle class, health care and education–and they will articulate those issues with a competency and passion that will drive the debate for other candidates and campaign surrogates.

What is your 2008 operating budget?
$5.5 million

Looking out 2-3 years, how would you like to grow/change your organization?
Our goal is to continue to implement the Candidate Recruitment and Development Program in two to three new states every two years until it is part of the permanent political infrastructure in 23 states. As it grows, the program will not only expand across the nation but will also increase in depth within each state. Progressive Majority is also laying the groundwork now to build a Leadership Institute. This would provide comprehensive personal and political leadership development training to candidates, campaign workers and elected officials who come out of the recruitment program.

Progressive Majority's "great eye for talent" is "winning elections across the country." They are "the pipeline."

What do you need to do that?
By 2011, Progressive Majority needs to increase its annual budget from $5.5 million to approximately $7 million to facilitate programmatic growth. To build the Leadership Institute, Progressive Majority needs to establish the appropriate organizational legal structure, raise training money and hire top quality staff to conduct the leadership development work.

How will your organization change if progressives win in November? If they lose?
Our program is designed to withstand political trends. When Democrats were still losing at the federal level in 2004, Progressive Majority saw its candidates get elected and take majorities at the state level. In 2006, we capitalized on the Democratic trend by putting even more races in play. In 2008 and beyond, Progressive Majority will continue its work to build a large "farm team" of political leaders; those leaders will go on to win election and pass progressive legislation—no matter the outcome of any one election.

If you had to offer some advice to fellow progressives what would it be?
Run for office (well, not *everyone* should, so at least consider it)! Recruit someone else to run for office. Support progressive candidates by volunteering or donating money. Pay attention to the state and local races—they control more and more resources and pass many more laws that affect you—as closely as the presidential and federal campaigns. Never believe that a progressive agenda is not a winning agenda—we have hundreds of candidates proving every day that it works.

Please list your board of directors and their affiliations.

Karen Ackerman
Political Director, AFL-CIO

Robert Borosage
Co-Director, Campaign for America's Future

Beth Broderick-Paetty
Actress/Activist, Regardless Films

Dan Carol
President, The Cause Company

Edmund Cooke
Partner, Thelen Reid Brown Raysman & Steiner, LLP

Michael Lux
President, Progressive Strategies, L.L.C.

Tom Matzzie
Fund for America

Julie Martinez Ortega
Director of Research, American Rights at Work

Steve Phillips
President, PowerPAC.org

Jack Polidori
Director of Legislation and Political Organizing, Delaware State Education Association

Fran Rodgers
CEO, WFD, Inc. (formerly Work/Family Directions)

Jon Youngdahl
National Political Director, SEIU

PROGRESSIVE STATES Network

101 Avenue of the Americas
New York, NY 10013

☎ 212-680-3116
🖨 212-680-3117
✕ Georges Berges,
   Development Director
@ gberges@ progressivestates.org

🖥 progressivestates.org
🔑 2005
📊 $2,000,000
🔗 501 (c)(3)

Joel Barkin
Executive Director

As the Executive Director of the Progressive States Network, Joel Barkin works with state and national organizations on key progressive policy issues by providing guidance on strategy and message to key legislative campaigns. Under his leadership, the Progressive States Network has become one of the key meeting spaces for progressive legislators, activists and citizens interested in state policy. Barkin also served as Communications Director and Special Advisor to Senator Bernie Sanders (I-VT) and in the Communications Department for the American Israel Public Affairs Committee (AIPAC). He's worked on a number of campaigns and progressive initiatives at the state and national level.

What does your organization do and how does it do it?
Progressive States Network aims to transform the political landscape by supporting state legislators who can promote positive change, while providing strategic support in defeating rightwing movements operating at the state and local levels.

We do this by integrating multiple issues into a broad framework for promoting a government more accountable to its citizens. We help track the best legislation and practices around the country, promote them to state legislators and local advocates, build national legislative networks to support peer education among legislators and provide technical and strategic support for legislators both through our own work and the work of others. The key to our strategy is to get things started at the grassroots level, while facilitating a multi-state exchange of ideas that builds a groundswell of interest as ideas become reality.

How will your organization impact the public debate in 2008?

Given the fact that it's an election year and there is divided power in Washington, states are the hotbed for legislative action in 2008. Whether it is immigration, election reform, health care or the environment, states are setting the debate as we move towards the election. PSN is helping pass and promote a wide range of bills in state legislatures across that country that is creating the momentum for national reform.

What is your 2008 operating budget?

$2 million

Looking out 2-3 years, how would you like to grow/change your organization?

Progressive States Network is growing at an unprecedented pace, within the coming years we expect to increase staff and, more importantly, open regional offices. PSN's regional offices will enable us to provide direct day to day on the ground support that will be reinforced by our main office in New York. Through a combination of infrastructure, networks and access to New York staff, the regional offices will create the kind of on the ground momentum necessary to change state, regional and, ultimately, the national narrative of how and what issues are debated.

What do you need to do that?

Currently, PSN is working to secure, local, state and national support from likeminded individuals, organizations and foundations. In addition, we are creating the necessary local and state partnerships that will be the bedrock to establishing multiple regional offices.

How will your organization change if progressives win in November? If they lose?

If Progressives win back the White House and increase their majorities in the Congress, there will be an unprecedented opportunity for the states and the federal government to colloroabate on moving a national progressive agenda. The fight over SCHIP is a perfect example that, for progressives, federalism is not an either- or- question (federal OR state policy) but a question of finding the best model for effective collaboration. Should progressives win in November, PSN will continue to work with our national partners to address key issues of how to fund programs, build strong national standards on state success and limit federal preemption.

If you had to offer some advice to fellow progressives what would it be?

Progressives must cut through the media hype and glam politics, and try to figure out where real change is made and where it isn't, and then go there and work our butts off. Social change isn't about one election or one candidate, but rather a long

PSN "thinks big" but "starts local." Barkin's leadership is "a force to be reckoned with."

term vision that requires getting in the trenches, organizing people and articulating a message that connects with real people's lives.

Please list your board of directors and their affiliations:

Executive Director, Joel Barkin

Founding Co-Chair, Steve Doherty

Founding Co-Chair, David Sirota

Sen. Joe Bolkcom
Iowa State House

Wes Boyd
President, MoveOn.org

David Brock
President and CEO, Media Matters for America

Anna Burger
Secretary-Treasurer, SEIU

Rep. Morgan Carroll
Colorado State House

Rep. Garnet Coleman
Texas House of Representatives

Asm. Adriano Espaillat
New York Assembly

Leo Gerard
International President, United Steelworkers

Lisa Seitz Gruwell
Political Director, Skyline Public Works

Steve Kest
Executive Director, ACORN

George Lakoff
Senior Fellow, Rockbridge Institute

Ned Lamont
Founder, Lamont Digital Systems

Robert McChesney
Founder and President, Free Press

Rep. Hannah Pingree
Maine House of Representatives

John Podesta
President and CEO, Center for American Progress

Lee Saunders
Executive Assistant to the President, AFSCME

Naomi Walker
State Legislative Issues Coordinator, AFL-CIO

PROJECT VOTE

739 8th St SE
Washington, DC 20003

✆ 202-546-4173
🖨 202-546-2483
✂ Kevin Whelan, Director
   of Special Projects
@ voterengage@projectvote.org

🖳 projectvote.org
🔑 1982
📊 $17,057,677
🔲 501(c)(3)

Zach Polett
Executive Director

Zach Polett, Executive Director, has spent the past 28 years as a full-time community, labor and electoral organizer. In that time he has served as a community organizer, head organizer and regional director in several states and as ACORN's national director of political operations. In this capacity, he has coordinated voter registration drives and worked on a series of campaigns to eliminate obstacles to voter registration. Starting in 1985 he built a union of low-wage health care and service workers, Local 100A of the Service Employees International Union, AFL-CIO, that won the first homecare collective bargaining agreement in the South.

What does your organization do and how does it do it?
Project Vote's vision is full participation in the democratic process so that government is elected by and accountable to America's diverse population. We help Americans register to vote, connect voting with the everyday issues that affect their lives and dismantle barriers to political participation.

We develop customized Voter Registration programs, and Voter Education and Mobilization programs, providing management, tools and technical assistance to help local partners engage their communities. Through our Election Adminsitration program we work to make sure that election systems

Exceptional in it's GOTV effort. Their efforts are "unparalleled" with a staff that "reaches for the stars."

enable people to register, vote and have their votes counted.

How will your organization impact the public debate in 2008?

Project Vote's goal in 2008 is to help register, mobilize and protect the voting rights of millions of citizens who have historically been left out of the electorate—low income Americans, minorities, immigrants and youth. We will help shape the national debate around elections policy with research on issues like voter caging and voter suppression. We fight against unfair voter restrictions and we hold states accountable for failing to live up to their legal responsibilities to offer citizens the chance to register under the National Voter Registration Act.

What is your 2008 operating budget?

$17,057,677

Looking out 2-3 years, how would you like to grow/change your organization?

We will expand our Civic Engagement efforts, and deepen our strategic leadership in 27 or more states. We will also expand our Election Administration program to address systemic issues and improve election infrastructure. Even as we support community-based efforts to register disenfranchised voters, we will continue to push for the government to live up to its obligations to make voting convenient and accessible to all Americans.

What do you need to do that?

We will require new resources to help our community partners fully engage

their communities and constituencies, and we will need the attention of dedicated people who care about justice and understand the importance of voter participation and the need to protect voter rights.

How will your organization change if progressives win in November? If they lose?

Project vote is a non-partisan organization dedicated to full civic participation for all, and this mission will continue regardless of who holds office. We hope elected officials become educated about—and committed to—the impact of civic participation, and will work with us to remove barriers to this participation. Additionally, the next Justice Department—regardless of party—needs to do a better job of recognizing that politically motivated efforts to disenfranchise voters are civil rights violations and responding to them accordingly.

If you had to offer some advice to fellow progressives what would it be?

Take voter participation seriously. Real change will only happen when people demand it, and right now the people who need and want change the most—low-income Americans, minorities, immigrants and youth—are being left out of the discussion. The electorate going to the polls is disproportionately old, wealthy and white, and our national agenda public policy agenda is skewed accordingly.

Progressives should speak out clearly against efforts to maintain the status quo by excluding voters through illegal restrictions, intimidation, manipulation or misinformation. We have to take a stand for fair and accessible elections, and recognize that efforts to curb so-called "voter fraud" are in reality attempts to disenfranchise and silence our least powerful citizens.

Please list your board of directors and their affiliations.

The members of Project Vote's Board of Directors are not political professionals or philanthropists but leaders from the low-income communities and communities of color which the organization works to empower. They provide strategic direction and oversight for the organization.

President, Maxine Nelson

A registered nurse in Pine Bluff, Arkansas with over 35 years of experience as a leader for social justice and civil rights in Arkansas and the United States.

Vice-President, Donna Massey

A life-long resident of Arkansas. An employee at a FedEx shipping center, she is a member of the Pulaski County Quorum Court, Justice of the Peace for the 6th District.

Julie Smith

A former single mother, trained in 2006 as a Precinct Voter Action Network Leader and was a leader in efforts to increase Ohio's minimum wage. Now a nationally recognized leader on the minimum wage issue, she is also a member of Ohio ACORN's Board of Directors.

Cleo Mata

From Houston, TX, Cleo is a Latino woman in her late fifties. A former welfare recipient, currently chairperson of Pecan Park, she is very active in the community, volunteers as senior aide at the area Constable's office, volunteers as an income tax preparer with AARP and is a member of the fundraising committee at her church.

Mary Alvarez

From the Bronx, NY, Mary a Latina women in her early 60s. Ms. Alvarez has been a teacher in the New York City Schools for over 20 years, volunteers with her church and is well-known in her community for her activist work on affordable housing and investing in programs for youth.

CLEAN
MONEY
CLEAN
ELECTIONS

Public Campaign (c3), Public Campaign Action Fund (c4)
Campaign Money Watch (527)

320 19th St NW
Ste M-1
Washington, DC 20036

📞 202.293.0222
🖨 202.293.0202
✂ William Ewing
@ wewing@publicampaign.org

💻 publicampaign.org
🗓 January 1997
📊 $6,013,035*
🗂 501(c)(4), 527

Nick Nyhart

President and CEO,
Public Campaign
Executive Director,
Public Campaign Action Fund
(above)

David Donnelly
Director, Campaign Money Watch
(not shown)

A three decade veteran of social change politics, issue advocacy, grassroots organizing and non-profit management, Nyhart brings a wealth of experience to the national reform movement. Following the 1992 elections, Nyhart became Director of the Northeast Action Money and Politics Project, a six-state venture that laid the groundwork for Maine's 1996 breakthrough full public financing victory. In January 1997, Nyhart joined scores of state and national money and politics activists to found Public Campaign, where he served as National Field Director and Deputy Director before assuming the group's helm in 2000.

At Public Campaign, Nyhart has worked to win cutting edge state reform efforts across the country and has organized a number of innovative national collaborations to promote publicly financed elections at the federal level.

What does your organization do and how does it do it?
Public Campaign's organizations advocate and organize to transform, through publicly financed elections, the nation's privately funded campaign system into one that levels the political playing field, gives voters more choices and leaves elected officials accountable to their constituents. We believe this is not simply a "process"

---

* Public Campaign (c3): $1,635,800; Public Campaign Action Fund (c4): $377,235;
Campaign Money Watch (527): $4,000,000+

THE PRACTICAL PROGRESSIVE

issue but one of power, policy and inequality. Public Campaign's soul is in community organizing, popular democracy, issue advocacy and electoral politics revolving around social and economic justice. We successfully work with lawmakers, opinion leaders, grassroots activists, local, state and national constituency organizations and influential civic leaders across the country, supporting cutting-edge state and local campaigns to win full reform either by ballot initiative or legislative action while pressing for sweeping change at the federal level. The PC Action Fund's Campaign Money Watch project raises the issue of undue influence of wealthy interests with voters during the election cycle.

How will your organization impact the public debate in 2008?
Campaign Money Watch will take politicians to task for connections between campaign cash and their policy decisions. Exposing the excesses and abuses of a privately funded campaign system, while pointing the way to the publicly-financed alternative will help energize grassroots activists and organizations and empower a base for change. Public Campaign will seek new supporters from economically disadvantaged, racial and ethnic minority communities by demonstrating the political, social and economic justice benefits of publicly financed elections.

What is your 2008 operating budget?
Public Campaign (c3): $1,635,800;

Public Campaign Action Fund (c4): $377,235; Campaign Money Watch (527): $4,000,000+

Looking out 2-3 years, how would you like to grow/change your organization?
We would like to secure sufficient staff and financial resources to aid additional local and state efforts to pass, implement and defend Clean Elections reform while at the same time playing a lead role in organizing the winning campaign for public financing of federal elections. We will need to expand the Clean Elections movement by integrating publicly financed elections reform into the priority list for national and local grassroots issue advocacy organizations. We also need to better analyze and then publicize the impact of Clean Elections where it now exists.

What do you need to do that?
Increased capacity to reach out to new allies and supporters and better vehicles for telling our story. More than 70 percent of Americans favor enactment of publicly financed elections, including nearly every demographic imaginable. Increased financial support from individual and institutional donors will enable us to reach out to key constituencies.

This "brave" organization "will not give up." Nick Nyhart "keeps 'em honest."

How will your organization change if progressives win in November? If they lose?

The nation will elect a president in 2008 with a track record of support for public financing. Given numerous conservative incumbent retirements and continuing scandals, the new Congress will have 35 to 60 new members, which will increase the power of public financing's lead sponsors, Asst. Senate Majority Leader Dick Durbin (D-IL), and House Democratic Caucus Vice Chair John Larson (D-CT). For the first time since Watergate, public financing will be on the table in Congress and a federal victory will be within reach. If progressives lose, the fight for federal public financing will be waged on far more difficult terrain.

If you had to offer some advice to fellow progressives what would it be?

Movements for change require an inclusive and diverse community of activists and an environment where the open exchange of ideas from a variety of voices and perspectives is encouraged. A willingness to adapt strategic approaches without sacrificing core beliefs, persistence in fighting for the best solution consistent with values without rigid adherence to unattainable goals, and an honest recognition of the fundamental worth of all citizens regardless of ideology, creed or partisan alignment.

Please list your board of directors and their affiliations.

George Christie
Director of Programs & Outreach, Engage Maine

Zack Exley
Political and technology consultant

Becky Glass
Executive Director, Midwest States Center

Chair, Joan Mandle,
Executive Director, Democracy Matters; Associate Professor of Sociology, Colgate University

William McNary
President, U.S. Action

Dan Petegorsky
Executive Director, Western States Center

Richard Romero
Retired, Assistant Superintendent of Schools, Albuquerque, New Mexico; Former President Pro Tem, New Mexico State Senate

Whitney North Seymour, Jr.
Attorney at law; Former U.S. Attorney, Southern District of New York

Tracy Sturdivant
Michigan Programs Director

Jon Stryker

Pushback
NETWORK
All. Together. Now.

	✆ 323-737-7884	🖥 pushbacknetwork.org
	📠 323-735-3286	2005
4801 Exposition Blvd	✂ Rodney McKenzie, Jr.	📊 $2,500,000
Los Angeles, CA 90016	@ Rodney@pushbacknetwork.org	501(c)(3)

Rodney McKenzie, Jr.
Coordinating Director

Rodney McKenzie, Jr. is the Coordinating Director for The Pushback Network. The Pushback Network is a collaborative of independent, grassroots organizations committed to building and increasing electoral power for communities of color, low-income, young people and working communities.

For a total of four years, Rodney was a Project Director in the Organizing & Training Department at the National Gay and Lesbian Task Force. McKenzie's work focused on building grassroots political power in gay, lesbian, bisexual and transgender communities across the country. During his tenure at the Task Force, he played a key role in defeating historic anti-gay

ballot measures in Miami, Florida, Tacoma, Washington and Ypsilanti, Michigan. In 2004, McKenzie was the deputy field director of the No on 36 Campaign in Portland, Oregon.

From 2005-2006, he served as Program Director at Freedom to Marry, the gay and non-gay coalition to win the right to marry for all people. He was charged with the overall programmatic direction of the organization and was responsible for a $300,000 regranting program, providing grassroots organizing technical assistance to key state and national partners.

Rodney has taught hundreds of people the skills needed to build grassroots LGBT political power. His trainings have focused on building a multi-

This group is "an engine of ground up government." They are "building a real representative democracy."

racial organization, recruiting and motivating a large volunteer base, creating a clear and honest message and using a variety of organizing tools to ensure a win.

What does your organization do and how does it do it?

The Pushback Network (PBN) is a national collaboration of indigenous, grassroots organizations and networks committed to building bottom-up, state-based alliances that change both the composition and levels of participation of the electorate. We emphasize strategies to empower underrepresented constituencies: people of color, poor and working class communities and young people.

How will your organization impact the public debate in 2008?

In 2008, Pushback is seeking to enhance and strengthen its state-alliance work in order to achieve new levels of scale and strategic coherency in local, state and national arenas. Currently operating in 6 states, and expanding to 10 in 2008, Pushback is putting forth a series of actions and efforts that will not only strengthen state-wide infrastructures, but will ultimately identify and address issues of public concern, remove barriers that prevent marginalized people from participating in issues that affect their lives and facilitate the overall participation of people of color, low income and working-class people and young people in civic and voter-engagement processes.

What is your 2008 operating budget?

$2.5 million.

Looking out 2-3 years, how would you like to grow/change your organization?

PBN has developed measurable goals designed to have lasting impact on bringing to realization our vision for an authentic, participatory democracy. Our goals for the next few years include:

Goal #1: Demonstrate a meaningful and substantially increased level of voter participation in 10 targeted states; Goal #2: An established national infrastructure that increases the capacity for training and leadership development at the grassroots, and for mobilizing thousands of indigenous grassroots precinct (and other area) leaders; Goal #3: Increased Capacity for Strategic Communications; Goal #4: Increased Capacity for State-Based, Peer-to-Peer Learning and Evaluation.

What do you need to do that?

Pushback is seeking additional resources to fund and provide direct assistance to the important local and statewide work that is happening on the ground. Over the next year, PBN will be diversifying its donor base by targeting individual and corporate donors with a clear message of the importance of civic participation work on election day and beyond.

How will your organization change if progressives win in November? If they lose?

PBN believes that whatever victories are secured on a national level–they must be protected on the local level. Our work is about building power from the ground up to ensure that everyday people, from Eastern Kentucky to Harlem, are protected by a government that is in theory for all people. Regardless if a progressive wins or loses in November, Pushback will continue its commitment to building the leadership capacities of people who've been historically pushed to the margins. It's this commitment to on-going politically conscious base building among people of color, young people and poor and working class people that will ensure that who ever is elected to office is held accountable to its constituencies.

If you had to offer some advice to fellow progressives what would it be?

In the words of Robby Rodriguez, Pushback Network's Chair and Executive Director of Southwest Organizing Project (SWOP), "Democracy doesn't end on Election Day."

Please list your board of directors and their affiliations.

PBN Steering Committee Members:

Hill Carmichael
Campaign Coordinator, Constitutional Reform Education Campaign, Greater Birmingham Ministries, AL

Scott Douglas
Director, Greater Birmingham Ministries, AL

Kimble Forrister
Executive Director, Arise Citizens' Policy Project, AL

PBN Secretary
Rudy Gonzalves
Coordinator, California Alliance, CA

Darnell Johnson
Kentucky Jobs with Justice, KY

PBN Treasurer
Leroy Johnson
Director, Southern Echo, MS

Keegan King
Co-Director, New Mexico Youth Organized, NM

Burt Lauderdale
Executive Director, Kentuckians for the Commonwealth, KY

Carl Lipscombe
Organizer, New York Jobs with Justice, NY

Robby Rodriguez
PBN Co-Chair, Director, Southwest Organizing Project, NM

Mike Sayer
Senior Organizer and Training Coordinator, Southern Echo, MS

Micaela Shapiro-Shellaby
Organizer, New York Jobs with Justice, NY

ROCK THE VOTE

1505 22nd St NW
Washington, DC, 20037

☎ 202- 719-9910
🖷 202-719-9952
✂ Chrissy Faessen
@ Chrissy@rockthevote.com

🖥 rockthevote.com
⚷ 1980
📊 more than $5,000,000
🖧 501(c)(3)

Heather Smith
Executive Director

Heather Smith is the Executive Director of Rock the Vote. In this capacity, she has been profiled by *The Washington Post,* and was named by *Esquire* magazine as one of the "Best and Brightest" of her generation. Smith comes to Rock the Vote from Young Voter Strategies (YVS), where Smith served as Executive Director and lead a nonpartisan effort to re-energize our democracy through engaging young voters. In 2006, Smith, together with the Young Voter Strategies team, coordinated a national non partisan project to register 350,000 young voters using innovative and replicable methods of voter outreach. The project registered 500,000 young voters ages 18-30 and played a large role in young voter increase in 2006. Prior to launching Young Voter Strategies, Smith served as the national field director for the PIRGs New Voters Project, the largest nonpartisan grassroots effort ever undertaken to register and mobilize young voters. Across the country, the New Voters Project, under Smith's direction, registered nearly 600,000 voters and conducted an intensive, multi-faceted get-out-the-vote effort to bring these newly registered voters to the polls on Election Day. Youth turnout was 11 percentage points higher than in 2000. Prior to her work at the New Voters Project, Smith was an organizing director for Green Corps' Field School for Environmental Organizing in Boston. Smith received a B.A. with honors in economics and public policy from Duke University. In 2006, Smith was named one of *Campaign & Elections* magazine's Rising Stars for her work with young voters.

Rock the Vote makes "voting cool" and "moblizes the masses."

What does your organization do and how does it do it?

This year, Rock the Vote will register two million young Americans, between the ages of 18 and 29 to vote, and mobilize many more to the polls.

Our hybrid use of an online voter registration tool, online social networks, print, radio and television PSAs, mobile technology and peer-to-peer contact, is redefining the way we reach young voters.

Rock the Vote also commissions polls that examine young people's political attitudes, and civic engagement, and highlights the best practices for campaigns looking to mobilize young voters. We then use our findings to educate campaigns on these best practices, and to persuade those in power to focus on the needs and priorities of the Millennial Generation.

Hand-in-hand with our online, on-the-ground and political outreach methods, RTV utilizes the power of music and musicians to engage, motivate and inspire action among young people.

How will your organization impact the public debate in 2008?

Our registration and mobilization efforts will continue the push away from the conventional wisdom that young people "don't care" and "don't vote" to the reality and promise of young people's civic engagement and electoral participation. Once the electoral power of this generation is fully realized, Millennials' priorities–progressive priorities–will begin to take center stage in our national debate.

What is your 2008 operating budget?

More than $5 million

Looking out 2-3 years, how would you like to grow/change your organization?

Rock the Vote is currently developing a progressive platform that reflects the values and priorities of young people. During non-election years, Rock the Vote will use new technologies, social networking and culture to engage our online network in advocacy for change on issues of greatest importance to them. We will support our network of young people and our trusted political advisors to voice the needs, concerns and priorities of young people across America. It is our hope that in the next few years, Rock the Vote will represent a defacto "AARP" for the Millennial Generation.

What do you need to do that?

Rock the Vote will only be fully effective in promoting a progressive agenda once elected officials in Washington and party leaders recognize the power of the youth vote. We need elected officials to join with us in engaging young people in the political process during on and off cycles.

How will your organization change if progressives win in November? If they lose?

When progressives win in November it will be young people who have put them in power; and it will become our organization's job to hold those leaders accountable on behalf of young America. Should progressive not win, we will continue to push our agenda, and refocus on 2010.

If you had to offer some advice to fellow progressives what would it be?

Go after young voters! We're hungry for change. Join us in registering two million young people to vote by utilizing our online voter registration tool on your webpage. It makes voting easy. Check it out at www.rockthevote.com/partners.

Please list your board of directors and their affiliations.

Jeff Ayeroff
Co-President, Shangri-La Music

Treasurer, Kevin Murray
Senior Vice President,
William Morris Agency

Deborah Rappaport
President/CEO, Skyline Public Works

Secretary, Jon Rubin
Co-President, Shangri-La Music

Ex-Officio member, Heather Smith
Executive Director, Rock the Vote

THE ROOSEVELT INSTITUTION

1527 New Hampshire Ave NW
4th Flr
Washington, DC 20036

☏ 202-483-2512, ext. 124
🖷 202-483-2657
✂ Sarah Suniti Bal,
Communication Director
202-483-2512, ext. 124
@ sarah.bal
@rooseveltinstitution.org

🖳 rooseveltinstitution.org
🗝 November, 3 2004
📊 $580,000
🖧 501(c)(3)

Nate Loewentheil
Executive Director

Nate Loewentheil is a proud son of Baltimore, Maryland. He graduated cum laude from Yale University in 2007, majoring in the Program in Ethics, Politics and Economics with distinction. He has previously worked for a number of nonprofits in economic and community development and currently serves as the executive director of the Roosevelt Institution, which he helped found in his sophomore year of college. Since taking over as Executive Director in August, Nate has doubled the national staff, tripled the annual budget and more broadly helped link the progressive youth organizations with the flourishing 'ideas sector.' Nate has published on housing policy and urban planning in the *Review of Policy Research* as well as with the Center for American Progress, and wrote his thesis on public transportation in his hometown.

What does your organization do and how does it do it?
The Roosevelt Institution is the nation's first student think tank. Our organization comprises more than 8,000 students, professors and policymakers at more than 70 campus-based chapters across the country. We educate students about progressive politics, encouraging them to research and write on important policy issues, leveraging the academic resources of our colleges and universities. We then disseminate the products of that work to policymakers and media outlets on the local, state and national level. At the same time we connect our students to progressive organizations, helping to

develop the next generation of active citizens and leaders. As part of our work we offer internship programs, conferences and training workshops throughout the year, publishing a series of journals and white papers in print and through our website.

How will your organization impact the public debate in 2008?
Through our alumni network, student members, policy journals, website and media partnerships we reach a broad audience. Each year we focus on three challenges selected by our members. This year we decided to address: community development, democracy and criminal justice. These challenges address policy areas our members felt were especially significant this election year. Through our work on each challenge we educate students about important issues, spur social innovation and influence policy makers and the media. As this year marks the 75th anniversary of FDR's New Deal we are particularly conscious of preserving and promoting his legacy: an affective government providing security and opportunity for all citizens.

What is your 2008 operating budget?
$580,000

Looking out 2-3 years, how would you like to grow/change your organization?
Over the next three years, we will build on the resources we've already developed: a strong chapter network, capacity for policy dissemination, student interest in commentary, a terrific talent pool and relationships with other progressive organizations. We will expand our chapter network and provide more resources; not only money and staff time, but stronger training programs for our students. We believe that to have the best ideas we must have a broad range of voices and so we are committed to expanding the diversity of our network. In the years to come we hope to venture into international affairs and possibly start chapters abroad. We also hope to expand our presence in the media and bring fresh student voices into the mainstream.

What do you need to do that?
In order to achieve our goals we need to build and leverage partnerships with other progressive organizations, strengthen our media influence and continue to expand our fundraising capacity. We also need the active help of the media and other progressive organizations to help better train our students and circulate our policy.

How will your organization change if progressives win in November? If they lose?

If progressives were to win, our students would have renewed enthusiasm because our policies would reach a more receptive legislative audience. However, regardless of the

We should "keep an eye out" for the new progressive intellectuals that will emerge from this group.

outcome of this year's elections our long-term goal of fostering the future leaders of the progressive movement remains vital.

If you had to offer some advice to fellow progressives what would it be?
Take the voices of young people seriously. The Millennial generation is on the rise; we have come out in record numbers during this primary season and continue to play an active role in this election. We encourage progressive organizations to create opportunities to incorporate our generation's ideas and energy. Connecting now to the next generation of citizens ensures the future of the progressive movement.

Please list your board of directors and their affiliations.

The Roosevelt Institution merged with the Franklin and Eleanor Roosevelt Institute in July 2007. A committee of the FERI board governs the Roosevelt Institution.

Anne Roosevelt
Director of Community and Education Relations, Boeing

Alison Overseth
President, Board of Directors, Partnership for After-School Education; Vice-Chair, FERI Board of Directors

Dr. Robert Curvin
Former Vice-President, Ford Foundation; Member, *The New York Times* Editorial Board

Joe Barrow
Executive Director, The First Tee; Senior Vice-President, World Golf Foundation

Dan Appelman JD, PhD
Partner, Heller, Ehrman, White, & McAuliffe, Berkeley, CA

Neil Proto
Partner, Schnader Harrison Segal & Lewis

Elizabeth Coleman
President, Bennington College; Chair Vermont Rhodes Scholarship Trust

Sarah Brown
NYU Grad Political Director for DNC's Chief Counsel

David Merchant
Executive Director, Policy Studies Organization

Mattie Hutton
Policy Analyst, Governor O'Malley; B.A. & M.A. from Stanford

Mark Newberg
Director Special Projects, RNN Television

Marian Breeze
Communications & Development consultant

SEIU
SERVICE EMPLOYEES INTERNATIONAL UNION

1800 Massachusetts Ave, NW
Washington, DC 20036

📞 202-730-7000 (general)
   202-730-7234 (M. Ringuette)

🖨 202-429-5563

✂ Michelle Ringuette, Assistant
   Director of Communications

@ michelle.ringuette@seiu.org

🖥 seiu.org

🔑 1921

🗂 501(c)(5)

Andy Stern
President

Andy Stern is the president of the 1.9 million member Service Employees International Union (SEIU), the fastest-growing union in North America.

As both a labor leader and an activist, Stern is a leading voice and aggressive advocate for practical solutions to achieve economic opportunity and justice for workers; to ensure affordable, quality health care for all; to promote quality public services; and to guarantee that globalization benefits not just big corporations but also working people. To that end, Stern has spearheaded bold new partnerships with community allies, employers and other worker organizations, and he has helped elect officials of both major parties.

Called "a different kind of labor chief" and a "courageous, visionary leader who charted a bold new course for American unionism," Stern began working as a social service worker and member of SEIU Local 668 in 1973 and rose through the ranks before his election as SEIU president in 1996. After launching a national debate about the fundamental change needed to unite the 9 out of 10 American workers who have no organization at work, Stern led SEIU out of the AFL-CIO and founded Change to Win, a new six-million member federation of seven major unions dedicated to giving workers a voice at their jobs.

This strong union is of "tantamount importance" to the progressive infrastructure.

Stern is the author of the book, *A Country That Works* (Free Press), which offers a fresh prescription for the vital political and economic reforms America needs to get back on track.

What does your organization do and how does it do it?
SEIU takes a broad view of what it means to improve the lives of workers and the services they provide.

Healthcare, public sector and building service workers come together in SEIU to win industry-leading pay and benefits; quality, affordable healthcare; a secure retirement; and health and safety in the workplace.
- SEIU members team up with workers in other countries that share common employers;
- In our communities, we build long-term, mutually beneficial relationships with allies;
- We find common issues with partners to build greater political strength;
- We articulate our vision, plan and strategy with a 21st Century, multi-channel communications system that reaches audiences in multiple ways, including web sites, e-mail, text messaging, video, mainstream and progressive media and direct marketing.

In giving workers a stronger voice in our communities, the workplace and the political arena, SEIU ensures that working families–not just CEOs–benefit from today's global economy.

How will your organization impact the public debate in 2008?

SEIU members have made workers' issues the issues of this presidential election–from access to health care for everyone to economic solutions that benefit all working people.

We began influencing the 2008 public debate long before this year, and we haven't stopped. In March 2007, SEIU hosted the first presidential candidates' forum on healthcare; in the months following, every major Democratic candidate spent a day on the job and at home with an SEIU member.

Looking out 2-3 years, how would you like to grow/change your organization?
In the months ahead, we seek to increase SEIU member participation, streamline and modernize our member resource services and help make sure that everyone who wants to join a union has the freedom to do so.

What do you need to do that?
Unions are the best anti-poverty, equal opportunity, family security and middle class-building programs for working people in America today. As a leading voice for working people, SEIU is committed to seeing that all working people who want to join a union have the freedom to do so and that all working families have the chance to achieve the American Dream.

To help make this a reality, we need to pass the Employee Free Choice Act, a law that will restore democracy in the workplace. With passage of this important law, workers will be able to exercise their freedom to choose to join together and share in the prosperity they have done so much to create.

How will your organization change if progressives win in November? If they lose?

Regardless of who wins in November, we will launch an extensive effort to ensure that those in Washington work with us to bring about the change workers need. We will continue to fight in the public and private sectors, and at the global, federal, state and local levels for:

- Quality, affordable heath care for all;
- Workers' freedom to form a union;
- Income equality and a fairer tax system;
- Comprehensive immigration reform; and
- Retirement security.

If you had to offer some advice to fellow progressives what would it be?

We're all stronger when we work together to achieve the change our country needs. We can't let our differences detract from our shared goal of creating a new American Dream for all working people in this country. We're also stronger when we hold our elected officials accountable to the promises they make before they're elected. They have to know that the only way to earn our support is to take action on our issues.

Please list your board of directors and their affiliations.

Tom Balanoff
SEIU Local 1

Alice Dale
SEIU Local 49

Tom DeBruin
SEIU Local 1199P

Mike Fishman
SEIU Local 32BJ

Leslie Frane
SEIU Local 503

Tyrone Freeman
SEIU Local 6434

Mike Garcia
SEIU Local 1877

Annelle Grajeda
SEIU Local 721

George Gresham
Local 1199
SEIU Healthcare Workers East

Jim Hard
SEIU Local 1000

David Holway
SEIU Local 5000

Danielle Legault
SEIU Local 298

Valarie Long
SEIU/SEIU Local 32BJ

Bob Moore
Local 1199
SEIU Healthcare Workers East

Roberto Pagan Rodríguez
SEIU Local 1996

Dave Regan
SEIU Local 1199WVKYOH

Dennis Rivera
SEIU Healthcare Chair

Sal Rosselli
SEIU Local 2005UHW

Monica Russo
SEIU Florida Healthcare Union

Kristy Sermersheim
SEIU Local 521

Sharleen Stewart
SEIU Local 1.on (Ontario)

Mitch Ackerman
SEIU Local 105

Marshall Blake
Local 1199SEIU Healthcare
Workers East

Christine Boardman
SEIU Local 73

Carmen Boudier
SEIU Local 1199NE

Kenneth Brynien
SEIU Local 4053

Maria Castaneda
Local 1199SEIU Healthcare
Workers East

Kim Cook
SEIU Local 925

Merle Cuttitta
SEIU Local 500

Damita Davis-Howard
SEIU Local 1021

Randy Dorn
SEIU PSE of WA

Don Driscoll
NAGE

Marc Earls
Retired, from SEIU Local 6

Juan G. Eliza Colon
SEIU Local 1199UGT

George Francisco
SEIU NCFO

Cathy Hackett
SEIU Local 1000

Byron Hobbs
SEIU Local 20

Bruce Hodsdon
SEIU/MSEA Local 1989

Rickman Jackson
SEIU Local MIHU

Kathy Jellison
SEIU Local 668

Keith Kelleher
SEIU Local 880

Eileen Kirlin
SEIU International Headquarters

Raymond Larcher
SEIU Local 800

Stephen Lerner
SEIU International Headquarters

Jane McAlevey
SEIU Local 1107

Josie Mooney
SEIU Local 1021

Javier Morillo-Alicea
SEIU Local 26

Rahaman Muhammad
SEIU Local 617

Mike O'Brien
SEIU Local 2001

Dian Palmer
SEIU Local 1199WI

Janice Platzke
SEIU Local 336

John Reid
SEIU 1199UHE

David Rolf
SEIU Healthcare 775NW

Rocio Saenz
SEIU Local 615

Julie Schnell
SEIU Local 113

Susana Segat
SEIU Local 888

Cathy Singer Glasson
SEIU Local 199

Gary Smith
SEIU Local 1984

Diane Sosne
SEIU Local 1199NW

Phil Thompson
SEIU Local 517M

Celia Wcislo
Local 1199 SEIU Healthcare
Workers East

Norman Yen
SEIU Houston Office

Andy Stern
SEIU International, President

Anna Burger
SEIU International, Secretary-Treasurer

Eliseo Medina
SEIU International,
Executive Vice President

Mary Kay Henry
SEIU International,
Executive Vice President

Gerry Hudson
SEIU International,
Executive Vice President

Tom Woodruff
SEIU International,
Executive Vice President

SIERRA CLUB
FOUNDED 1892

	✆ 415-977-5729	🖳 sierraclub.org
	🖨 415-977-5788	⚷ 1892
85 Second St·	✄ Jacquelyn Brown	📊 $81,217,000
2nd Flr	@ Jacquelyn.brown@	🖧 501 (c)(4)*
San Francisco, CA 94105	sierraclub.org	

Carl Pope
Executive Director

Carl Pope was appointed Executive Director of the Sierra Club in 1992 and over a 30+ year tenure has served as Associate Conservation Director, Political Director and Conservation Director. He has served on the boards of the California League of Conservation Voters, Public Voice, National Clean Air Coalition, California Common Cause, Public Interest Economics, Inc. and Zero Population Growth, and was also Executive Director of the California League of Conservation Voters and the Political Director of Zero Population Growth. Pope is the author of three books: *Sahib, an American Misadventure in India* (1971);

Hazardous Waste in America (1981); and *Strategic Ignorance: Why the Bush Administration Is Recklessly Destroying a Century of Environmental Progress*. He graduated summa cum laude from Harvard College in 1967.

What does your organization do and how does it do it?

• The Sierra Club's 1.3m members and supporters lobby representatives, write letters, sign on-line petitions, testify at hearings, educate the media and help create policy.

• Our network of 32,000 activist leaders fight polluting industry, educate communities about clean energy, attend local and state hearings, hold rallies, lead outings to threatened places and hold leaders accountable for decisions on the environment.

• Our legislative staff and volunteers in every state legislative and congressional district help pass pro-environment bills, like the recent federal increase in fuel economy standards, and block bad ones.

• Our Legal Program is a national

THE PRACTICAL PROGRESSIVE

leader in litigating environmental cases from county courthouses to the Supreme Court, where our recent victory required the EPA to regulate greenhouse gas emissions.

- Our political program boasts "the biggest return on its investment" (*The Economist*) in electing pro-environment candidates. We turn out voters, give money and staff to campaigns and endorse bipartisan environmental champions.

How will your organization impact the public debate in 2008?

The Sierra Club will focus non-partisan grassroots political action in 10 key states during the 2008 election cycle. Our experienced DC staff and volunteers will lobby Congress to pass important global warming and energy-related bills. And our primary charitable campaigns will litigate to stop the new coal rush, increase the use of clean renewable energy and preserve America's wild legacy–all within the scope of addressing climate change.

What is your 2008 operating budget?

$81,217,000

Looking out 2-3 years, how would you like to grow/change your organization?

Under our new priority Climate Change Initiative, the Sierra Club will dramatically cut carbon emissions and jumpstart renewable energy and efficiency programs across the country–to slow and stop global warming. In particular, we will stop construction of new coal plants, defend clean-car laws, put teeth in municipal plans to reduce global warming emissions and support biofuels and wind power. We will also restore and protect ecosystems to help capture carbon and help species adapt to and survive climate change.

What do you need to do that?

We need strong donor commitment to these programs. With full funding, we can stop the next wave of 50 coal plants and channel investments into clean energy, give communities the tools they need to address the effects of climate change and ensure that our national legacy of wild places lives on for future generations.

How will your organization change if progressives win in November? If they lose?

If progressives win, the Sierra Club will have a good shot at enacting strong federal solutions to climate change. We will initiate a nationwide grassroots and communications campaign designed to focus public pressure on decision-makers. If progressives lose, we will still continue our federal work, but will emphasize more heavily our work at the local and state levels.

This "behemoth" of environmental advocacy is "driving home the problems of ours and the generations to come" and "tirelessly" devising ways to combat them.

If you had to offer some advice to fellow progressives what would it be?

The progressive vision of justice, fairness and a healthy environment is one of our greatest assets. Articulating that vision clearly, powerfully and consistently is one of the foremost challenges for progressive leaders. The progressive movement has made considerable strides in the past few years—for example, the Sierra Club's Blue-Green Alliance with the United Steelworkers to push for a new energy economy. We must avoid relying on stopping threats, such as coal plants being built, even though they are worthwhile, short-term victories. The lasting success of the progressive movement depends on our ability to powerfully convey our vision for society.

Please list your board of directors and their affiliations.

Joni Bosh
Phoenix, Arizona; Vice President, Finance, American Solar

Jim Catlin
Salt Lake City, Utah; scientist, project director, Wild Utah Project

Allison Chin
Stanford, California; scientist, cancer/AIDS drug development

Robert Cox
Chapel Hill, North Carolina; communication professor, environmental author, activist

Jim Dougherty
Washington, DC; environmental lawyer and landscape photographer

Jennifer Ferenstein
Missoula, Montana; grassroots organizer, The Wilderness Society

Barbara Frank
La Crosse, Wisconsin; environmental activist, artist, former teacher

David Karpf
Philadelphia, Pennsylvania; doctoral candidate, University of Pennsylvania

Robin Mann
Rosemont, Pennsylvania; environmental activist

Ellen Pillard
Reno, Nevada; university faculty emerita; community activist

Rafael K. Reyes
San Mateo, California; Associate Director, As You Sow

Sanjay Ranchod
Atlanta, Georgia; attorney

Lisa Renstrom
Charlotte, North Carolina; environmental activist

Marilyn Wall
Cincinnati, Ohio; Retired, former technical manager

Bernie Zaleha
Boise, Idaho; environmental attorney and activist

SOJOURNERS

3333 14th St NW
Ste 200
Washington, DC 20010

☎ 202-328-8842
🖨 202-328-8757
✂ Chuck Gutenson
@ cgutenson@sojo.net

🖥 sojo.net
🗝 1971
📊 approx. $6,000,000
🔗 501c3

Jim Wallis
President/CEO

Jim Wallis is a best-selling author, public theologian, speaker, preacher and international commentator on religion and public life, faith and politics. His latest book is *The Great Awakening: Reviving Faith & Politics in a Post–Religious Right America* (HarperOne, 2008). His previous book, *God's Politics: Why the Right Gets It Wrong and the Left Doesn't Get It* (Harper Collins, 2005), was on *The New York Times* best-seller list for four months. He is president and chief executive officer of *Sojourners*, where he is editor-in-chief of *Sojourners* magazine, whose combined print and electronic media have a readership of more than 250,000 people. Wallis speaks at more than 200 events a year and his columns appear in major newspapers, including *The New York Times*, *The Washington Post*, the *Los Angeles Times*, and both *Time* and *Newsweek* online. He regularly appears on radio and television, including shows like Meet the Press, The Daily Show With Jon Stewart and The O'Reilly Factor. Jim is also a frequent guest on the news programs of CBS, NBC, ABC, CNN, MSNBC, Fox and National Public Radio. He has taught at Harvard's Divinity School and Kennedy School of Government on "Faith, Politics and Society." Jim has written eight books, including: *Faith Works, The Soul of Politics Who Speaks for God?*, and *The Call to Conversion*.

Jim Wallis is "outstanding." Sojourners unites people across the religious spectrum, a "brilliant" group that "inspires a new outlook" on religion and politics.

Jim Wallis was raised in a Midwest evangelical family. As a teenager, his questioning of the racial segregation in his church and community led him to the black churches and neighborhoods of inner-city Detroit. He spent his student years involved in the civil rights and anti-war movements at Michigan State University. While at Trinity Evangelical Divinity School in Illinois, Jim and several other students started a small magazine and community with a Christian commitment to social justice which has now grown into a national faith-based organization. In 1979, *Time* magazine named Wallis one of the "50 Faces for America's Future."

Jim lives in inner-city Washington, DC, with his wife, Joy Carroll, one of the first women ordained in the Church of England and author of *Beneath the Cassock: The Real-life Vicar of Dibley*; and their sons, Luke (9) and Jack (4). He is a Little League baseball coach.

Visit Jim Wallis and Sojourners at their Web site, www.sojo.net, and read his daily blog at www.GodsPolitics.com.

What does your organization do and how does it do it?
Our mission is to articulate the biblical call to social justice, inspiring hope and building a movement to transform individuals, communities, the church and the world.

In response to this call, we offer a vision for faith in public life by:
• publishing *Sojourners* magazine,

SojoMail and other resources that address issues of faith, politics and culture from a biblical perspective;
• preaching, teaching, organizing and public witness;
• nurturing community by bringing together people from the various traditions and streams of the church;
• hosting an annual program of voluntary service for education, ministry and discipleship.
In our lives and in our work, we seek to be guided by the biblical principles of justice, mercy and humility.

How will your organization impact the public debate in 2008?
We'll continue to actively seek out opportunities for our executive director, Jim Wallis, to share our vision in print, radio and television interviews. We'll get out the word through our magazine, our blog at www.GodsPolitics.com, organizing toolkits, other content at www.sojo.net and networking with partner organizations. We are also organizing a series of Justice Revivals—events at which thousands of people gather for three nights of inspiring preaching, music and a call to do justice.

What is your 2008 operating budget?
Around $6 million.

Looking out 2-3 years, how would you like to grow/change your organization?
We want to keep expanding our presence by putting out great content from a progressive, Christian viewpoint and by calling together

disparate groups, helping individuals develop a commitment to social justice and impacting public policy. We also want to provide more multimedia content—primarily audio and video, such as mp3 podcasts and YouTube videos—to respond to breaking events and articulate our message to new audiences.

A new initiative which we have launched is the Windchangers program, which convenes regional teams of committed activists whom we empower with intensive training to build and maintain a movement for social justice.

What do you need to do that?
We will need to expand our budget to hire excellent new staff members who can help us realize our mission. We will also synergistically bring together staff members and others in the faith community, including those who attend our Justice Revivals, our readers, online constituency, Windchangers and others.

How will your organization change if progressives win in November? If they lose?
If they win, we will actively call officeholders to faithfully enact a progressive agenda, particularly around the issues of poverty and peace-making. If they lose, we will continue to work at bridge-building with the goal of realizing as many of our strategic policy objectives as possible. Either way, our goal will be to help our nation's policies serve "the least of these," and we will continue to be non-partisan in pursuing those goals.

If you had to offer some advice to fellow progressives what would it be?
Sadly, too many progressives seem unaware of how powerful a force religious belief can be in political, cultural and economic matters. We'd like to encourage our fellow progressives to be willing, indeed eager, to make common cause with progressive religious persons whenever possible.

Please list your board of directors and their affiliations.

Tom Allio
Executive director, Cleveland Diocesan Social Action Office, Cleveland, Ohio

Dr. David Batstone
Coordinator, Not for Sale Campaign; professor of ethics, the University of San Francisco, California

Rev. Dr. Michael Battle
Priest in charge, Church of Our Saviour, San Gabriel, California

Angela Glover Blackwell
Founder and CEO, PolicyLink, Oakland, California

Rev. Peter Borgdorff
Executive director emeritus, Christian Reformed Church, Grand Rapids, Michigan

Sunlight Foundation

1818 N St NW
Ste 410
Washington, DC 20036

📞 202-742-1520
🖨 202-742-1524
✳ Gabriela Schneider,
   Communications Director
@ gschneider@
   sunlightfoundation.com

🖥 sunlightfoundation.com
🔑 2006
📊 $6,200,000
🔗 501(c)(3)

Ellen S. Miller
Co-Founder/Executive Director

Ellen S. Miller is the Co-Founder and Executive Director of the Sunlight Foundation, a Washington-based, non-profit catalyst that is using new technology to open up Congress. In just two years, Sunlight has created more than two dozen Web sites, databases, distributed research projects, tools and widgets to make information about Congress' activities more accessible through the Internet. She is the founder of two prominent Washington-based organizations in the field of money and politics—the Center for Responsive Politics and Public Campaign—and a nationally recognized expert on campaign finance and ethics issues. Ms. Miller is a well-recognized public speaker, commentator and writer on the issues of money, politics and power. Her experience as a Washington advocate for more than 35 years spans the worlds of public interest advocacy, grass roots activism and journalism. In addition to her more than two decades of work on the issue of money in politics, Ms. Miller served as Deputy Director of Campaign for America's Future, where she directed its Project for an Accountable Congress, the publisher of TomPaine.com and a senior fellow at *The American Prospect*. She spent nearly a decade working on Capitol Hill. She blogs regularly at the Sunlight Foundation site and has written frequently for TomPaine.com, *The Hill*, *The American Prospect* and *The Nation*.

What does your organization do and how does it do it?
The Sunlight Foundation was founded in January 2006 with the goal of using the revolutionary power of the Internet and new information technology to enable citizens to learn more about what Congress and their elected representatives are doing,

and thus help reduce corruption, ensure greater transparency and accountability by government, and foster public trust in the vital institutions of democracy. We are unique in that technology and the power of the Internet are at the core of every one of our efforts.

We have liberated megabytes of important political data from basements, paper, .pdfs and other non-searchable and non-mashable formats. These efforts, combined with our own innovative distributed investigative research projects, and community-based engagement with Congress to demand changes in how and what Congress makes publicly available online, have created here-to-fore unprecedented access and demand for more: more information, more transparency and more easy-to-use tools.

How will your organization impact the public debate in 2008?
Since our founding in 2006, we have achieved more than we imagined possible. The information online now about lawmakers and their activities is routinely viewed by hundreds of thousands. There have been millions of searches of the data that we have enabled to be put online in the last year. Tens of thousands, on a daily basis, rely on the facts of our databases and Web sites, participate in our online discussions, contribute to our ongoing distributed research projects and follow our investigative work.

What is your 2008 operating budget?
$6.2 million

Looking out 2-3 years, how would you like to grow/change your organization?
While our 2008 organizational objective is to continue to support the development, improvement and maintenance of cornerstone databases built by Sunlight and our current major grantees, by 2009 we want to firmly position Sunlight as the main platform or engine for obtaining critical data about Congress. We are also interested in launching several experiments in e-government, with the aim of helping elected representatives and constituents better communicate with each other, and are considering whether we should take everything we are learning and doing with respect to the legislative branch and focus as well on the executive branch agencies of government.

What do you need to do that?
Sunlight's goals presuppose that increasing amounts of resources are available so all of our projects continue to develop and thrive, with significant support from Sunlight and other philanthropic partners.

This group is "magnificent."

How will your organization change if progressives win in November? If they lose?

As Sunlight is a non-partisan organization, the political affiliation and ideology of the Administration will not affect Sunlight's work and future plans. However, depending on the outcome of the presidential election, there may be all kinds of fresh opportunities to push the envelope of federal transparency which could fall into three categories: developing government data for disclosure (meaning the data is not currently available even by the Freedom of Information Act); making existing government data searchable; and improving access to data already online.

If you had to offer some advice to fellow progressives what would it be?

Progressive organizations advocate on behalf of a variety of issues affected by legislation and the work of Congress. Transparency is key to creating better congressional accountability about all the issues progressives care about. Sunlight urges progressives to make use of the growing number of free resources now available that offer access to legislative, civic and political information with Web 2.0 ease of use so progressives can keep tabs on what is really happening on Capitol Hill. A resource guide to these 'insanely useful' Web sites is available at www.sunlightfoundation.com/resources.

Please list your board of directors and their affiliations.

Board of Directors

Chairman, Michael R. Klein

Sec-Treasurer, Ellen S. Miller

Esther Dyson
ED Venture

Craig Newmark
CraigsList

Nicholas J. Klein

Advisory Board

Yochai Benkler
Yale University

Lawrence Lessig
Stanford University

Charles Lewis
former director, Center for Public Integrity

Kim Scott
Google

Jimmy Wales
Wikipedia

ThirdWay

1025 Connecticut Ave NW
Ste 501
Washington, DC 20036

✆ 202-775-3768

🖨 202-775-0430

✄ Jill Pike, Deputy Director for
Public Affairs

@ jpike@thirdway.org

🖥 thirdway.org

🔑 January 2005

📊 $4,500,000

⊟ 501(c)(4) and
a 501(c)(3) component

Jonathan Cowan
Co-founder

Mr. Cowan, like the other co-founders of Third Way, has over 15 years experience at senior levels of progressive politics and government. Prior to co-founding Third Way, Mr. Cowan founded and ran Americans for Gun Safety, which *The Washington Post* dubbed the "dominant" group on the gun safety side of that debate. In the spring of 2000, Mr. Cowan was a Visiting Fellow at Harvard's Institute of Politics, teaching a course on youth and political advocacy. During the second Clinton administration, Mr. Cowan served as Chief of Staff of the U.S. Department of Housing and Urban Development, helping to manage a federal agency of 9,000 employees with a $27 billion annual budget. Previously, he was Senior Advisor to

the HUD Secretary and was Acting Assistant Secretary for Public Affairs. In 1992, he co-founded Lead...or Leave, which became the nation's leading Generation X advocacy group. He was featured on the cover of *U.S. News & World Report*, in *Time*, on Nightline, 60 Minutes, Today and in many other media outlets as a generational spokesperson. He also co-authored *Revolution X* and has published op-eds in *The New York Times*, *The Washington Post* and *Los Angeles Times*.

What does your organization do and how does it do it?
Third Way, described by *Newsweek* as an "influential Democratic think tank," is advancing a 21st Century progressive agenda by working with elected officials, candidates and advocates

Third Way "never strays." "Excellent" and "focused."

to create policies and market those ideas in the public debate. Our work is structured into three program areas:

- National Security
- Middle Class Economics
- Culture

How will your organization impact the public debate in 2008?
Third Way will play an active role this year in helping congressional leaders and candidates to offer fresh policy ideas that truly resonate with the American public. This will include the development of highly targeted, modular policy initiatives for candidates that will provide them with fresh policy ideas that are targeted at significant security, cultural or economic problems, along with campaign event ideas, talking points and background materials. We also will conduct a series of interactive, hands-on trainings for both current Members and congressional candidates.

What is your 2008 operating budget?
$4.5 million

Looking out 2-3 years, how would you like to grow/change your organization?
In our first three years, we became one of the "go-to" idea groups for Senators, candidates and a limited number of House Members. Because of our high-impact track record and the effectiveness and pragmatic nature of our products, the demand for our work required that we expand our work into the House of Representatives and to some select work with governors.

Consequently, the demand for our products and trainings now exceeds our capacity; thus, our objective for 2008-10 is to expand our organization sufficiently to serve Congress more completely, make further inroads in establishing a robust program of work with the nation's governors and, if progressives take control of the Executive Branch, do extensive work there too.

What do you need to do that?
To fully meet demand for our products, Third Way would need to grow, from our current size of 21 FTEs to approximately 30-35 FTEs (plus contractors). To come to that scale would require that we increase our annual budget to around $7 million by 2010.

How will your organization change if progressives win in November? If they lose?
We do not anticipate any fundamental structural changes to our organization regardless of the outcome in November. However, if progressives win we will certainly seize the opportunity to move our policy and message ideas through leaders in the Executive Branch–we would work closely with the White House and relevant agencies on budget and policy development, rollout and communications strategies. If progressives lose, we will continue doing what we're doing today–working closely with leaders in Congress and the states to modernize and move a progressive agenda.

If you had to offer some advice to fellow progressives what would it be?

We would urge our fellow progressives to continually challenge their own assumptions about how to put our core values into practice. Our movement must be seen as dynamic and adaptable–we must not fall back on 20th Century ideas to meet modern challenges. On national security, we cannot be simply an anti-Iraq War movement–we must emphasize changing direction in Iraq to fight terror more effectively. On economics, we must understand that middle class families today face a whole new set of rules, bringing with them new anxieties and challenges. And on cultural issues, we must look for new areas of shared values with the vast majority of Americans who seek an end to the culture wars.

Please list your board of directors and their affiliations.

Dwight Anderson
Principal/portfolio manager, Ospraie Management, LLC

Georgette Bennett
Founder/President, Tanenbaum Center for Interreligious Understanding

Lewis B. Cullman
Founder/President, Cullman Ventures, Inc.

Beth Dater
Chief Investment Officer, AG Asset Management

Scott Delman
Managing Partner, DGZ Capital

John Dyson
Chairman, Millbrook Capital Management, Inc.

Robert R. Dyson
Chairman/CEO, Dyson-Kissner-Moran Corp.

Michael B. Goldberg
Partner/Managing Director, Kelso & Company

David Heller
Global head of equity trading, Goldman, Sachs

Peter Joseph
Managing Director, Palladium

Lieutenant General Claudia Kennedy (USA ret.)
Deputy Chief of Staff for Army Intelligence, 1997 to 2000; Chair, First Star, a nonprofit corporation

Derek Kirkland
Managing Director/Co-head, Global Financial Institutions Group, Morgan Stanley's Financial Institutions Group in Investment Banking

Reynold Levy
President, Lincoln Center for the Performing Arts

Thurgood Marshall, Jr.
Partner at Bingham McCutchen LLP, and a principal of Bingham Consulting Group

Truman National Security Project

1 Massachusetts Ave NW
Ste 333
Washington, DC 20001

📞 202-216-9723
🖨 202-682-1818
✂ Aiste Ray
@ info@trumanproject.org

💻 trumanproject.org
🔑 2005
📊 $1,000,000
🔗 501(c)4 with sister 501(c)3

The Rachel Kleinfeld
Executive Director/Co-Founder

Rachel Kleinfeld is the co-founder and Executive Director of the Truman National Security Project. Rachel previously served as a Senior Consultant at Booz Allen Hamilton, where she worked on information-sharing across the military, intelligence, law enforcement communities, homeland security and trade and security issues. She has also been a consultant to the Center for Security and International Studies writing with Richard Danzig, former Secretary of the Navy, on bioterrorism. Rachel currently serves as an independent member of the Board of Trustees for the Blue Fund, a progressive mutual fund.

Rachel maintains a strong interest in efforts to strengthen weak states through the rule of law, human rights, security and development. She has consulted for the World Bank, the U.S. Department of State, the Open Society Institute and other organizations regarding building strong police, judicial and legal structures in weak states. She has also worked in India, Israel and Eastern Europe for human rights, economic development and rule of law building nonprofit organizations. Rachel's commentary has appeared in radio, television and in multiple books, journals and newspapers, including *The Washington Post*, the *LA Times*, and *The Wall Street Journal*.

A Rhodes Scholar and a Truman Scholar, Rachel received her B.A.

The Truman Project is "ahead of the curve." It is "the future" of progressive national security policy.

from Yale University and her M.Phil in International Relations from St. Antony's College, Oxford.

What does your organization do and how does it do it?
The Truman Project has a clear and simple vision: to make a strong, smart, principled security tradition preeminent across America again. As the nation's premier progressive security training institute, we are creating a national force of progressive leaders trained in national security and able to speak with credibility to the American public, so that we own this issue for decades to come.

The Truman Project provides a continuum of battle-tested training programs to educate a new generation of progressive leaders across the country, from future Members of Congress to state and local leaders under 40, Congressional staffers and recent college graduates. Our leadership development programs build a powerful national network of politically-astute, influential change-agents who understand hard security challenges and talk about national security in ways that make Americans feel safe. Operating behind the scenes, leaders we train staff political candidates, run for office themselves, appear in the media and move strong progressive policy ideas into the political mainstream.

How will your organization impact the public debate in 2008?

Our trained leaders include speechwriters for Barack Obama, traveling press lead for Hillary Clinton and other high-profile positions already influencing the debate. Our message development work provides the arguments that progressive candidates and surrogates are using today to reframe the national security debate on our terms. We engage in message development with other leading progressive organizations to spread these ideas, and were the only security group chosen by the Senate to assist them in messaging national security this year.

What is your 2008 operating budget?
$1,000,000

Looking out 2-3 years, how would you like to grow/change your organization?
Today, we are the nation's premier training institute for training progressive leaders in security and communication. But the media still frames security in a simplistic, strong vs. weak dichotomy, which progressives often lose. Our next step is to make strong security progressives a major, mainstream voice in American public opinion. Over the next three years, we will increase our trainings, while expanding the "battle-think tank" side of our organization. A writing fellowship program will create a generation of politically savvy foreign policy writers producing a stream of popular writing, our communications shop will saturate the media and leaders we have trained will speak across the country.

What do you need to do that?
Our budget would need to grow to approximately 2.5 to 3 million dollars. We have had immense success in fundraising, having started from nothing just three years ago, and are now bringing on a Director of Development to help us reach the next level.

How will your organization change if progressives win in November? If they lose?
Our mission will be doubly needed if progressives win, because released from power, conservatives will be free to wholly focus their arsenal on attacking progressives in office–and Karl Rove has already told us they will target how progressives undermine America's security. We will need a growing set of trained leaders around the country who will fight back against these right-wing attacks. In Washington, we expect that many of leaders we've trained will be in the next Administration; so we will need to expand the pipeline of progressives who can fill security positions in Congress, other progressive organizations and can step into Administration jobs as others leave.

If you had to offer some advice to fellow progressives what would it be?
To convince the persuadable center, we don't have to triangulate our policies or abandon our values. We do need to empathize with other Americans in their hearts and guts, not their heads. Policy alone has no power to move men's (and women's) souls. The basic lesson of persuasion is to connect with people where they are emotionally—to acknowledge the fear, anger, insecurity, pride or happiness they are feeling—and only then to lead them to our ideas. We cannot denigrate or dismiss others' emotions and expect them to hear our policies.

Please list your board of directors and their affiliations.

Board of Advisors

**The Honorable
Dr. Madeleine K. Albright**
Principal, The Albright Group LLC

Dr. Kurt M. Campbell
CEO and Co-Founder, Center for a New American Security

Gregory B. Craig
Partner, Williams and Connolly LLP

Dr. Leslie H. Gelb
President Emeritus, Council on Foreign Relations

William Marshall
President, Progressive Policy Institute

The Honorable Dr. William J. Perry
Professor and Senior Fellow, Hoover Institution on War, Revolution, and Peace, Stanford University

John D. Podesta
President and CEO, Center for American Progress

The Honorable Wendy R. Sherman,
Principal, The Albright Group LLC

Dr. Anne-Marie Slaughter,
Dean, Woodrow Wilson School,
Princeton University

Board of Directors

Stephen Bailey
Senior Vice President, Frontier
Strategy Group

Pierre Chao
Senior Associate, Center for Strategic
and International Studies

Derek Chollet
Senior Fellow, Center for a New
American Security

Joy Drucker
Senior Vice President, Glover
Park Group

Sally Painter
Principal, Dutko Worldwide

Jamie Smith
Deputy Traveling Press Lead,
Hillary Clinton for President

Rachel Kleinfeld
Co-Founder and Executive Director,
Truman National Security Project

Dr. Matthew Spence
Co-Founder and Director, Truman
National Security Project

 **ACTION**

1825 K St NW
Ste 210
Washington, DC 20006

📞 202-263-4528
🖨 202-263-4530
🗯 Marti Rosenberg,
   Development Director
@ mrosenberg@usaction.org

💻 usaction.org
🔑 1999
📊 $5,000,000, plus our sister
   organization's $9,00,000
🔗 501(c)(4)

Jeff Blum
Executive Director

Jeff Blum, as Executive Director, helps shape USAction's belief in the value of community responsibility and government's powerful role to create an America that is truly committed to liberty and justice for all. He manages USAction's and USAction Education Fund's staff of 25 and works especially intensely to ensure their financial stability and growth.

Blum's experience in grassroots organizing is extensive. He founded and directed Pennsylvania Citizen Action; worked for Massachusetts Fair Share, People for the American Way (where he co-coordinated the campaign to establish AmeriCorps), Surface Transportation Policy Project, Chesapeake Bay Foundation and

Citizens Fund; and was Transportation Policy Director for Citizen Action, where he led the first-ever national campaign to promote public transit and Amtrak in the highway law reauthorization. Blum has also served as President of Maryland Citizen Action, founder and member of the Advisory Board of the Jewish Fund for Justice and as a member of the board of Citizens for Tax Justice. In Pennsylvania, he ran for state Senate in 1990 and was the Northeast Pennsylvania Regional Director of the Clinton/Gore Campaign in 1992.

What does your organization do and how does it do it?
Through cutting edge field and messaging, on-line and on-the-ground, USAction advances three of the most important issues for people in

USAction is "harnessing the power" of communities. A "cornerstone" of grassroots politics.

PAGE 311

America: safely ending the war in Iraq; winning quality, affordable health care for all; and overturning the upside-down priorities of the Bush Administration to create economic opportunity and security for low- and middle-income Americans.

We lead some of the nation's strongest coalitions on our top issues, both at the national and state levels, creating unified alliances of diverse organizations.

USAction recruits and trains people to be grassroots activists within our network of state affiliates, in half the states in the country. We carry out strategic and tech-savvy civic engagement programs, attracting members whom we educate, ID and mobilize to the polls.

All of our field work is aimed at winning victories on our critical issue campaigns, to create an America that works for all of us.

How do we do it?

USAction has helped create a new model for legislative campaigns that uses the energy of political campaigns, but values tailoring the work to each state's strengths.

We create national messaging through polling and research. Then, we train our state affiliate staff and leaders, and with our national coalition partners, create a campaign plan aimed at maximizing grassroots power. Each state affiliate then carries out the campaign tactics

and gets state-level press in the way that works best in their state.

How will your organization impact the public debate in 2008?
USAction's leaders and our members will bring our critical issues to the candidates–making a wave of demand for safely ending the war, creating a high-quality health care system and prioritizing economic opportunity for all.

We will focus on protecting our legislative allies, criticizing our opponents and creating Legislative Champions, who will take responsibility for highlighting our agenda publicly in Congress in 2009.

What is your 2008 operating budget?
$5M, plus our sister organization's $9M.

Looking out 2-3 years, how would you like to grow/change your organization?
In 2011, USAction wants to be a stronger part of the progressive movement–and to do that we need to be more financially sustained by our members. We also want to make our state affiliates more powerful, both as forces for change in their state legislatures and in Congress. When we do this, we will be able to point to significant policy victories that we will have helped achieve–which will help us recruit more new members and activists, and become increasingly visible movement leaders.

What do you need to do that?
In order to achieve our vision, we need:

- Investment of resources from diverse sources
- Members who will support us financially and will take action to make progressive change
- Partnerships with other national organizations for economic and political efficiency and power

How will your organization change if progressives win in November? If they lose?

If progressives win in November, we're positioned to lead three urgent national campaigns–safely ending the war; winning health care for all; and changing federal budget priorities by rolling back the tax breaks for corporations and the rich and creating economic opportunity and security for all in America.

If progressives lose in November, we'll work harder than ever to blunt the mandate that a new conservative President has to turn his views into law. We'll force the President's hand case by case on issues like SCHIP expansion, and turn to the states for innovative policy and progressive gains.

If you had to offer some advice to fellow progressives what would it be?

Build for power, and organize, organize, organize.

Create infrastructure, so that we never have to reinvent the wheel.

Share information and work closely together, so we learn from each other. Only working together will our movement be able to define politics and win. Be creative.

Reach for a bold vision of hope and progress, to continue to inspire those who are coming into the political process now for the very first time.

Please list your board of directors and their affiliations.

Board President, William McNary
Co-Director, Citizen Action/Illinois

External Vice President, Heather Booth
National Healthcare Campaign Director, AFL-CIO

Internal Vice President, Betty Ahrens
Executive Director, Iowa Citizen Action Network

Secretary-Treasurer, Deana Knutsen
President, Washington Community Action Network

James Johnson
Board member, Colorado Progressive Action

Phyllis Salowe-Kaye
Executive Director, New Jersey Citizen Action

Jesse Graham
Executive Director, Maine People's Alliance

Richard Kirsch
Executive Director, Citizen Action of New York

Linda Honold
Executive Director, Citizen Action of
Wisconsin

JoAnn Bowman
Executive Director, Oregon
Citizen Action

LeeAnn Hall
Executive Director, Northwest
Federation of Community Organizations

Vinod Seth
Grassroots, NDPeople.org

Debra Nixon
Grassroots leader, Michigan
Citizen Action

Lonnie Thompson
Grassroots, Florida Consumer
Action Network

John Cameron
Coalition Director, Council 31 of
national affiliate AFSCME

Khalid Pitts
Director, Political Accountability at
national affiliate SEIU

Duane Peterson
Immediate Past Board President,
TrueMajority Action

Gabe Pendas
President, United States Student
Association

Marvin Randolph
Director of Organizing and Politics,
Center for Community Change

VoteVets.org
The Voice of America's 21st Century Patriots

303 Park Ave South
#1293
New York, NY 10010

📟 646-415-8429
📠 646-924-3262
🔖 Peter Mellman
@ pmellman@votevets.org

💻 votevets.org
🔑 February, 2006
📊 $4,000,000
🔀 501(c)(4) and PAC

Jon Soltz
Co-Founder/Chairman

Jon Soltz is a leader in the Iraq and Afghanistan Veterans community and is originally from Pittsburgh, Pennsylvania. From May to September 2003, Soltz served as a Captain during Operation Iraqi Freedom, deploying logistics convoys with the 1st Armored Division. During 2005, Soltz was mobilized for 365 days at Fort Dix New Jersey, training soldiers for combat in Afghanistan and Iraq. He also served his country with distinction in the Kosovo Campaign as a Tank Platoon Leader between June and December 2000. Soltz is a graduate of Washington & Jefferson College with dual degree in Political Science and History. He has completed graduate work at the University of Pittsburgh Graduate School of Public and International Affairs.

Jon Soltz has quickly become one of the most authoritative voices on veterans' issues and military issues. He has been interviewed by national outlets such as the *Associated Press*, *The Washington Post*, *The New York Times*, *Los Angeles Times*, *TIME*, *Newsweek*, among others and in dozens of local outlets. He has made numerous media appearances including Jim Lehrer's Newshour on PBS, CNN, MSNBC, FOX News, ABC News, Nightline and national radio programs including Air America

VoteVets achieves an "incredible impact" through "extremely articulate and effective" advocacy. They "changed the debate" on the military and national security.

Radio, the Ed Schultz Show, the Bill Press Show, Alan Colmes Show and Mancow in the Morning. Jon is a frequent contributor to Countdown with Keith Olbermann.

What does your organization do and how does it do it?
VoteVets.org is the largest political group of Iraq and Afghanistan veterans, representing over 1,000 veterans of the wars, over 14,000 other veterans and their families and over 60,000 civilian supporters. It organizes veterans nationwide to press elected officials to support progressive and responsible use of our military, while holding elected officials accountable, and electing Iraq and Afghanistan veterans to public office.

How will your organization impact the public debate in 2008?
VoteVets.org will flip the conventional wisdom that conservatives are "pro-military." Through hard-hitting ads and field organizing, VoteVets will make clear that conservatives are hurting our military and security.

What is your 2008 operating budget?
$4 million

Looking out 2-3 years, how would you like to grow/change your organization?
Through the next few years, VoteVets.org has an ambitious field plan to drastically grow its active membership and state chapters, giving progressives a permanent military/veterans organization.

VoteVets.org will also play a bigger role on policy discussions on the Hill on such issues as fully funding the VA, GI Bill of Rights and many other issues that relate to our soldiers and their families.

What do you need to do that?
VoteVets.org will need more paid veteran organizers, who work full-time on growing our national network. We will need to hire some key legislative aides as part of the VoteVets.org team to work on the issues of concern to all veterans and their families. In addition, VoteVets.org wants to expand its outreach efforts to other progressive causes so that we can work together to bring veterans into the progressive political structure. This will require a budget increase of $250,000 per year.

How will your organization change if progressives win in November? If they lose?
If progressives win the White House and Congress, VoteVets.org will focus its national network on lobbying centrist Democrats and Republicans to join and expand the majority to responsibly draw down forces from Iraq as soon as possible, creating a filibuster-proof coalition. If progressives lose, VoteVets.org will continue to expose what conservative policies are doing to our military and security, not allowing them to claim "progress" if none is really there, setting the table for the 2010 election.

If you had to offer some advice to fellow progressives what would it be?

Progressives must take a greater interest in our military, how it works and what military members think and feel. Too often, military members and veterans feel that they have no home in the progressive community, because the community doesn't understand the institution from which they came. We need to get back to FDR/JFK liberalism, which not only embraced the military, but also served. The result was a military that represented progressive values, at all levels, and veterans that found a home among liberals.

Please list your board of directors and their affiliations.

Chairman, Jonathan Soltz
Iraq War veteran; Co-Founder of VoteVets.org

Chairman, Richard Beattie
Simpson, Thatcher & Bartlett LLP

Bill Belding
U.S. Navy veteran; President, Vietnam Veterans of America Foundation

Gen. Wesley K. Clark (ret.)
Former NATO Supreme Allied Commander

Tammy Duckworth
Iraq War veteran

Maj. Gen. Paul D. Eaton (ret.
Iraq War veteran

Leslie H. Gelb
President Emeritus, Council on Foreign Relations

Paul Hackett
Iraq War veteran

Prof. Elaine Kamarck
Harvard University, Kennedy School of Government

Fmr. Sen. Bob Kerrey
Vietnam veteran, President of The New School, fmr. NE Sen.

Dr. Lawrence J. Korb
Senior Fellow, Center for American Progress

William E. Little
U.S. Navy veteran, former Chairman of George Little Management

Lawrence E. Penn III
U.S. Army veteran, Managing Director, The Camelot Group

Edward Vick
U.S. Navy veteran, former Chairman, Young & Rubicam

Western Progress

Arizona office:
345 E Palm Lane
Phoenix, AZ 85004

Colorado office:
1536 Wynkoop St, Ste 510
Denver, CO 80202

Montana office:
526 E. Front Street
Missoula, MT 59802

📟 Arizona: 602 254-2244
Colorado: 303 454-3368
Montana: 406 829-6603
🖶 Arizona: 602 254-2922

🖥 Cathy Carlson,
Outreach Director
@ ccarlson@westernprogress.org
🖥 westernprogress.org
🔑 January 2007
📊 $1,700,000
🗂 501(c)3

Alan Stephens
Executive Director

Alan Stephens has joined Western Progress as its first permanent executive director, and he brings a lifetime of public experience and policy skills to the task. Most recently co-chief of staff for Arizona Governor Janet Napolitano, Stephens has worked for decades on interests that closely align with the mission of Western Progress, a policy institute advancing progressive strategies in the eight Rocky Mountain States.

Prior to becoming co-chief of staff for Governor Napolitano, Stephens served in the Arizona legislature as both senate majority leader and minority leader, focusing on agriculture, water, health, housing and economic development. He also pursued his commitment to behavioral health.

What does your organization do and how does it do it?
Western Progress is an independent, non-partisan public policy institute dedicated to advancing progressive policy solutions in the eight states of the Rocky Mountain West. Across the region, we are promoting progressive policy initiatives, countering conservative rhetoric and creating coalitions to develop pragmatic results. We aim to achieve these goals with substantive policy research, aggressive media outreach and innovative solutions.

How will your organization impact the public debate in 2008?
Western Progress will work throughout 2008 to promote progressive ideas and attack conservative rhetoric wherever it appears in the region. We will specifically focus on the debate around renewable energy, declining water supplies and the restoration economy. Given the West's expected prominent role in the presidential contest, we also intend to work with regional and national media outlets to discuss how western issues and voters will affect the race.

What is your 2008 operating budget?
$1.7 million

Looking out 2-3 years, how would you like to grow/change your organization?
We would like to play a significant role in advancing a range of progressive policies in all eight of the Rocky Mountain states and in building a close-knit community of progressive activists that reaches across state borders in our region. We want to help develop a robust policy and communications foundation so that the ranks of enlightened lawmakers in our state capitals will grow and move their states forward.

What do you need to do that?
We need the additional resources to build up our staff, our policy expertise and our communications network so we can move closer to the vision outlined above.

How will your organization change if progressives win in November? If they lose?
Our long term mission will not change regardless of the outcome of November's election. We will continue to work with elected officials of all partisan stripes to promote progressive change on our issues in the Rocky Mountain West. We will also continue to build coalitions to promote progressive ideas and progressive policies in the region.

If you had to offer some advice to fellow progressives what would it be?
To remember that the West was once a center of American progressivism and to believe that it can be again.

Please list your board of directors and their affiliations.

Chairman, Fred DuVal
Mr. DuVal is the president of DuVal and Associates, a Phoenix consulting firm focusing on intergovernmental relations

Anna Whiting Sorrell
Ms. Sorrell is a policy advisor to Montana Governor Brian Schweitzer with areas of responsibility for

This group is "essential" to the spread of progressivism across the nation. They are "singular" in their region.

health and human services,
corrections and labor.

Bill Roe

Mr. Roe is the Chair of the Pima County
Conservation Acquisition Commission,
and a member of the Tucson Regional
Economic Opportunities Economic
Steering Committee and Arizona
League of Conservation Voters.

Edward Romero

Mr. Romero is a native New Mexican
who served as U.S. ambassador to
Spain in 1998 and headed several
delegations to Mexico to forge the
relationships necessary to expand
business opportunities.

Frankie Sue Del Papa

Ms. Del Papa lives and practices law
in Reno, Nevada and is active in many
environmental and other civic issues.

John Leshy

Mr. Leshy is one of the nation's leading
legal and policy experts in areas
including natural resources, water and
Native American law.

Maggie Fox

Ms. Fox is a conservationist and
attorney from Boulder, CO.

Marc Johnson

Mr. Johnson is President of The Gallatin
Group, a strategic communications
consulting firm, and a Partner in the
Boise office.

Ned Farquhar

Mr. Farquhar is the western energy
and climate advocate for the Natural
Resources Defense Council, where he
develops strategies to support regional
climate and renewable energy policies.

Alice Madden

Ms. Madden has served in the
Colorado legislature since 2000 and is
currently House Majority Leader.

WOMEN'S VOICES.
WOMEN VOTE.

1707 L St
Ste 750
Washington, DC 20036

☎ 202-659-9570
🖷 202-833-4362
✕ Sarah Johnson,
  Communications Director
@ sarah@wvwv.org

🖳 wwwv.org
🕰 2004
📊 $14,600,000;
  Action Fund: $10,000,000
🖧 501(c)(3)

Page Gardner
Founder/President

Page S. Gardner conceived of and founded Women's Voices. Women Vote. She is an expert in the voting patterns of women voters, with a particular expertise in unmarried voters. She began this project dedicated to increasing the share of unmarried women in the electorate.

During her twenty years experience as a political and communications manager and strategist, Ms. Gardner has worked at senior levels for the most competitive presidential, senatorial, gubernatorial and congressional campaigns in all parts of the country. Ms. Gardner also has managed some of the most hotly debated national public policy issue campaigns, including those related to reproductive rights, civil rights, national budget priorities, technology and trade. Ms. Gardner has been credited with designing and implementing some of the most creative and successful issue and legislative campaigns, as well as staging come-from-behind candidate victories in key battleground races. She is regarded as one of the top strategists in the country.

Ms. Gardner has a magna cum laude degree from Duke University. She lives with her husband and two daughters in Virginia.

What does your organization do and how does it do it?
WVWV adopts new approaches to civic engagement.

WVWV is fulfilling a "vital role." They are "strategic" and "creative." "The best ROI in politics."

Specifically we:

- Identified unmarried women as a key demographic under-represented in our democracy, an untapped resource for social and political change and the fastest growing large demographic. As 26% of eligible voters, they are equal in size to married women yet less likely to register, and vote.
- Were first to identify the marriage gap as the defining dynamic of the 21st Century. The marriage gap–the difference between how married and unmarried individuals live and participate–defines civic participation.
- Pioneered research-tested registration and turnout programs, proven to be cost effective in adding net additional voters. We created innovative approaches to civic engagement, relying on strict metrics and measurements of success. We apply lessons learned about unmarried women to other under-represented constituencies.
- Created a demographic approach providing more than 80% reach versus a geographic concentration, which yields a 15-20% reach.

How will your organization impact the public debate in 2008?

Through changing who participates in America's democracy by helping unmarried women and others bring their voices to the process and public policy debates. We produce groundbreaking public policy and survey results through our registration, turnout and advocacy programs and activate unmarried women into debates. Our research identifies the issues of utmost importance to women on their own. We also produce different, more culturally based communications that reflect the lives and interests of our audience.

What is your 2008 operating budget?

Women's Voices. Women Vote: $14.6 million; Women's Voices. Women Vote Action Fund : $10 million

Looking out 2-3 years, how would you like to grow/change your organization?

We want to expand the sweep and scope of our work. We are currently in the process of developing a public policy arm of WVWV so that we can begin to realize the public policy agenda of unmarried women. As part of this effort, we plan to test and improve new ways to encourage unmarried women to participate in public debates and decisions year-round, as well as registering and voting.

In addition, we intend to function in more states and to reach more under-represented populations using our direct marketing techniques.

What do you need to do that?

Expanding our base for capital resources and maintaining established partnerships is fundamental for continued growth at WVWV. As a research based organization that tests and evaluates all of our programs, continual incoming resources are essential for not only conducting our work, but also for expanding our knowledge base.

How will your organization change if progressives win in November? If they lose?

If progressives win, we will develop appeals that emphasize not only the urgency of the problems facing unmarried women but also the prospect of achieving solutions for these women and other Americans who struggle to make ends meet and realize the American dream. We will work with public officials to develop new programs and improve existing ones to address the needs of unmarried women.

If progressives lose, we will do even more to examine and highlight how we and our allies fell short of mobilizing those who are most likely to share our values and our goals.

If you had to offer some advice to fellow progressives what would it be?

The future of progressive politics depends largely on increasing the participation of under-participating progressive groups. Our ability to do this is enhanced by bringing civic engagement into the homes of people whose lives are very stretched.

We have found that people want factual, empowering information –not overblown rhetoric. They want communications that reflect their lives and their popular culture and they want activism and voting to fit into their lives.

We would also say test, test, test and never accept conventional wisdom about who can be activated and how. So called conventional wisdom is never wise.

Please list your board of directors and their affiliations.

Page Gardner
Founder and President, WVWV

Chris Desser
Fellow, Tomales Bay Institute

Ashley James
Student Activist, Howard University Law School

Michael Lux
President, American Family Voices

Mimi Mager
Partner, Heidepriem & Mager

Nancy McDonald
Resource Development Director, WVWV

William McNary
President, USAction

John Podesta
President and CEO, Center for American Progress

Maggie Rheinstein
Community Activist

YDA

Young Democrats of America

PO Box 77496
Washington, DC 20013

☏ 202-639-8585

🖨 202-318-3221

✳ Alexandra Acker

@ aacker@yda.org

🖥 yda.org

🔑 1932

📊 $3,000,000

🔗 527

Alexandra Acker
Executive Director (above)

David Hardt
President (not shown)

Alexandra Acker

Alexandra joined the Young Democrats of America (YDA) as Executive Director. YDA is a national, partisan youth-led political organization aimed at turning out the youth vote for Democrats and building a youth voting bloc. Alexandra oversees YDA's 10 national and state staff and supports YDA's 1,500 chapters in all 50 states. Alexandra is also a recognized youth vote expert who appears frequently in national and local media outlets, including as a regular commentator on Fox News Channel.

Prior to joining YDA, Alexandra was the Campaign Manager for the National Campaign for Fair Elections (an initiative of the Lawyers' Committee for Civil Rights Under Law), worked with national and state coalition partners to advance election reform legislation. In 2004, Alexandra served the National Youth Outreach Director for the John Kerry for President Campaign and the Democratic National Committee, culminating in the highest young voter turnout since 1972 and a 9-point advantage for the Kerry-Edwards ticket among young voters. As the Campus Outreach Manager for Planned Parenthood Federation of America (PPFA), Alexandra worked with PPFA affiliates across the country on campus organizing for public policy initiatives. During the 2002 election cycle, Alexandra worked for the Democratic Congressional Campaign Committee (DCCC) as the Assistant to the Chair, Congresswoman Nita Lowey (D-NY). She joined the DCCC after working for Rep. Lowey in her Congressional office.

Alexandra graduated magna cum laude from the State University of New York at Binghamton with a B.A. in political science. She grew up in Nyack, NY.

David Hardt

In the summer of 2002, David Hardt walked into the office of Pauline Dixon, a retired schoolteacher and longtime Democratic activist who was running for Congress against powerful Republican incumbent Pete Sessions. Over the course of the campaign, David helped Pauline raise thousands of dollars and became her most loyal volunteer. Pauline was unable to defeat the Republican incumbent, but the lessons David learned on that campaign strengthened his commitment to the Democratic Party.

David was driven to join Pauline's campaign because, as a gay man living in a conservative state, David recognizes that America is a nation in need of progressive change. Hoping to make a difference in his community, David joined the small, local Young Democrats chapter. By mid-2004, he was the club's treasurer and de-facto leader. Under David's guidance, which continued through 2005-06 during his term as President, the Dallas County Young Democrats grew to become the most important Democratic organization in Dallas and one of the largest YD chapters in the nation.

Since 2003, David has served on the Young Democrats of America National Committee as the male representative for Texas. In 2006, he served as chair of the YDA Site Selection Committee for the 2007 National Convention. Under David's leadership, the DCYDs were a key component of the surprising countywide victories won by Dallas Democrats in 2004 and later to the local party's sweep of all contested countywide races in the 2006 elections.

While most active within the Young Democrats, David Hardt has also been a leader and organizer within other parts of the local party, as a member of the Dallas County Democratic Party's Finance Council, a leader within Dallas's GLBT community, a board member of the Stonewall Democrats of Dallas, and supporter of the local branch of the Human Rights Campaign. He was a delegate to the 2004 Democratic National Convention in Boston.

David is currently the Chief Financial Officer of a manufacturing company and lives in Dallas, Texas, with his Partner Steven, a lawyer, their dog and two cats.

Youth is "critical." YDA is "making it happen."

What does your organization do and how does it do it?
The Young Democrats of America (YDA) is the largest youth-led, national, partisan political organization. YDA mobilizes young people under the age of 36 to participate in the electoral process, influences the ideals of the Democratic Party, and develops the skills of the youth generation to serve as leaders at the local and national level.

YDA has over 1,500 local chapters in all 50 states. Our 150,000+ members –including middle school, high school and college students as well as young workers, young professionals and young families–reflects the broad diversity of our nation and the Democratic Party. Our programs engage Young Democrats through their local county, college or high school chapters, through state and regional programming, and nationally through events like our national convention and issue advocacy work.

YDA's campaigns and programs are aimed at building a sustainable youth movement. Through trainings, hands-on campaign experience and leadership opportunities, YDA provides the infrastructure for young people to engage in partisan civic participation and prepares the youth generation to serve as leaders at the local, state and national level.

State Executive Directors oversee all aspects of our campaign programs and chapter building activities in their state, as well as the financial and administrative duties related to organizing and overseeing a state-wide network of high school, college and young workers/young professionals. State EDs create a year-long strategic plan and work with YDA national staff to create an effective campaign plan to target young voters.

How will your organization impact the public debate in 2008?
The 2008 election cycle is crucial to the consolidation of a Democratic youth base. Studies have shown that if a voter casts a ballot for one political party three elections in a row, they are likely to remain a loyal party voter for the rest of their lives. In this crucial election cycle, we will successfully create a bloc of young voters who make voting–and voting for Democratic candidates–part of their civic identity.

In 2004, 2006 and even now in the 2008 primaries, young people are voting in record numbers and are voting for Democrats. YDA's goal is to build a permanent bloc of young Democratic voters. Our Young Voter Revolution campaigns use a tested field model that identifies young voters, engages them in peer-to-peer communication and education, and then uses traditional and innovative methods to turn out the vote.

What is your 2008 operating budget?
$3 million

Looking out 2-3 years, how would you like to grow/change your organization?

State-based and local organizing are the cornerstones of our efforts to build a permanent bloc of young Democratic voters. YDA has evolved our campaign model into a year-round effort to grow and sustain our chapter network with direct financial support and staff assistance. Dubbed the State Partnership Program, YDA has created a matching grant program to assist state and local chapters with everything from hiring full-time Executive Directors to running voter contact programs to organizing trainings to developing websites.

In the coming years, YDA will continue to expand this program, growing chapters and electing Democrats in red, blue and purple states, incorporating constituency-based outreach programs into our model as well.

What do you need to do that?

With over 1,500 chapters in all 50 states, we have the network of activists needed to build a permanent infrastructure for the youth movement. We need additional resources–people, money, time–to help train all of our local leaders with the skills they need or organize and win.

How will your organization change if progressives win in November? If they lose?

YDA is focused on building a permanent bloc of young, Democratic voters, so we always look on to the next election cycle and the next cause. Our organization will work to bring in the new young, voters who were energized by the 2008 election for the important issue advocacy work that still lies ahead. We will also start planning for 2009 elections, 2010 elections and the crucial redistricting work to be done in key states. Most importantly, we will work, regardless of the outcome, to keep Young Democrats focused on the issues Americans care about, the solutions we can work towards and the skills, training and leadership development we need to meet those goals.

If you had to offer some advice to fellow progressives what would it be?

Practical advice for young progressives would be to work in all areas of the progressive movement. If you are a campaign hack, try a non-profit for a year or two. If you have never worked as a campaign staffer, give it a go for a cycle. Try raising money, earning media and organizing on behalf of a cause or candidate. On a larger scale, in order to sustain a true movement, we must always include new ideas and new leaders. We need to be creative and try new ideas!

Please list your board of directors and their affiliations.

President, David Hardt

Executive Vice-President, Chris Anderson

Democratic National Committeeman,
Crystal Strait

Democratic National Committeeman,
Francisco Domenech

1st Vice-President,
A'Shanti Fayshel-Gholar

2nd Vice-President, Omar Khan

3rd Vice-President, Josh Blevins

Secretary, Stephanie Hausner

Treasurer, Amy Lewis

Sasha Bruce

Veronica de la Garza

Vanessa Kerry

Orson Porter

Paul Yandura

YOUNG PEOPLE FOR

149 Fifth Ave

Seventh Flr

New York, New York 10011

📞 212.420.0440

🖨 212.420.7540

 Iara D. Peng

212.420.0440 x16

@ ipeng@pfaw.org

💻 yp4.org

🔑 Novemberzz 3, 2004

📊 $2,436,364

🏛 501(c)(3)

Iara D. Peng
Founder/Director

Iara D. Peng is the founder and director of Young People For, a program of People For the American Way Foundation (PFAWF) that identifies, engages and empowers new generations of young progressive leaders and activists. Before joining PFAWF, she served as the Executive Director of the Youth Justice Funding Collaborative, Vice President of Doble Research Associates and Vice President of Marga, Inc. Iara holds a Master of Public Administration degree with a concentration in nonprofit management from Columbia University's School of International and Public Affairs. She serves on the boards of Tides Advocacy Fund, the Youth Justice Funding Collaborative and the Beatitudes Society.

What does your organization do and how does it do it?
Young People For is diversifying the face of the progressive movement, identifying and training new generations of leadership and teaching young people to create positive social change in their communities. We provide personalized technical assistance and up to $2,000 in financial support for more than 200 fellows a year who are working to put their innovative ideas into action through self-designed social justice action plans. We select fellows from more than 90 campuses in at least 20 states each year, from community colleges to technical colleges to tribal colleges, historically black colleges and universities, Hispanic-serving institutions, state universities, conservative campuses and private

They are a "unique" group, proving that "young idealism need not be abstract." This organization is "cutting edge" in its approach.

universities. We provide a series of advanced leadership opportunities for fellows, including internship programs, one-on-one coaching, group coaching, mentorship, online courses, paid fellowships and retreats–all designed to help young people engage as leaders in the progressive movement over the long term.

How will your organization impact the public debate in 2008?
We provide support for young people's participation in the public debate through our blog, media training and local media outreach–all designed to ensure that diverse young people have the opportunity to be idea leaders in their communities. Throughout 2008 we will work to ensure that campaigns do not repeat their traditional abandonment of young people after the election cycle but instead plan to engage young people as leaders on an ongoing basis.

What is your 2008 operating budget?
$2,436,364

Looking out 2-3 years, how would you like to grow/change your organization?
We want to scale the work of YP4 to serve up to 1,000 fellows a year in 50 states, develop the management systems to connect with these leaders over the long term and continue supporting their leadership development beyond campus and beyond their first professional placements and continue to build a strong nationwide network of innovative, effective leaders working toward positive social change in all sectors: electoral, nonprofit and private.

What do you need to do that?
1. Growth capital support of at least six million dollars per year for the next four years to get the program to scale.
2. Sustainable revenue of at least that amount to support the program.
3. Nonprofits and businesses in all states to serve as host organizations for interns, fellows and full-time staff.

How will your organization change if progressives win in November? If they lose?
Our organization will not change if progressives win or lose in November. In either scenario, we will continue to focus on developing a network of diverse progressive leaders to serve in positions of power across sectors.

If you had to offer some advice to fellow progressives what would it be?
Young people are key agents of social change and have a deep commitment to progressive values of fairness, justice and equality. Young people lead with values of transparency, accountability and rigor. When taken seriously and provided with the resources they need, young people will help transform our nonprofit, private and electoral sectors. Make an intentional decision to invest in young leaders through providing mentorship, offering increased leadership opportunities and supporting youth leadership development as a key leverage area for social change.

Please list your board of directors and their affiliations.

Co-Chair/Founder, Norman Lear

Co-Chair, Ronald Feldman

David E. Altschul

James A. Autry

Alec Baldwin

Barbara Bluhm-Kaul

Blair Brown

The Hon. John H. Buchanan, Jr.

Robert L. Burkett

Julius L. Chambers

Susan Claassen

Bertis Downs

Tom Fontana

Judy Goldenberg

Joan Harris

Bianca Jagger

Daniel Katz

Howard G. (Blackie) Krafsur

Rev. Timothy McDonald

Dr. Jack L. Melamed, M.D., F.A.C.R.

Mary M. Middleton

Anthony T. (Tony) Podesta

Deborah Rappaport

David S. Rose

Joshua Sapan

Rabbi David Saperstein

Clyde (Ev) Shorey

Margery Tabankin

Kathleen Turner

Ruth B. Usem

THE
CONTRIBUTORS

ERIC ALTERMAN

Eric Alterman is a Distinguished Professor of English and Journalism, Brooklyn College, City University of New York, and Professor of Journalism at the CUNY Graduate School of Journalism. He is also "The Liberal Media" columnist for *The Nation*, and a fellow of the Nation Institute, a senior fellow and "Altercation" weblogger for Media Matters for America, (formerly at MSNBC.com) in Washington, DC, a senior fellow at the Center for American Progress in Washington, DC, where he writes and edits the "Think Again" column, a senior fellow (since 1985) at the World Policy Institute in New York and a history consultant to HBO Films.

Alterman is the author of seven books, including the just-published, *Why We're Liberals: A Political Handbook for Post-Bush America* (2008), and the national best-sellers *What Liberal Media? The Truth About Bias and the News* (2003, 2004), and *The Book on Bush: How George W. (Mis)leads America* (with Mark Green, 2004). The others include: *When Presidents Lie: A History of Official Deception and its Consequences*, (2004, 2005). *His Sound & Fury: The Making of the Punditocracy* (1992, 2000), won the 1992 George Orwell Award and his *It Ain't No Sin to be Glad You're Alive: The Promise of Bruce Springsteen* (1999, 2001), won the 1999 Stephen Crane Literary Award, and *Who Speaks for America? Why Democracy Matters in Foreign Policy*, (1998).

Termed "the most honest and incisive media critic writing today" in the *National Catholic Reporter*, and author of "the smartest and funniest political journal out there," in *The San Francisco Chronicle*, Alterman is frequent lecturer and contributor to virtually every significant national publication in the US and many in Europe. In recent years, he has also been a columnist for: *Worth*, *Rolling Stone*, *Mother Jones* and *The Sunday Express* (London). A former Adjunct Professor of Journalism at NYU and Columbia, Alterman received his B.A. in History and Government from Cornell, his M.A. in International Relations from Yale and his Ph.D. in US History from Stanford. He lives in New York, where he is at work on a history of postwar American liberalism.

PAUL BEGALA

From the White House's Situation Room to CNN's news program of the same name, Paul Begala's experience gives him an unmatched perspective on politics and the media as he comments on the 2008 political season. As a political strategist or pundit, Paul has been at the center of every election cycle of the last 20 years.

The CNN political analyst and former top aide to President Clinton was reportedly the first person to predict the Democratic takeover of the House in 2006, and as senior strategist to the campaign of Pennsylvania Democrat Bob Casey he helped unseat the third-ranking Republican in the US Senate, allowing the Democrats to take control of that chamber as well.

Paul served as Counselor to President Clinton in the White House, where he helped define and defend the Administration's agenda, from the State of the Union Address to the economic, domestic and international issues the White House faces each day. With his partner James Carville he was a senior strategist for the Clinton-Gore Presidential Campaign in 1992, and he has helped direct the political strategy of numerous other campaigns across the country and around the world, including advising politicians in Europe, Latin America, the Caribbean and Africa.

He helped his friend John F. Kennedy, Jr. launch the political magazine *George* and wrote the "Capitol Hillbilly" column. He is the author of several *New York Times* best-selling books, including *Is Our Children Learning?*, *The Case Against George W. Bush*, *Buck Up, Suck Up, Come Back When You Foul Up* and *Take It Back: Our Party, Our Country, Our Future*—the latter two he co-authored with Carville.

Begala is a research professor at Georgetown University's Public Policy Institute, and in 2007 was named the prestigious Carl Sanders Distinguished Scholar in Political Leadership at the University of Georgia School of Law. Paul received his BA in Government and his law degree from the University of Texas at Austin, where he was student body president.

SERGIO BENDIXEN

Sergio Bendixen is recognized as the preeminent expert in Hispanic public opinion research in the United States and Latin America. Bendixen's proficiency originates from his unique ability to merge a diverse set of experiences in public opinion research, communications, politics and public policy to strategically address the varied portfolio of his clients.

With over 25 years of polling experience, Bendixen is undoubtedly an expert in public opinion research. He has mastered research methodologies and has implemented detailed techniques to formulate studies and polls that accurately gauge public opinion. Bendixen has provided primary research and advice for clients both on a national and international level and has directed hundreds of demographic and attitudinal survey projects for statewide and congressional political races, major corporations and not-for-profit organizations.

Drawing from his experiences in most Latin American countries and throughout the rapidly growing Hispanic populations in the U.S., Bendixen specializes in gathering information about Latino public opinion. *The South Florida Sun-Sentinel* reported that Bendixen "has earned the undisputed title of being the leading pollster of Hispanics in the country." *The Columbia Journalism Review* identifies Bendixen as the pioneer of multilingual polling with surveys conducted in as many as 12 different languages. Bendixen's public opinion research surpasses his counterparts because early on he recognized that the power of multilingual polling rests in its ability to yield a depth and richness of opinion that is missing in English-only polls.

In addition to the expertise he has built in opinion research, Bendixen's background in the media, and the editorial praise he has received in recognition of the thoroughness, accuracy and ingenuity of his work, testify to his credibility. Bendixen is credited with helping put Spanish-language news on the map. He spent 14 years working as a national-television political analyst for four chief Spanish-language television networks: S.I.N. (1985-86), Univisíon (1987-92), CNN en Español (1993) and Télemundo (1994-98).

He has also provided commentary for countless radio shows and print stories. Bendixen's polls and writings have been featured in *Newsweek*, *The New York Times*, *The Wall Street Journal*, the *Los Angeles Times*, *The Washington Post* and *The Miami Herald*.

Bendixen's knowledge of, and contacts among, print and broadcast media enable him to take his expertise in public opinion research to a higher level where he can better suit the needs of his clientele. He understands how to craft his research findings into a potent message that is regarded as both understandable and credible by his clients, the media and their desired audiences.

This unique service is a Bendixen and Associates trademark and it is unparalleled.

The eight years that Bendixen spent in Washington, DC as Chief of Staff and Press Secretary to U.S. Representative William Lehman allowed him to develop a broad understanding of political and public policy issues. A native of Peru, Sergio Bendixen is the first and only Hispanic to have ever run a national campaign for U.S. President and has served as a senior consultant to two other presidential campaigns in both Costa Rica and Venezuela. The extensive political experiences that Bendixen brings to opinion research allow him to devise effective strategies to positively influence either electoral campaigns or public policy.

For example, after conducting a poll for the Children's Services Council that revealed a tax-averse climate in Miami-Dade County, Bendixen successfully devised a campaign strategy that persuaded county voters in September 2002 to adopt a property tax that provides $55 million a year to fund the Children's Trust.

Bendixen graduated from the University of Notre Dame in 1970 with a degree in chemical engineering. Following his studies at

Notre Dame, he was employed by the Atlantic Richfield Corporation in Corpus Christi, Texas. However, a fascination with politics and a desire to understand how to shape public policy drew Bendixen into the political arena, opinion research and the media. These experiences furnish him with a diversified perspective that enables him to gather, to observe and to strategically present both accurate and marketable information to his clientele.

WES BOYD

Wes Boyd is the co-founder of MoveOn.org, a progressive political action organization dedicated to promoting broad public participation in political discourse. Mr. Boyd is a software industry veteran, having founded a leading entertainment software company, Berkeley Systems. Berkeley Systems is best known for Flying Toaster screen savers, and You Don't Know Jack, an award-winning CD-ROM and online game. Prior to his work in consumer software, Mr. Boyd authored software for blind and visually impaired users allowing full access to computers with a graphical user interface.

JOE CONASON

A highly experienced journalist, author and editor, Joe Conason has served as Director of the Nation Institute Investigative Fund since November 2006. For the prior two years, he worked as investigative editor at *The American Prospect* magazine. The late Molly Ivins once described him as "one of the best investigative reporters in the country."

For the past 15 years, Conason has written a popular political column for *The New York Observer*. Creators Syndicate distributes his column nationally. He served as the *Manhattan Weekly's* executive editor from 1992 to 1997. Since 1998, he has also written a column that is among the most widely-read features on Salon.com.

Conason's most recent book is *It Can Happen Here: Authoritarian Peril in the Age of Bush* (St. Martins Press 2007), which the New York Review of Books called a "pithy…well-written account of an administration bent on establishing authoritarian executive power." He is also the author of *Big Lies: The Right-Wing Propaganda Machine and How It Distorts the Truth* (St. Martin's Press, 2003), a *New York Times* and Amazon.com bestseller, and co-author (with Gene Lyons) of *The Hunting of the President: The Ten-Year Campaign to Destroy Bill and Hillary Clinton* (St. Martin's Press, 2000), which appeared on both *The New York Times* and *Los Angeles Times* bestseller lists. Conason co-produced a 2004 documentary film, The Hunting of the President, which was based on the book and was selected as a special screening by the festival director at the Sundance Film Festival.

Conason began his career as a reporter for the *East Boston Community News*, a small neighborhood newspaper, in 1976. From there he went on to join *The Real Paper*, an alternative weekly published in Cambridge, Massachusetts as a staff writer. He covered environmental, racial and political issues for both papers.

From 1978 to 1990, he worked for *The Village Voice* as a columnist, staff writer and national correspondent. During his twelve years at the *Voice*, he covered beats ranging from national political campaigns, City Hall scandals and the Iran-contra affair to major foreign stories in the Philippines and China.

In 1985, he co-authored the *Voice* expose of Ferdinand and Imelda Marcos's hidden Manhattan real estate holdings. That worldwide scoop led to Congressional hearings, and provoked the election that preceded the Philippine dictator's overthrow. During the two years that followed, Conason made several trips to the Philippines to cover that election and subsequent events, including two coup attempts against President Corazon Aquino. In 1989, he arrived in Beijing, China, on the night after the Tiananmen Square massacre and reported on its tragic aftermath for the *Voice*.

Prior to joining the *Observer* in 1992, he spent two years as editor-at-large for Conde Nast's *Details* magazine. During the Clinton administration, his investigative reporting on the Whitewater affair and the Office of Independent Counsel for *The Nation* and *The New York Observer* brought him national media attention. He revealed the existence of the "Arkansas Project," a secret, multi-million-dollar effort funded by a conservative Pittsburgh billionaire to find or invent negative material about the Clintons. In 2004, Conason was one of the first journalists to delve into the background and finances of the so-called "Swift-Boat Veterans for Truth" and its campaign against John Kerry for Salon.com.

Conason's articles and reviews have appeared in *The New York Times*, *The Washington Post*, the *Los Angeles Times*, *Esquire*, *Harpers*, *The Nation*, *The New Republic*, *The Guardian* (London) and *The New Yorker*, among many other periodicals in the US and abroad. His December 2005 *Esquire* cover story on Bill Clinton's post-presidency was anthologized in *The Best American Political Writing* 2006 (Thunder's Mouth Press). He appears frequently as a commentator on television and radio. A winner of the New York Press Club's Byline Award, he has covered every American presidential election since 1980. He graduated from Brandeis University in 1975 with honors in history. He was born in New York City, where he lives today with his wife, Elizabeth Wagley, and their two children.

KELLY CRAIGHEAD

Kelly Craighead came to the Democracy Alliance with extensive knowledge and experience in politics, media and business. After joining the Alliance team as a consultant in 2004, she was promoted to Vice-President of Partner Services in 2005 and was responsible for recruiting Alliance Partners, managing Partner engagement and aligning millions of dollars in Alliance Partner investments.

In January of 2007, Kelly was named Managing Director and is charged with strengthening the Alliance community of donors and organization leaders, all of whom are committed to making our progressive vision of America a reality. Kelly joined the Democracy Alliance after working as a strategic consultant to Media Matters for America during its start-up phase. Prior to that, Kelly worked for Senator Hillary Rodham Clinton, during both her tenure as First Lady and later at her leadership PAC. In the White House, with the rank of Deputy Assistant to the President, Kelly directed all aspects of the First Lady's travels abroad and in the United States as well as managing many special domestic and international initiatives. She and her husband live in Washington, DC.

GAIL FURMAN

Dr. Gail Furman is a child psychologist, currently in private practice in New York City. In addition to her practice she is involved in a wide range of civic and professional activities. She serves on the Board of the Women's Commission for Refugee Women, and IRC's Leadership Council of Children in Armed Conflict and has participated in a number of fact finding missions, examining children's programs in Angola, Rwanda, Uganda, Kosovo and the Thai/Burma border.

Dr. Furman also serves on the boards of the Brennan Center for Social Justice at the NYU Law School, Human Rights First and the Democracy Alliance. She is also a member of the Council on Foreign Relations and is very involved in the Face to Face Program at Auburn Seminary, a program that fosters conflict resolution for youth in the Middle East.

ALISON GREEN

Alison Greene is the chief of staff for the Marijuana Policy Project, where she oversees the day-to-day management of the staff. Before taking on her current role, Alison served as MPP's director of membership and publications, overseeing revenue-raising programs and printed and online materials.

Prior to coming to MPP, Alison worked as the communications director and publications director for two grassroots advocacy organizations and spent six years as a staff writer and campaign coordinator for People for the Ethical Treatment of Animals (PETA), where her accomplishments included making headlines for an effort that resulted in Procter & Gamble placing a moratorium on animal testing; designing and launching a campaign to reach college students; teaching students how to work with the media and organize on campuses; and bringing the animal rights message into the pages of many conservative newspapers.

Her writings on an array of topics have been published in *The Washington Post*, *The New York Times*, *The Wall Street Journal*, *Maxim* and more than 250 other newspapers.

JERRY HAUSER

Since its inception in 2006, Jerry has served as the Chief Executive Officer of The Management Center, a nonprofit providing management assistance and coaching to make it easier for leaders of progressive advocacy organizations to achieve outstanding results. He brings to the role his dual passions for promoting social justice and creating high-performing organizations.

Prior to his current role, Jerry was the President and CEO of the Advocacy Institute, and before that he served as the Chief Operating Officer at Teach For America. During his seven years at Teach For America, Jerry helped the national nonprofit expand its reach significantly: applications increased from 3,000 to 17,000 per year and annual fundraising went from $8 million to $38 million. Jerry also learned about creating strong organizations while working as an associate at

the management consulting firm of McKinsey & Company in Washington, DC, where he served Fortune 500, state government and nonprofit clients. He holds a J.D. from Yale Law School, where he was a Senior Editor of the Yale Law Journal and he earned his undergraduate degree in political science from Duke University. Jerry has appeared on a variety of panels regarding nonprofit leadership; his article on "Organizational Lessons for Non-Profits" appeared in The McKinsey Quarterly in 2003.

GARA LAMARCHE

Gara LaMarche is President and CEO of The Atlantic Philanthropies. The Atlantic Philanthropies are dedicated to bringing about lasting changes in the lives of disadvantaged and vulnerable people. Atlantic focuses on four critical social problems: Ageing, Disadvantaged Children & Youth, Population Health and Reconciliation & Human Rights. Programmes funded by Atlantic operate in Australia, Bermuda, Northern Ireland, the Republic of Ireland, South Africa, the United States and Viet Nam. LaMarche joined Atlantic in April 2007 to lead the organisation through its final chapter as the foundation disburses its remaining $4 billion endowment and completes active grantmaking by 2016.

Before joining Atlantic, LaMarche served as Vice President and Director of U.S. Programs for the Open Society Institute (OSI), a foundation established by philanthropist George Soros. LaMarche joined OSI in 1996 to launch its U.S. Programs, which focuses on challenges to social justice and democracy.

LaMarche previously served as Associate Director of Human Rights Watch and Director of its Free Expression Project from 1990 to 1996. He was Director of the Freedom-to-Write Program of the PEN American Center from 1988 to 1990, when PEN played a leading role in campaigns to lift Iran's fatwa against Salman Rushdie and challenged restrictions on arts funding in the United States.

He served in a variety of positions with the American Civil Liberties Union (ACLU), with which he first became associated at age 18 as a member of its national Academic Freedom Committee. He was the Associate Director of the ACLU's New York branch from 1979 to 1984 and the Executive Director of the American Civil Liberties Union of Texas from 1984 to 1988. At the Texas ACLU, he led campaigns to provide adequate representation for death row inmates and oppose discriminatory treatment of persons with AIDS in the early days of the epidemic.

LaMarche is the author of numerous articles on human rights and social justice issues and is the editor of *Speech and Equality: Do We Really Have to Choose?* (New York University Press, 1996). He teaches a course in philanthropy and public policy at New York University's Wagner School of Public Service, and was an adjunct professor at New School University and The John Jay College of Criminal Justice.

LaMarche serves on the boards of PEN American Center and The White House Project, as a member of the Advisory Committee for the Sundance Documentary Fund and on the Leadership Council of Hispanics in Philanthropy.

A Westerly, R.I. native, LaMarche graduated from Columbia College in New York.

BRIAN MATHIS

Brian Mathis is a Managing Director of the Provident Group Limited and a Manager Partner of Provident Group Asset Management, LLC. Mr. Mathis has 10 years of alternative asset investment experience, including fund of hedge fund, hedge fund and private equity experience, globally.

Prior to joining Provident Group, Mr. Mathis was a Managing Director at Advent Capital Management, LLC ("ACM") responsible for the business development and marketing of ACM's hedge fund and long-only strategies. Prior to joining ACM, Mr. Mathis was a Director at Pacific Alternative Asset Management Company, LLC ("PAAMCO"), a fund of hedge funds with over $9 billion of assets under management.

He was a member of the Investment Management Committee, with responsibilities including evaluating directional hedge fund strategies, asset allocation among hedge fund strategies and guiding strategic initiatives of the firm, including establishing PAAMCO's London office. Prior to joining PAAMCO, Mr. Mathis was a Vice President from 1995 to June 2002 in various private equity groups at J.P. Morgan Chase & Co., including LabMorgan, focusing on investments in the hedge fund space, and managing LabMorgan's existing portfolio, J.P. Morgan Capital, investing in later-stage venture/growth capital and mid-cap leveraged buy-outs and Private Equity Placements, raising capital for private equity deals as well as private equity funds. Mr. Mathis served on the Board of Directors/Advisors for PlusFunds (observer), Eastport Operating Partners LP, ICV Capital Partners, Edison Schools, LinksCorp and Bell Sports.

Mr. Mathis began his career as a political appointee of President Clinton at the U.S. Department of the Treasury. He is a member of the Council on Foreign Relations and serves on the Board of Directors for the Children's Museum of Manhattan. Mr. Mathis received a B.B.A. from the University of Michigan Business School and a J.D./M.P.A. from Harvard Law School and the John F. Kennedy School of Government, Harvard University, respectively.

ALEXIS MCGILL

Alexis McGill is a political strategist, educator, writer and a passionate organizer around issues of social justice facing her generation and community. Throughout her work, Alexis has explored the shifting paradigms of identity politics in the post-civil rights era, increasing civic engagement among youth and people of color, and the implications for demographic and ideological changes of these constituencies on national politics.

Upon earning her undergraduate degree in politics from Princeton University in 1993, Alexis enrolled in the doctoral program of the Department of Political Science at Yale University. Not satisfied with the insular boundaries of the Ivory Tower, Alexis decided to explore other venues and audiences to discuss the real life concerns and experiences of her generation.

In March 2002, she found such an outlet in *Savoy Magazine* where she wrote an article about mobilizing the Hip-Hop Generation—raising the question—"Can the Hip Hop Generation become the Next NRA?" An interview for that article with Russell Simmons, the legendary "Godfather of Hip Hop," created a unique opportunity to begin work as Political Director of the Hip-Hop Summit Action Network, Simmons's voter mobilization organization. From July 2003 through the following year, she worked with Mr. Simmons and his national network of artists and cultural participants to devise the strategic plan for the Hip-Hop Summit's voter registration and mobilization initiatives.

In July 2004, Alexis became Executive Director of Citizen Change, a national, non-partisan and non-profit organization founded by Sean Combs which launched an unprecedented media and marketing campaign to educate, motivate and empower young people through voting. This campaign was marked by the now ubiquitous slogan "Vote or Die!" Mixing traditional grassroots mobilization with non-traditional consumer based marketing methodology, she created a new model for reaching young people and people of color and helped lead the most massive grassroots mobilization this generation has ever seen.

Since 2004, Alexis has developed a media and marketing consulting practice which applies the same mix of traditional grassroots organizing with the non-traditional consumer based model used in Vote or Die! for issues, candidates and corporate pro-social initiatives. She has worked with: Ned Lamont for Senate, WE tv, American Federation of Teachers and the Democratic Senate Campaign Committee.

She remains a committed political activist and strategist for a variety of organizations and continues to research, write, lecture and build coalitions with other artists, foundations and activists while taking time to think broadly and decisively about how to harness the power of this great generation in our nation's service.

ROBERT L. MCKAY

Rob is the president of the McKay Family Foundation, which supports community-based organizations working for long-term social, economic and political progress in California and New Mexico. In July 2006, Rob was elected Board Chair of the Democracy Alliance.

The Alliance is a network of over 100 partners committed to financing the national political infrastructures of the progressive movement. Priorities for long-term investment include media capacity, leadership development and think tanks.

In 2002, Rob was the author and principal funder of a California ballot initiative to promote election day voter registration. He is the managing partner for McKay Investment Group, which provides venture capital for early-stage technology and consumer product companies.

Rob was Chair of the 2004 California HAVA Advisory Committee, and is active on many corporate and non-profit boards, including Ms. Foundation for Women, San Francisco Art Institute, Salon Media Group and *Mother Jones* magazine.

MINYON MOORE

Minyon Moore heads Dewey Square's successful state and local affairs practice. Moore is considered one of Washington's top strategic thinkers.

Moore formerly served as the Chief Operating Officer of the Democratic National Committee, the world's oldest, continuing political party, before joining DSG. Moore was directly responsible for the day-to-day management and oversight of the Party's activities, including political operations, communications, research strategy and fund-raising, as well as fiscal and administrative operations with an operating budget of $60 million. She was appointed to the position by Chairman Terence R. McAuliffe after serving as Transition Director following his election as Party Chair in February 2001.

Prior to directing DNC operations, Moore served as Assistant to the President of the United States and Director of White House Political Affairs. In this capacity, she served as the principal political adviser to the President, Vice President, First Lady and senior White House staff, with primary responsibility for planning and directing the political activities of the President. Moore began her White House career as Deputy Director of Political Affairs. In this position, she managed the regional political operation, which monitored local political activity and worked with state and local elected officials in each region.

Before joining the Clinton Administration, Moore was National Political Director for the Democratic National Committee ("DNC") during the 1996 election cycle. In conjunction with the Democratic Congressional and Senatorial Campaign Committees, and the Democratic Governor's Association, she developed the framework and infrastructure for the DNC's 1996 Coordinated Campaign base vote activities in all fifty states. Moore also served on the 1984 and 1988 presidential campaigns. In 1988, she served as the National Deputy Field Director for Reverend Jackson. She served as Convention Coordinator for the 1988 Jackson campaign and was a special assistant to Jackson's Convention Manager, Ronald H. Brown, who later became U.S. Secretary of Commerce. During the 1988 general election, she served as Governor Michael Dukakis' National Deputy Field Director, with primary responsibility for managing the Dukakis field operations and coordinating Get-Out-The-Vote campaign activities across the country.

Moore is a native of Chicago, Illinois and attended the University of Illinois at Chicago where she majored in sociology. Moore has been a guest lecturer at the Harvard University Kennedy School of Government.

JORGE MURSULI

Jorge Mursuli—Vice President, People For the American Way Foundation; National Executive Director, Democracia USA. Born in the province of Sancti Spiritu, Cuba, Jorge Mursuli immigrated with this family to Brooklyn, New York in 1967. He received his Bachelor of Science degree from the University of Florida.

In 1993 Jorge Mursuli joined SAVE Dade (Safeguarding American Values for Everyone), an organization whose goal, among other things, was to secure the passage of an amendment to the Miami-Dade County Human Rights Ordinance that would include sexual orientation as a category protected by law from discrimination in employment, financing, public accommodation and housing. In 1997, Jorge took over SAVE Dade as Executive Director; in December 1998, the Miami-Dade County Commission adopted the amendment.

In 2001, Jorge joined PFAW Foundation and PFAW and as the Florida State Director. In September 2002, People For the American Way, together with SAVE Dade, led the fight, and was victorious against a repeal of the sexual orientation clause in Miami-Dade's Human Rights Ordinance. During the 2002 and 2004 elections, he helped organize PFAW Foundation's Election Protection program.

In 2004 PFAW Foundation, in partnership with the Center for Immigrant Democracy, launched Democracia U.S.A. with Jorge as the National Executive Director. In August 2005 Jorge Mursuli was promoted to Vice President of PAFW and PFAW Foundation while maintaining his role as Florida Director of PFAW and PFAW Foundation.

In the four years that Jorge has been at the helm of D-USA, the program has grown to be one of the most effective Hispanic civic engagement, voter empowerment and leadership training programs in the nation, moving from its home at PFAW Foundation in 2008 to begin a new partnership with the National Council of La Raza, where the program will become an affiliated corporation of NCLR with Jorge Mursuli as its President and CEO.

Jorge Mursuli served on the Board of the Greater Miami Convention and Visitor's Bureau. He is the former Chair of the Miami-Dade County Community Relations Board Task Force on Police/ Community Relations. Currently, he serves on the National Board of the League of Conservation Voters.

As a result of Jorge Mursuli's community-building endeavors and as an advocate for education and immigration throughout the years, he has been the recipient of the United Way of Miami-Dade's 1999 Elsie Silva Community Builder Award, the 1999 Dade Human Rights Foundation Award, the 2003 Mother's Voices Extraordinary Voice Award and the recipient of the United Teachers of Dade Unity Caucus' 23rd Annual Dr. Martin Luther King, Jr. Award. In 2004

Jorge received "The Plumed Warrior" award from The National Latina/o Lesbian, Gay, Bisexual & Transgender Organization (LLEGO) for his leadership in grassroots organizing on issues of concern to members of the Hispanic community and to members of the LGBT community.

JOHN PODESTA

John Podesta is the president and CEO of the Center for American Progress and visiting professor of law at the Georgetown University Law Center. Podesta served as chief of staff to President William J. Clinton from October 1998 until January 2001, where he was responsible for directing, managing and overseeing all policy development, daily operations, Congressional relations and staff activities of the White House.

He coordinated the work of cabinet agencies with a particular emphasis on the development of federal budget and tax policy, and served in the President's Cabinet and as a principal on the National Security Council. From 1997 to 1998 he served as both an Assistant to the President and deputy chief of staff. Earlier, from January 1993 to 1995, he was Assistant to the President, Staff Secretary and a senior policy adviser on government information, privacy, telecommunications security and regulatory policy.

Podesta previously held a number of positions on Capitol Hill including: counselor to Democratic Leader Senator Thomas A. Daschle; chief counsel for the Senate Agriculture Committee; chief minority counsel for the Senate Judiciary Subcommittees on Patents, Copyrights, and Trademarks; Security and Terrorism; and Regulatory Reform; and counsel on the Majority Staff of the Senate Judiciary Committee.

Podesta is a graduate of Georgetown University Law Center and Knox College.

SASHA POST

Sasha Post is the Program Officer for the Open Society Institute's Global Fellows Program. From 2005 through 2007, as Special Assistant to the Director of US Programs, he helped oversee many of OSI's Progressive Infrastructure grants to think tanks, publications and organizing efforts in the United States.

A Berkeley native, he graduated from Harvard College in 2005 and now lives in Brooklyn.

ANDREW RICH

Andrew Rich is Associate Professor of Political Science at City College of New York and the CUNY Graduate Center. He is also Deputy Director and Director of Programs at the Colin Powell Center for Policy Studies at CCNY. He is the author of *Think Tanks, Public Policy and the Politics of Expertise* (Cambridge University Press, 2004), a book about the proliferation of think tanks in U.S. national policymaking and the ways that research and research-based nonprofit organizations influence contemporary decision-making.

Rich has worked as a consultant or adviser to a number of foundations and organizations, including the Open Society Institute, Ford Foundation and Pew Charitable Trusts. Rich received his Ph.D. in political science from Yale University.

CECILE RICHARDS

Cecile Richards is president of Planned Parenthood Federation of America (PPFA) and the Planned Parenthood Action Fund. Over the course of her career, she has become a nationally recognized progressive leader and a fierce advocate for reproductive health and rights. Since coming to Planned Parenthood in February 2006, Ms. Richards has led the organization to many significant achievements, including its success in ensuring FDA approval of over-the-counter status for emergency contraception, and the launch of a nationwide campaign to provide comprehensive, medically accurate sex education for all young people in America.

Ms. Richards leads a federation of more than 100 Planned Parenthood affiliates that manage more than 860 health centers nationwide, providing high-quality family planning and reproductive health care services, education and information to millions of women, men and young people each year.

For more than 90 years, Planned Parenthood has led the movement to improve women's health and safety, prevent unintended pregnancies and sexually transmitted infections, and advance the right and ability of individuals and families to make informed and responsible health care decisions. That effort takes place in Washington, DC, and in all 50 states where Planned Parenthood advocates for positive, commonsense policies that address the health priorities of individuals and families, including support for medically accurate, age-appropriate sex education. Planned Parenthood also works with allies in other countries to help provide and protect sexual and reproductive health care for women and men worldwide.

Before joining Planned Parenthood, Ms. Richards served as deputy chief of staff for Democratic Leader Nancy Pelosi and played a key role in her election as the first woman speaker of the House.

Ms. Richards has a long history of organizing in support of reproductive freedom and social justice. In 2004, she founded and served as president of America Votes, a coalition of 42 national membership-based organizations, that works to maximize voter registration, education and mobilization efforts at the grassroots level.

Ms. Richards began her career organizing low-wage workers in the hotel, health care and janitorial industries throughout California, Louisiana and Texas. Prior to her national advocacy work, she established the Texas Freedom Network, a grassroots organization that has grown to include more than 28,000 clergy and community leaders, to advance a mainstream agenda of religious freedom and individual liberties across the state.

The daughter of former Texas Governor Ann Richards, Ms. Richards was raised in a family committed to social justice and public service. She worked side by side with her mother on her very first campaign—the successful election to the state legislature of Sarah Weddington, the lawyer who successfully argued the landmark 1973 U.S. Supreme Court case *Roe v. Wade*, which legalized abortion nationwide. Cecile Richards and her husband, Kirk Adams, have three children. They currently reside in New York City.

BERNARD L. SCHWARTZ

Bernard L. Schwartz is chairman and CEO of BLS Investments, LLC, a private investment firm. He also manages the investments of the Bernard and Irene Schwartz Foundation, which mainly supports higher education, medical research and New York City-based cultural organizations. He promotes the development of U.S. economic policy initiatives through investment in educational institutions, think tanks and advocacy organizations. Mr. Schwartz is also an active supporter of the Democratic Party.

Prior to establishing BLS Investments in March 2006, Mr. Schwartz served for 34 years as chairman of the board and chief executive officer of Loral Space & Communications and its predecessor company, Loral Corporation. In 1972, Mr. Schwartz took the helm at Loral which became, under his leadership, a Fortune 200 designer and manufacturer of advanced, state-of-the-art systems, hardware and systems integration for the defense and aerospace industries.

Through its successful strategy of acquisition and internal development, the company achieved extraordinary growth, posting 96 consecutive quarters of increased earnings from 1972 to 1996. Over that period, Loral made more than 40 acquisitions and its market value rose from $7.5 million to $15 billion. At its height, the company employed more than 30,000 employees in numerous countries around the world. In 1996, Mr. Schwartz directed the divestment of Loral's defense businesses and formed Loral Space & Communications, one of the world's largest satellite manufacturing and satellite services companies. In connection with this transaction, Loral collectively paid a dividend to its shareholders of more than $9 billion, primarily in cash and the balance in stock of the new Loral Space & Communications. In addition, Bernard Schwartz personally established a fund of more than $18 million for distribution to employees of Loral to mitigate any negative effects on those employees from the sale of Loral's defense businesses.

In recognition of his achievements and extensive experience in industry and global finance, Mr. Schwartz is often called upon to express his views or provide counsel on matters ranging from U.S. economic growth and competitiveness to technology and infrastructure investment. At a number of institutions, he has initiated programs that rigorously examine current U.S. economic performance, in the process challenging current orthodoxy to arrive at innovative policy proposals that will further U.S. economic and technological preeminence.

The programs employ lectures, position papers, conferences and debates and tap the expertise of leading economists, business people and policy makers. The policy proposals that emerge from these programs are broadly distributed to government officials, members of Congress, educators, researchers, the media and the general public.

Mr. Schwartz graduated from City College of New York with a B.S. degree in finance and holds an honorary Doctorate of Science degree from the college. He and his wife live in New York City and have two daughters, three granddaughters and one grandson.

FRANK SMITH

Frank Smith has been involved in political and public policy issues throughout his career. He is President of a Cambridge, Massachusetts consulting firm specializing in elections, non-profit and election law and public policy. He has a varied client list including foundations, individuals and the Democracy Alliance.

He has served as an Assistant District Attorney in Boston and worked on a number of political campaigns, including two Presidential elections. He is co-author of a recent book on the American healthcare system and writes a monthly newsletter on American politics. He is a graduate of Georgetown University and Boston College Law School, and a member of the Massachusetts Bar. He has served on a number of non-governmental organization boards.

ROB STEIN

Mr. Stein's critical research about the funding, management and overall infrastructure of the conservative movement over the last three decades led to the formation of the Democracy Alliance. An attorney, Mr. Stein served as chief of staff of the U.S. Department of Commerce and chief of staff at the Washington office of the Clinton-Gore Transition.

He also was a senior strategic advisor to Ron Brown, Chairman of the Democratic National Committee

(1989-1992), and has founded and led several non-profit organizations. Mr. Stein currently is actively involved, as both Founder and board member, in the Democracy Alliance.

KATRINA VANDEN HEUVEL

Katrina vanden Heuvel is Editor and Publisher of *The Nation*. She is the co-editor of *Taking Back America— And Taking Down The Radical Right* (NationBooks, 2004).

She is also co-editor (with Stephen F. Cohen) of *Voices of Glasnost: Interviews with Gorbachev's Reformers* (Norton, 1989) and editor of *The Nation: 1865-1990*, and the collection *A Just Response: The Nation on Terrorism, Democracy and September 11, 2001*.

Her book, *A Dictionary of Republicanisms, (An Indispensable Guide to Their Doublespeak)*, was published in November 2005.

She is a frequent commentator on American and international politics on ABC, MSNBC, CNN and PBS. Her articles have appeared in *The Washington Post*, the *Los Angeles Times*, *The New York Times* and *The Boston Globe*.

Her weblog for thenation.com is "Editor's Cut."

She is a recipient of Planned Parenthood's Maggie Award for her article, *"Right-to-Lifers Hit Russia."*

The special issue she conceived and edited, *"Gorbachev's Soviet Union,"* was awarded New York University's 1988 Olive Branch Award. Vanden Heuvel was also co-editor of *Vyi i Myi*, a Russian-language feminist newsletter.

She has received awards for public service from numerous groups, including The Liberty Hill Foundation, The Correctional Association and The Association for American-Russian Women. In 2003, she received the New York Civil Liberties Union's Callaway Prize for the Defense of the Right of Privacy. She is also the recipient of The American-Arab Anti-Discrimination Committee's 2003 "Voices of Peace" award, and the Asian American Legal Defense and Education Fund's 2006 "Justice in Action" award.

Vanden Heuvel also serves on the boards of The Institute for Policy Studies, The Campaign for America's Future, The Correctional Association of New York, The Franklin and Eleanor Roosevelt Institute and Princeton Progressive Nation. She is a member of the National Advisory Board of The Roosevelt Institution, *Facing South* (online) magazine and the Progressive Book Club Editorial Board.

She is a summa cum laude graduate of Princeton University, and she lives in New York City with her husband and daughter.

MAUREEN WHITE

Maureen White is currently Chairman of the Board of Overseers of The International Rescue Committee (IRC) and a National Finance Chair of the Hillary Clinton for President Campaign.

She served as the National Finance Chair of the Democratic National Committee (DNC) from March 2001 until April 2006.

Ms. White was the United States Government Representative to the United Nations Children's Fund (UNICEF) from 1997 until January 2001. For the better part of the last decade, she has worked with a number of organizations dealing with international humanitarian issues, human rights, refugees and children affected by armed conflict. She is on the Board of the International Women's Health Coalition (IWHC) and the Chatham House Foundation. She is a member of the Council on Foreign Relations.

Prior to that Ms. White had a career in international economic research. From 1978 to 1982 she was at the Royal Institute of International Affairs in London and the Nomura Research Institute in Tokyo. She spent eight years from 1983 to 1991 in investment banking research in London and New York with First Boston Corporation and Globe Finlay International.

She was educated at Mount Holyoke College (BA) and the London School of Economics (MSc). She is married to Steven Rattner and they have four children.

ABOUT THE EDITOR

One of the most innovative political strategists in the country, **Erica Payne** is at the forefront of an effort to build a modern progressive movement.

Payne is the Founder and Principal of **The Tesseract Group** a boutique consulting firm that provides strategic counsel and communications expertise to major foundations, private philanthropists, and select organizations. Prior to founding Tesseract, Payne co-founded the Democracy Alliance, a donor collaborative whose partners have invested over $100 million in progressive organizations.

Prior to this, Payne served as Deputy National Finance Director for the Democratic National Committee during the 1996 presidential re-election campaign and as a consultant to a number of campaigns and political organizations. In addition to her public sector work, Payne has held senior marketing positions in the private sector.

Payne has an MBA from the Wharton School of Business at UPenn and a BA from the University of North Carolina at Chapel Hill. She has appeared on MSNBC and has written for the Huffington Post. She lives in New York.

Endnotes for The Conservative Infrastructure (pages 31-40)

[1] *United States Presidential Election*, 1964. Wikipedia.org. July 12, 2007.
<http://www.en.wikipedia.org/wiki/U.S._presidential_election,_1964.

[2] *People and Events; The 1964 Republican Campaign*. PBS Online. Accessed July 13th,
2007. www.pbs.org/wgbh/amex/rockefellers/peopleevents/e_1964.html.

[3] *People and Events; The 1964 Republican Campaign*.

[4] *1964: Election triumph for Lyndon B Johnson*. BBC Online. Accessed July 13, 2007.
<http://news.bbc.co.uk/onthisday/hi/dates/stories/november/3/newsid 3641000/3641464.stm>.

[5] Fox, John. *Lewis Franklin Powell Jr*. Biographies of the Robes. December, 2006
<http://www.pbs.org/wnet/supremecourt/rights/robes_powell.html>.

[6] Powell, Lewis. *Attack of the American Free Enterprise System*. August 23, 1971.
<http://www.tesseractllc.com/images/stories/suggestedmedia/the%20powell%20memo.pdf>

[7] Powell.

[8] Powell.

[9] Powell.

[10] Powell.

[11] Powell.

[12] Powell, Lewis. *Attack of the American Free Enterprise System*. August 23, 1971.
<http://www.tesseractllc.com/images/stories/suggestedmedia the%20powell%20memo.pdf>.

[13] Powell.

[14] Powell.

[15] *About Us*. The Heritage Foundation. Accessed July 20, 2007.
<http://www.heritage.org/about/>.

[16] *About Us*.

[17] Heritage Foundation Mission Statement.

[18] Paul Weyrich. dKosopedia. Accessed July 31st 2007.
<http://www.dkosopedia.com/wiki/Paul_Weyrich>.

[19] *The Heritage Foundation*. Media Transparency. Accessed July 31st 2007.
<http://www.mediatransparency.org/recipientprofile.php?recipientID=153>.

[20] *Heritage Foundation*. dKosopedia. Accessed July 13th 2007.
<http://www.dkosopedia.com/wiki/Heritage_Foundation>.

[21] *The Heritage Foundation*.

[22] *Heritage Foundation*. dKosopedia. Accessed July 13th 2007.
<http://www.dkosopedia.com/wiki/Heritage_Foundation>.

[23] *Heritage Foundation*. SourceWatch. Accessed July 31st 2007.
<http://www.sourcewatch.org/index.php?title=Heritage_Foundation>.

[24] dKosopedia.

[25] dKosopedia.

[26] Stein, Rob. *The Conservative Message Machine's Money Matrix*. PowerPoin v Presentation. Viewed on July 13, 2007.

[27] Represents 2002 organizational budgets.

[28] *American Enterprise Institute*. SourceWatch. Accessed July 31st 2007. <http://www.sourcewatch.org/index.php?title=American_Enterprise_Institute>.

[29] *Cato Institute*. Wikipedia. Accessed July 31st 2007. <http://en.wikipedia.org/wiki/Cato_Institute>.

[30] *Cato Institute*. Wikipedia. Accessed July 31st 2007. <http://en.wikipedia.org/wiki/Cato_Institute>.

[31] *Hoover Institution*. Wikipedia. Accessed July 31st 2007. <http://en.wikipedia.org/wiki/Hoover_Institution>.

[32] *Right Web Profile: Hoover Institution*. Right Web. Accessed July 31st 2007. <http://rightweb.irc-online.org/profile/1479>.

[33] *Right Web Profile: Hoover Institution*.

[34] Stein, Rob. *The Conservative Message Machine's Money Matrix*. PowerPoint Presentation. Viewed on July 13, 2007.

[35] Stein.

[36] Represents 2002 organizational budgets.

[37] Represents 2002 organizational budgets.

[38] Stein.

[39] Alterman, Eric. *Think Again; Money Matters Part II*. Center for American Progress. October 20th, 2004. <http://www.americanprogress.org/issues/2004/10/b225778.html>

[40] Represents 2002 figures.

[41] Stein.

[42] Berkowitz, Bill. *Team Schiavo's Deep Pockets*. Media Transparency. <http://www.mediatransparency.org/storyprinterfriendly.php?storyID=56>.

[43] Capital Research Center . Wikipedia. Accessed July 31st 2007. <http://en.wikipedia.org/wiki/Capital_Research_Center >. 50 Leo, John. U.S. News & World Report; 3/7/2005, Vol. 138 Issue 8, p60-60, 1p, 2c.

[44] Ambinder, Marc. *Inside the Council for National Policy*. ABC News Online. May 5, 2002 <http://abcnews.go.com/Politics/Story?id=121170&page=2>.

[45] Ambinder.

[46] Learning, Jeremy. *Behind Closed Doors*. Americans United For the Separation of Church and State. October 2004. <http:// www.au.org/site/News2?page=NewsArticle&id=6949&abbr=cs_>.